Gilbert Elliot Minto

Lord Minto in India

Life and Letters of Gilbert Elliot, first Earl of Minto from 1807 to 1814

Gilbert Elliot Minto

Lord Minto in India

Life and Letters of Gilbert Elliot, first Earl of Minto from 1807 to 1814

ISBN/EAN: 9783337135409

Printed in Europe, USA, Canada, Australia, Japan

Cover: Foto ©ninafisch / pixelio.de

More available books at **www.hansebooks.com**

LORD MINTO IN INDIA

LIFE AND LETTERS

OF

GILBERT ELLIOT, FIRST EARL OF MINTO

FROM

1807 TO 1814

WHILE GOVERNOR-GENERAL OF INDIA

BEING A SEQUEL TO HIS "LIFE AND LETTERS" PUBLISHED IN 1874

EDITED BY HIS GREAT-NIECE

THE COUNTESS OF MINTO

LONDON
LONGMANS, GREEN, AND CO.
1880

All rights reserved

PREFACE.

In one of Lord Minto's letters from India he says, in reference to a recent publication, that, in his judgment, a biography should not be made to contain all that can be told about a man, but should rather aim at giving a judicious selection of what is calculated to represent his actions and character.

Upon this principle the selection from his letters and papers now published has been made.

It has no pretension to historical comprehensiveness. The historians of British India have treated the period of Lord Minto's administration with a weight of authority, and in a spirit of candour, leaving nothing to be desired.

Many important transactions are recorded in their pages which find no place in this correspondence, and others again are brought prominently forward in the letters which heretofore have been well nigh overlooked.

Nevertheless, the life of a statesman floats on the tide of history, and his public conduct cannot be fairly judged, apart from the conditions of the time in which he lived.

When Lord Minto landed in India in 1807, fifty years had barely elapsed since the British merchants of Calcutta had become sovereigns of Bengal. One of his aides-de-camp who visited the battle-field of Plassy in 1808 was conducted over the ground by an eye-witness of that memorable victory. In the period that followed it, the genius of Clive and of Warren Hastings extended the Company's rule.

Within a decade of Lord Minto's assumption of the Governor-Generalship the victorious arms of Lord Wellesley had asserted the supremacy of the British Power over the greater part of the Peninsula. But his policy was disapproved at home; his career of victory was arrested while his conquests were still unconsolidated; and the services which had been the instruments of his success were subjected to a somewhat drastic treatment of retrenchment and reform.

On Lord Minto's arrival in India, he found a condition bordering on anarchy in the newly ceded territories; a barely suppressed rebellion among the newly subjugated races; discontent in the Company's services; and a general objection to the restraints of legality.

Within two years of his instalment in the seat of

government, he came into conflict with pretensions of all others most dangerous to an infant State—those engendered by religious bigotry, and by the spirit of military ascendancy. How unflinchingly he asserted the paramount authority of the civil power, while never forgetting that law and justice are the only stable foundations of government, may be seen in the correspondence now published.

N. M.

Minto: *November* 8, 1879.

Note.—In the first pages of the Introduction to this volume, Lord Minto is stated to have left England in February 1807, whereas October 1806 is given as the date of his departure in the last volume of his 'Life and Letters,' published by me in 1874. It had been originally fixed for the earlier period, but was subsequently postponed ;—a fact of which I was ignorant when the volumes of his European correspondence were brought to a conclusion.

CONTENTS.

CHAPTER
I. INTRODUCTION 1

II. VOYAGE—MADRAS—CALCUTTA—CHANGE OF ADMINISTRATION—LADY MALMESBURY'S LETTERS . 13

III. STATE OF INDIA—EXTERNAL POLICY—INTERNAL POLICY—THE NATIVE RACES—THE MISSIONARIES 49

IV. FAMILY CORRESPONDENCE 83

V. POSITION OF ENGLAND—DEFENCE OF INDIA—RELATIONS WITH PERSIA AND TURKEY—MISSION TO PERSIA 97

VI. MISSION TO LAHORE 141

VII. MISSION TO CABUL 159

VIII. NEWS FROM EUROPE—MAY IN INDIA—DACOITIES . 179

IX. MUTINY OF MADRAS ARMY 197

X. FAMILY LETTERS—EDINBURGH IN 1809 . . . 228

CONTENTS.

CHAPTER		PAGE
XI.	FOREIGN POLICY—CONQUEST OF FRENCH ISLANDS	239
XII.	EXPEDITION TO JAVA	249
XIII.	CALCUTTA—OFFICIAL CORRESPONDENCE LETTERS FROM LONDON—FROM INDIA RECALL OF LORD MINTO—EARLDOM	318
XIV.	REVIEW OF LORD MINTO'S INTERNAL ADMINISTRATION—FINANCE—SCHEMES FOR RETRENCHMENT—FREE TRADE—MILITARY EXPENDITURE—BALANCE OF POWER—COLLEGE OF FORT WILLIAM—SCHEME FOR NATIVE COLLEGES	352
XV.	CONCLUSION—LORD MINTO'S RETURN TO ENGLAND—LONDON—MINTO—HIS DEATH	382

INDEX 395

LORD MINTO IN INDIA.

CHAPTER I.

LORD MINTO assumed the reins of government at Calcutta on July 3, 1807.

Before entering on this new chapter of his life it will be desirable to cast a retrospective glance over the circumstances which had led to his appointment to the government of India.

On the formation in 1806, of the Whig Ministry, called that of 'the Talents,' Lord Minto became President of the Board of Control, and in that capacity confirmed 'under reserve' the succession of Sir George Barlow to the office of Governor General which, vacated by the death of Lord Cornwallis, devolved as a matter of course upon Sir George as senior member of Council, until a fresh appointment could be made in England.

The death of Lord Cornwallis had occurred almost simultaneously with the advent of the Whigs to power. It will be remembered that the brilliant administration of Lord Wellesley was brought to a close by his recall.

While he was engaged in creating an empire, his masters in Leadenhall Street were learning to their dismay that the process was not a paying one. Impoverished finances with augmented responsibilities led them to the conclusion that the interests of a trading company might be placed in safer if not in abler hands. At their urgent desire Lord Cornwallis was prevailed on to return to India to inaugurate a reign of peace, and to observe a strict abstention from interference in the affairs of the Native States beyond the British frontier.

But Lord Cornwallis was old and infirm; he felt that he went out to die, and his death followed almost immediately on his arrival in India. When his authority fell to Sir George Barlow, the Directors were happy to find in him, though a quondam pupil of Lord Wellesley, a thorough-going supporter of the policy which they had committed to Lord Cornwallis, and would gladly have confirmed him in the office of Governor General; but such was not the intention of the Cabinet.

Early in February, Lord Minto was instructed to inform Sir George Barlow that the permanency of his appointment was not to be considered as determined, and on the 1st of April he wrote again to announce to Sir George the intended nomination of his successor; remarking at the same time that when in his former letter he had stated the King's Government to have reserved their ulterior judgment, he was not aware it was so near the point of decision, for had he known it he would, at once, have frankly and candidly imparted that information to Sir George himself.

Writing to his old friend Lord William Bentinck, Governor of Madras, on the same day, April 1, Lord Minto says:—'The arrangements with regard to the Government of Bengal are always considered as belonging to the Cabinet, in which I have not a seat. But in fact this particular measure has been settled and conducted I may say with the entire exclusion of my voice or judgment in the affair. It was determined upon some weeks before it reached my ears, and it was only communicated to me on the day on which I was desired to communicate it to the Chairs. I do not say this in the way of complaint, being assured that the perfect cordiality of Lord Grenville towards me precludes the possibility of intentional slight.'

Whatever the reasons may have been for the conduct of the Cabinet, it certainly had an appearance of want of candour that sufficiently accounted for the irritation manifested by the Court of Directors. They had not forgotten that the Prime Minister, Lord Grenville, had warmly approved of the administration of Lord Wellesley which they had condemned, and when the name of Lord Lauderdale was made known as that of the chosen successor to Sir George Barlow, they at once refused to consider the nomination. The Government, persisting in their measure, exercised a power given to the King by 33 Geo. III. c. 52, and vacated the commission of Sir George. Both parties being equally resolved, the quarrel grew hot and bitter. Mr. Fox supported the pretensions of Lord Lauderdale with that passionate carelessness of consequences where his feelings were concerned which made him so beloved as a friend and so distrusted as a statesman. He positively refused to listen to any other name, and somewhat autocratically desired that the Ministry should abandon the right of nomination altogether, rather than withdraw the one they had made in compliance with the objections of the Court of Directors. The discussions in the Cabinet were so prolonged and warm that Lord Minto appears to have had misgivings as to the extent to which the divergences of opinion manifested there might ultimately be carried. In the course of the summer he wrote to Lady Minto that, while believing Lord Lauderdale to have many qualifications for the office of Governor General which would justify the appointment, he should himself resign if the Government persisted in forcing on the Company an individual obnoxious to them. A rupture between the Directors and the controlling power was imminent when Lord Lauderdale suddenly withdrew his pretensions, induced by the serious illness of Mr. Fox to spare him further agitation on the subject.

Lord Grenville immediately nominated Lord Minto, and the appointment proved to be equally acceptable to the Directors and to the public.

'When the appointment of Lord Lauderdale became manifestly impossible,' wrote Lord Minto to Lord William Bentinck, 'the views of all parties turned towards me, and the accidental union which manifested itself on this choice seemed to make my nomination a sort of peace-offering on both sides, and a means of compromise and reconciliation which might solve a great difficulty. Under this inducement I accepted, not without a strong private and domestic struggle, nor without an anxious distrust of my qualifications for so weighty a burthen, a situation which, so far from seeking, I thought a week before no human persuasion could have led me to undertake.'

Though by no means an adherent on all points to Lord Wellesley's policy, Lord Minto was, as Lord Grenville well knew, second to no man in his devotion to the honour and interests of the Empire, while the natural moderation of his character convinced the Directors that no hankerings after a showy policy would prevent their instructions from being rigorously observed. If these were limited, as he afterwards playfully declared, to a general recommendation to maintain a system of non-intervention, and a more definite one to control the consumption of penknives, we may assume that their confidence in the new Governor General was complete.

With Lord Grenville he had many conversations in which were foreshadowed the main features of the policy that before the close of his administration left Great Britain without a rival in the Eastern hemisphere.

Such having been the circumstances that led to the appointment of Lord Minto to the government of India, a few words may be permitted to us on the personal conditions which pointed him out as singularly fitted for the post.

Lord Minto's early and intimate connection with Burke was the keynote of his political career. For that great man he formed an enthusiastic affection which was returned with so much tenderness and confidence that, when indulging after long years in a retrospect of their old friendship, he was able to say, ' I believe I was among those whom Burke loved best, and most trusted.'

Some of Burke's finest orations were due to the profound interest he felt in the relations of England and India, to the indignation with which he saw the interests of the native princes and people trafficked away by the servants of a trading Company, and to the disgust with which he recognised that the ruling powers in England had minds too small for the sphere of their duty. These sentiments were intensified by the natural bias of his intellect. There was an epic grandeur in the dramas enacting on that most ancient stage, a tragic dignity in the fallen estate of dynasties as ancient, a magnitude in the scale of the crimes and triumphs, the sorrows and sufferings of which India was the scene, that stirred his keenest sympathies, and called forth the scathing eloquence that imparts to those who hear it something of its divine fervour. Burke must be allowed the honour of having been the first to awaken in the British Parliament and people a sense of their duty to the native races of India; yet it cannot be denied that when the light of his imagination played over the stores of his knowledge, an ideal India was created, brilliant and unreal as the luminous pageants which Asiatics love to trace in lines of fire on midnight skies. The following passage from his speech on the East India Bill in 1783, curious for various reasons at the present day, may serve at once to confirm this assertion and to show the traditions of a school of which Burke was the master.

'This multitude of men does not consist of an abject and barbarous populace; much less of gangs of savages, like the Guaranis and Chiquitos, who wander on the waste borders of the river of Amazons or the Plate; but a people for ages civilised and cultivated; cultivated by all the arts of polished life, whilst we were yet in the woods. There, have been (and still the skeletons remain) princes once of great dignity, authority, and opulence. There, are to be found the chiefs of tribes and nations. There, is to be found an ancient and venerable priesthood, the depositary of their laws, learning, and industry, the guides of the people whilst living, and their consolation in death; a nobility of great antiquity and renown; a multitude of cities, not exceeded in population and trade by those of the first class in Europe; merchants and bankers, individual houses of whom have once vied in capital with the Bank of England . . . millions of ingenious manufacturers and mechanics; millions of the most diligent, and not the least intelligent, tillers of the earth. Here are to be found almost all the religions professed by men;

the Brahminical, the Mussulman, the Eastern and the Western Christians.

'If I were to take the whole aggregate of our possessions there, I should compare it as the nearest parallel I could find to the Empire of Germany; our immediate possessions I should compare with the Austrian dominions, and they would not suffer in the comparison. The Nabob of Oude might stand for the King of Prussia; the Nabob of Arcot I would compare, as superior in territory and equal in revenue, to the Elector of Saxony. The Rajah of Benares might well rank with the Prince of Hesse, at least; and the Rajah of Tanjore (though hardly equal in extent of dominion, superior in revenue) with the Elector of Bavaria. The Polygars and the northern Zemindars and other great chiefs might well class with the rest of the princes, dukes, counts, marquises, and bishops in the Empire; all of whom I mention to honour, and surely without disparagement to any or all of those most respectable princes and grandees.'[1]

It was no doubt due to Sir Gilbert's ardent sympathy with the views and the labours of his friend that in 1783 he was designated as one of the seven Parliamentary Directors (the Seven Kings as they were called) to be appointed under the provisions of Mr. Fox's India Bill.

The measure was lost, and as with it collapsed the Ministry and the reign of the Whig party, the honour was a barren one; but his first appearance on the

[1] Speech on the East India Bill. *Burke's Works*, vol. i. p. 338.

political stage in a leading part was nevertheless destined to be connected with the interests of India. Two sessions had passed since he and Mirabeau stood together at the Bar of the House of Commons to listen to the great tribunes of England, when Sir Gilbert himself made his first important effort in that formidable assembly, and moved the Impeachment of Sir Elijah Impey in a speech which elicited the warm admiration of its most illustrious members.

In the following year he became one of the managers in the trial of Warren Hastings. 'His earnest desire,' he said in his opening speech on that occasion, 'to befriend the natives of India had decided him to undertake a business in many respects most uncongenial to his nature.' But another determining cause was the urgency with which Burke besought him to throw off his modesty, ' his only fault,' and the warmth of encouragement which hailed his opening effort. A note, written in December 1787 and sent to Sir Gilbert with a book intended to be of use to him while engaged in the preparation of his charge against Sir Elijah Impey, ends thus :

'God bless you and forward your good undertaking. Stick to it. You have years before you, and if I were of your age, and had your talents and your manners, I should not despair of seeing India a happy country in a few years. Yours ever,

'E. BURKE.'

Having kept all these things in his heart he could

not but ponder on them at the moment when his destiny was about to lead him among the people to whom his early sympathies had been given; nothing could be more natural than that a few of his last hours in England should be spent with all that remained of his old friend. 'I paid my visit to Mrs. Burke yesterday,' he wrote to his wife a day or two before his embarkation, 'and took leave of the old groves as well as of herself by walking round the place which to me and a few other people is sanctified—as I am never there without feeling. Sitting there alone I thought of more things than even you would understand.'

From the groves which crown the heights of Beaconsfield it was only a pleasant drive to Taplow Court, where Lord and Lady Thomond (Sir Joshua Reynolds' niece) owned one of the loveliest places on the Thames; thence it was no 'far cry' to Dropmore, the home of the Grenvilles; nor to Park Place, that of the Malmesburys, with the little 'Lavender House'[1] nestling under its slopes. Of each and of all these familiar haunts he took a long farewell. While to some of those, for whose sake they were dear, the word itself remained unspoken.

A pathetic proof of its bitterness to others as well as to himself is given in a letter addressed to him at Portsmouth, by Lady Malmesbury.

[1] Belonging to Mr. and Mrs. Culverden, sister of Lady Palmerston.

'Spring Gardens: February 10, 1807.

'I must send you a few lines to *thank you* for sparing me the most wretched of all things—a parting scene. People feel so differently on these points that I would not ask you to do so, in case you felt differently, and no selfish feelings could be attended to by me on such an occasion. In youth one rather covets such things as call forth the feelings, but in later life there is less *spring* to support them, and I am inclined to believe that as the passions weaken the feelings strengthen. I therefore repeat that I thank you sincerely for *not* coming here, and that I consider the last squeeze of your hand as fully satisfactory. . . . I hope and pray that the sacrifice you have made may be rewarded in every possible shape, and that the interval may be as little irksome as it can be. I am sure that the retrospect of it will be one of its principal rewards, as the *will* of doing good will equal the power in your hands, and the latter is unequalled perhaps in any situation on the globe.'

Lord Malmesbury wrote in like strain :

'London : February 10, 1807.

'I really could not make up my mind to see you before you left London. I even studiously avoided it. The taking leave of an old and affectionate friend, going for several years to a very distant country, at my time of life and with my infirmities, is a very painful task, and calculated to raise so many melancholy sensations that I shrank from attempting it.

'I feel almost sure you guessed and understood the motives of my conduct, but there is a satisfaction in writing them to you, resting on the same feeling which made it so painful for me to express them personally.

> 'If we do meet again, why we shall smile,
> If not, why then this parting was well made.'

Before the frigate sailed which was to convey him to India, Lord Minto sent a few parting lines to his wife, in which the following passage occurs.

'February 6, 1807.

'I took leave of Gilbert [1] yesterday after sealing my letter to you, and I may reckon the worst moments of my probation over. The last was one of those of which it is impossible to say all that is felt, and if one could it is better to suppress it. Many people have said of their sons that they have never given them pain; I can say with perfect and literal truth that there has not been an instant of his life on which I have reflected without comfort and delight. So much for that. The wind has not been fair.'

[1] His eldest son, Gilbert Elliot, afterwards second Earl of Minto.

CHAPTER II.

THE voyage from England to Madras, in the 'Modeste' frigate commanded by George Elliot, Lord Minto's second son, took four months. As it neither produced a sea fight nor ended in disaster it was considered to have been favoured by fortune. The nearest approach to such naval adventures as Lord Minto had witnessed in the Mediterranean[1] was a chase after a couple of our own merchantmen, whence half-a-dozen sailors were extracted to make up the 'Modeste's' own very deficient complement, chiefly composed of raw landsmen. No less ill-fitted than ill-manned, the frigate after weathering a severe gale reached Madeira in need of serious repairs. 'A little more would have been too much for us,' wrote Lord Minto in the log kept for the benefit of the family circle at home; but he was comforted for the delay by a sight of scenery that reminded him of Nice and Bastia, and the enjoyment of a quiet morning, 'rusticating in all the ways I like, among flowering trees and shrubs regaling the air with perfume.' A pathetic interest is lent to these few lines by the circumstance that never again in his journal-

[1] When Viceroy of Corsica.

like letters is mention made of 'ways' hitherto so frequently recorded as to form part of his habitual life, whether the summer hours were spent on the craigs of Minto, under the chestnuts of Sheen, or by the bright waters of the Thames,—

> That, as they bicker'd thro' the sunny glade,
> Tho' restless still themselves, a lulling murmur made.

Of the log no more need be said than that no one of those for whom it was kept but could find some congenial topic there. For his son there were comments on soldiers and sailors, colonists and governors; for his daughters bright little word-pictures of Funchal and Cape Town—for the youngest, the only child left in the family, tales of the mids that came to his cabin for their daily treat of oranges, and of their pet playfellow, a goat that was born on board ship, rated herself one of them, and knew no more of craigs than the Minto pointers had told her.[1] Lastly, for his wife there was the constant recurrence of words showing how all his thoughts ended in her. 'Cape Town, May, 1807. In the country I am now driving through, there is a quarter called Franzneuk or French corner. It is so called from some French refugees, expelled by the edict of Nantes, who took refuge in South Africa, and obtained grants of land where they cultivated the vine, and I have no doubt advanced that art very materially. To what country has that event not brought some

---

[1] Lord Minto was carrying a couple of pointers to India as a present to his son.

precious acquisition?' It will be remembered that Lady Minto was descended from a Huguenot family.

After one of these playful entries he says: 'Heaven knows I am serious enough as the serious scene draws near.'

The next day he was at Madras.

The 'Modeste' anchored in the Madras roads on the evening of June 20, 1807. At six o'clock next morning Lord William Bentinck, and John Elliot [1] came on board to welcome him—'both unchanged, and unchangeable.' Though Lord Minto was detained at Madras for a fortnight by the necessity of having a new foremast for the 'Modeste,' he could take no official part there since his commission could only be opened on his arrival at Calcutta, but he profited by the opportunity to acquaint himself with the affairs of that perturbed Presidency where some of the mutineers of Vellore were still under sentence awaiting their fate.[2] As those parts of his letters which relate to that disastrous event contain little more than his personal opinion upon facts long since established they are omitted. His first impressions of Indian life have more interest.

[1] John Edmund Elliot, third son of Lord Minto, who had been appointed to a writership in 1805, and now became private secretary to his father.

[2] The European barracks at Vellore had been seized in the night of July 10, 1806, by two battalions of Sepoys, in the Company's service, and their inmates put to the sword. The mutiny was put down almost immediately, but a general revolt of the native troops was for some time apprehended. A proclamation of the Madras Government, dated December 3, 1806, states the cause of the mutiny to have been an unfounded belief that the Government meant to convert the native troops by forcible means to Christianity.

'Madras: June 29.

'The novelty of this scene exceeds even my expectations. I have already told you of our safe arrival and perfect health. I do not find the heat at all amiss, though it is the hottest season of the year. I never go out at all till five o'clock in the afternoon; it is then cool enough to drive in the curricle. John is my coachman. We take a *giro* on the Mount Road which is the general resort at that time of day, and strike off occasionally for variety into other roads. The roads are all as fine as the smoothest gravel walks, being composed of pounded brick; the dust of this is rather troublesome. They are extremely wide, with trees on each side, and are in effect handsome avenues. The whole of the Choultry plain, which extends seven or eight miles from Madras, is divided into villas and pleasure-grounds, and the grounds are so extensive that the houses are much farther from each other than on Putney Heath, or Wimbledon Common. These are the habitations of the English, and the higher class of natives. John and I finish our drive where we are invited to dine, the hour being seven o'clock. As yet I am in a round of great dinners, at which I meet the same thirty or forty grandees every day.

Most people come and go in their palanquins, and travel at the rate of five or six miles an hour, carried by four bearers, and attended by four more to relieve each other, all running and always singing some ditty or other. Indeed, in carriages, going a good round pace with four horses on a smooth road, you are always

attended by men on foot, one for each horse, and often
more for dignity—so that it is not one running
footman or two, with a fine gentleman or fine lady;
here and there one, as in Germany or Italy, but every
sort of person here is followed by a cloud of *volantes*.
This annoys me extremely, very much to John's amusement, who assures me that *they like* it, while I am
thinking how I should like it myself with my lungs in
this burning sun. They run thirty miles on end without thinking much of it, and will set off back again
with little or no rest. One advantage is that they are
not burdened with a heavy wardrobe. I was not prepared for the entire nakedness of the Gentoo inhabitants.
I mean the men, nine tenths of whom have literally no
clothes except only a narrow belt about the waist from
which another is passed between the limbs exactly as in
the South Sea Islands. In this attire crowds are in
the streets, and in the roads, and walk about your
house. It seems really strange to a *griffin*—the cant
word for a European just arrived, and would, I suppose,
seem still stranger to our countrywomen if these men
were white instead of black or bronze. The Queen (of
Naples) might here study figures without anything to
" abimer " her models. This race of men are not
exactly Academy figures, not being very muscular, but
their forms are remarkably delicate and elegant, and
many of their countenances uncommonly fine. . . The
habit of walking without clothes gives them a free and
manly as well as a graceful gait. The rest of the inhabitants, who are Moors, and the richer Gentoos, are

dressed in various degrees and fashions, but universally in white muslin, and mostly robed down to the feet. From that fortunate class to the lowest there is a regular gradation of dishabille. The women are almost universally very ugly. They certainly have none of them livers, for the vertical sun makes them no hotter than it makes a cucumber. They work hard in his very beams, and, when they may rest, lie in them on the baked sand even when shade is close to them.

'The Hindoos are all marked with the distinctive sign of their castes. These are painted or rather plastered on their foreheads with *chunam,* a sort of very fine plaster lime, for which Madras is famous. It is coloured in various ways, sometimes gilt, but generally of a yellow tint. The marks consist in a score or several scores upon the forehead, some horizontal, some vertical, some oblique, according to the caste. A very frequent mark is a round patch just above the nose. They all perform their ablutions every morning before they eat. The marks of caste are therefore effaced. They breakfast without them and renew them immediately afterwards. The best sort wash before each meal, morning and evening—and must renew their decorations therefore twice a day.

'There are two sorts of distinction amongst these people on perfectly separate principles, but both existing together in their full force; one, as in the rest of the world, consists in the difference of fortune and power; the other takes no notice of these vulgar sources of consideration, but sets them all at defiance, and maintains itself in spite of all worldly vicissitudes. A Brahmin of the highest caste may be the servant or at least the humble dependant of a man of an inferior caste; but the master, in such cases, must not presume to sit down or to eat in the presence of his servant, and the latter would think himself dishonoured by being even looked at by his rich superior while cooking his rice.

'All Christians and other pagans are classed with the lowest or Pariah caste. Sometimes people of this caste enlist in the Sepoy regiments, and Sir John Cradock, Knight of the Bath and Commander-in-chief, told me that a Pariah Sepoy had sometimes come to him for a furlough or some other small favour, and by way of recommending himself has said, "Master know I be Master's caste," and I daresay has paid master no small compliment by acknowledging him even for a Pariah.

'A thousand whimsical consequences, and ten thousand inconvenient, often ruinous, restraints, result from these original but firmly established institutions. One great convenience, however, of these singularities I must mention, which is that no servant is fed or even lodges in the house. They receive so much money, and very little it is, and provide for themselves. The coachmen alone wear liveries, and they are dressed exactly like English postilions; but, as soon as they leave their box, they strip off their European finery, and walk off stark naked to their own huts and dress their rice, and have no more to do with you till the carriage comes. The coachman would scorn to rub his horse down, and the horse-keeper would scorn to rub more than one horse; hence it is lucky that all these gentlemen have no religious prejudice against low wages: eight or ten shillings a month pays all wages.

. . . .

'I suppose there are fifty things in sight and hearing every minute that would amuse you in description, but my eye is spoilt already, and I hardly know what is strange and what is common.

'I have told you very little about the Nabob (of the Carnatic), although no day passes without messengers from him, in the morning to enquire how I slept, and in the middle of the day to present a gift of fruit and flowers. He insists on my seeing these messengers with great silver sticks and returning my salaams by them, which is a great and grievous bore twice a day. After my first visit he sent me a dinner of at least fifty dishes, each of which was brought on the head of a black damsel. This feast was displayed on the floor of the colonnade, and I was brought forth to see the rich embroidered covers taken off, and to admire the cook-shop. I made my salaam, and the repast was devoured by Lord William's body-guard. This present of a dinner is an established custom in the East. The Nabob is a very fat black-bearded person about thirty. At my first visit he received me at the door of my coach, having bargained that I should do the like when he returned my visit. He embraced me as soon as I was out of the coach with most affectionate hugs, saying each time, " How d'ye do, Governor General ? "

This I thought a very suitable salutation at our meeting, but it seemed less neat and appropriate at my departure, when, at the coach door, he repeated the four embraces with " How d'ye do, Governor General ? " four times again. During the reception he sat on a sofa in a great hall, in which was also the musnud or throne, I on his right, Lord William on his left. Then our interpreter made us mutually happy by assurances of each other's perfect health, and the Nabob returned thanks to God for the health of the King, the Queen, the Prince of Wales, all the Princes and Princesses, the Court of Directors, the House of Peers, and all the Members of the House of Commons, every one of whom I assured him I had left in the most blooming health. We were then still more deeply affected by our extreme attachment for each other, and by the singular felicity of beholding each other's faces. Many other similar affairs of state were transacted between us, and when the painful moment for parting arrived, His Highness dropt a few drops of attar of roses on my handkerchief, then sprinkled me profusely all over my best Vienna embroidered coat with rose-water, saying affectionately that he knew he was spoiling my coat (but what is a coat to the effusions of friendship?). Then he put on my neck a garland of white flowers; gave me two packets of betel-nut and then two roses. After which Lord William and all my family were treated in the same manner, and we retired.'

The next day the visit was returned, and on the

following one the Governor General was entertained at a Nautch—of which festivity he was quite unworthy—thinking he had never seen such a collection of hideous women in his life.

'I am sorry to say the season has been most calamitous here, from the entire failure of the usual monsoon, and a consequent loss of the crop. A sad famine is at this moment desolating several extensive districts; . . . thousands of country people have swarmed into Madras in quest of bread; thousands are employed on public works; to thousands who can't work rice is distributed gratis daily, by a public subscription. But some arrive too late and too much exhausted, others refrain too long from pride or scruples from accepting this relief, and it has been common to see famished wretches brought at last by friends to the Choultry, where the distribution is made, expire after the first mouthful of food which their stomachs could no longer receive in safety. It has been worse in the country. . . . It seems hard that the people of this country should experience distress, for none can experience fewer wants; a little rice is literally the only necessary of life. The man requires no clothes, the woman little more. Fuel to cook their rice is all they want, and they need pay no house-rent, for their habitations are huts composed of a few mats or hurdles fastened to upright stakes about four feet high, and a roof of as light timbers thatched with large leaves. These hovels can be run up in an hour, and are erected along the sides of the high roads or in any corner of waste land they like. The wind passes through them freely, which is all the better; but the rain enters with as little ceremony; and in all wet weather they must go out of their houses to have any chance of being dry. They enjoy the hottest sun and bask in the baked dust without shelter and for pleasure at noon-day, but they all look as miserable as cats in a shower.

'One thing I have forgotten to tell you of—the prickly heat. To give you some notion of its intensity, the placid Lord William has been found sprawling on a table on his back; and Sir Henry Gwillin, one of the Madras judges, who is a Welshman and a fiery Briton in all senses, was discovered by a visitor rolling on his own floor roaring like a baited bull. Here I must close the Madras chapter. I have been writing down to July 19, and must embark to-morrow morning.'

On Lord Minto's arrival in Calcutta Sir George Barlow resumed the position of senior member of Council vacated by him while holding the office of Governor General. After his appointment to the Government of Madras which took place a few weeks later, Mr. Lumsden, an experienced public servant, Mr. Colebrooke, 'a man of extraordinary talents and extremely agreeable manners,' and General Hewitt, Commander-in-chief, constituted the Council, in which there were no further changes during Lord Minto's administration. Mr. N. B. Edmonstone filled the post of Secretary to Government. Sir Edward Pellew

—afterwards Lord Exmouth—held the chief naval command, 'a sailor of the Nelson school,' and therefore particularly acceptable to the Governor General. Lord Minto was justified in saying that he found 'plenty of ability in all departments.'

'Calcutta: July 31, 1807.[1]

'To have arrived at our destination and all well, is so material a step, though the first one of our design, that I feel, perhaps more than I ever did before, grateful to Providence for this good beginning. . . . To return to the fussifications of my arrival and accession. When I found myself lost from my cobbler's stall in Arlington Street, seated in full possession of this noble and magnificent marble hall, the crowds of servants and attendants bowing round me in all the forms of Eastern prostration, I felt a little like Nell awaking in Lady Loverrule's bed, with the difference, however, that it is not at all like my notions of Paradise.'

'Calcutta: September 15.[2]

'Notwithstanding the awkward situation in which Sir G. Barlow and I are placed with regard to each other, I find no unpleasant consequences result from it. . . . His good sense and some other neutral qualities in his character have enabled him to act the part he had chosen with dignity and with many marks of real magnanimity. His good properties are of a high class.

[1] To Lady Minto. [2] To Hon. Gilbert Elliot.

A real attachment to his public duties, and, I have every reason to believe, a naturally sincere and honourable character, secure his best advice as a colleague. A constitutional coldness and apathy of temper, which has exposed him to the reproach of indifference to the interests of other men, and has enabled him to discharge many harsh duties pretty inflexibly, seems at the same time to have kept his personal feelings in a temperate state, and to render a second place less irksome and irritating than it would be to ninety-nine men in a hundred who had filled the first. He acknowledges, also, the great attention and delicacy I had shown towards his feelings from the beginning of the controversy concerning his office to the present time. I have omitted nothing, which a real and strong feeling for the unpleasantness of his situation can suggest, to diminish his own discomfort, and create a cordial instead of a jealous feeling between us.

'The situation of public affairs in this country is particularly favourable to the circumstances in which I am placed. There is in reality nothing of great moment depending, and nothing stirring in the great scale of politics on which I should desire to act on views and principles of *my own*, rather than on the mere experience and familiarity of other men with the subject. I have time, therefore, to form my views at leisure, and to acquire a little familiarity of my own with affairs before I need make free with them. In the meanwhile, my total inexperience in the details of current business makes the assistance of a colleague who has been living with them on the most intimate footing all his life particularly seasonable. The principal grievance I have to complain of is that the quantity and quick succession of current business is such as to employ every instant that I can command from ceremony, and the interruption of private solicitation, without affording any time for reading back, or looking forward, and acquiring general information. . . . The routine is this: the secretaries in the different departments send in circulation to me and the members of Council the despatches they have received since the last Council, and the documents relating to all business which arises in the interval. These are extremely voluminous, and would require pretty nearly the whole interval for mere perusal. The number and variety of affairs is also immense; for everything, small as well as great, must have the sanction of Government, and instead of being transacted by the secretaries, as in England, must be actually stated, and the orders given in Council. A declaration of war, and an estimate for an addition to a barrack a thousand miles off, may come next to each other in the secretaries' bundle. You may conceive the loads of such ware which such a country as this produces. The secretaries attend at Council, each department in its turn with its mountain of bundles. The secretary reads, or often only states shortly the substance of each paper, and the order is given on the spot. We are enabled to do this by having read these bundles at home. Now, our secretaries are all modest men, who scarcely read above their breath.

It is a constant strain of the ear to hear them; the business is often the heaviest and dullest kind, the voices monotonous, and as one small concern succeeds another, the punkah vibrates gently over my eyes; and in this warm atmosphere the whole operation has been found in the course of five hours somewhat composing. It is often a vehement struggle to avoid a delectable oblivious wink. But if the sovereign nods, the empire must fall to pieces; the fear of which has hitherto kept my fond eyelids from kissing each other, but not from most loving dispositions. However, if we nod and listen much, we have little occasion to write. The secretaries reduce all our orders into minutes of Council, letters, instructions, &c., and the different Boards and other executive officers carry the measures agreed upon into execution. We hold two Councils a week—Monday and Friday. We meet at ten and sit till three or four. From Friday to Tuesday I have my levées, audiences, dinners, and other personal communications, besides the reading of papers for Council.

'On Monday evening I go to Barrackpore, and remain there till Friday morning, when I return at five o'clock A.M. by water to Calcutta, and am there soon after seven. This division of the week, besides making half of it delicious, is of real advantage to business. At Barrackpore I can read, and really do so the livelong day.

'I can perceive nothing yet in any quarter that indicates a spirit of party, and there is certainly none now existing that leads to hostility towards me. If Sir G. Barlow had been a very popular character, the case might have been different; but he is not popular, and I believe his merits may have been the cause of it, or at least one among others. In truth, a Company's servant raised to the commanding height above his fellows which the Governor General holds here, excites envy rather than respect or love. They are all comparing themselves with him, and their own pretensions with his.

'I have never felt anything here equal to the heat of Bastia or even Vienna in summer. These are the most oppressive and most unhealthy weeks in the year —the end of September and beginning of October. Afterwards come four, or sometimes five delectable months. Barrackpore is really delicious, and takes the sting out of India.'

'Calcutta: September 20, 1807.'[1]

'The hours and occupations of Calcutta seem contrived to exclude women from society; and I hardly know how it can be helped; for in order to have any air or any exercise you must be riding or driving by five in the morning. This makes it necessary to most of us that we should be in bed by ten. In the evening between five and six, everybody is out again to get a gasp, by which means it is difficult to dine before eight. The only way of seeing ladies that I have discovered is

[1] To Hon. A. M. Elliot.

at table; the moment the meal is swallowed it is time to part. At table I have hitherto been allowed but one dish—namely the Burro Bebee, or lady of the highest rank, and to her, therefore, I am wedded, and care is taken that I should be a faithful husband. Since one cannot have one's own wife, I should think a little variety not amiss. Accordingly I am laying plans for that purpose, and have begun to invite small domestic sort of parties to dinner.

'I drive out almost every morning and evening. The formality of these airings is uncomfortable to me to a degree that I cannot at all accustom myself to. I am always followed by an officer and six troopers of the body-guard. These cannot be dispensed with. Four syces or horse-keepers with fly-flappers ran alongside of the horses till I positively rebelled against this annoyance. Everybody, European and native, salaams as I pass, and the natives, who swarm, draw up in lines and touch the ground almost with their heads. The consequence is that my right hand is never away from my head. I have had thoughts of sticking a wax hand in my hat. It is still worse with a palanquin. Thirty people go before in two lines which extend a great way forward. They carry gold and silver maces and halberds, and embroidered fans, and cows' tails to keep the flies off, besides two orderly Sepoys and two troopers. All these run on foot at a round trot, some of them proclaiming my titles; which, as the proclamation is rather long, I imagine must be Hindostanee for Gilbert Elliot, Murray of Melgund, and Kynynmound of that ilk.

The worst of all is the excessive annoyance at home by the same sort of crowd and incessant *entourage*. The first night I went to bed at Calcutta I was followed by fourteen persons in white muslin gowns into the dressing-room. One might have hoped that some of them were ladies; but on finding that there were as many turbans and black beards as gowns, I was very desirous that these bearded handmaids should leave me to single Tom, which with some trouble and perseverance I accomplished, and in that one room I enjoy a degree of privacy, but far from perfect. The doors are open, the partitions are open or transparent also, and it is the business of a certain number to keep an eye upon me, and see if I want the particular service which each is allowed by his caste to render me. It is the same in bed; a set of these black men sleep and watch all night on the floor of the passage, and an orderly man of the body-guard mounts guard at the door with Sepoys in almost all the rooms, and at all the staircases. These give you a regular military salute every time you stir out of your room or go up or down stairs, besides four or five with maces running before you. I have gradually got rid of this troublesome nonsense, but enough remains and must remain to tease me and turn comfort out of doors. As to John, he is orientalised already, and is mighty content to have five fellows attend his toilet; one holds a glass before him, one has hold of his foot, another of his knee, his hair, his body. I have a barber to shave me and a hair-dresser. Tom thought he ought to have some office also; and

after the man had dressed my hair he chose to tie my
cue, till I prevailed on him to be less oriental, and
leave the care of my cue to the hairdresser. I have
banished as much of this as possible from Barrackpore,
and we are more comfortable there; but after all, I
believe the best way will be to endure what it is impossible here to cure entirely. Barrackpore surpasses all
my expectations, in the beauty of the ground, the
beauty of the situation, and the comfort of its ways,
compared to Calcutta. The grounds are a mixture of
park and pleasure-grounds. They are laid out with
the greatest judgment and taste, and their extent
is very considerable. There is a great variety of
fine timber and curious ornamental shrubs and
flowering trees. Pools of water of very pretty forms
and certain inequalities of surface have been artificially
produced, but the real beauties consist in the rich
verdure which covers the whole, the magnificent timber, and the fine river which forms one side of the
place from end to end. Although it is a tide river,
there is no mud on the sides; the grass extends to low
watermark. The breadth of the Ganges here is sufficient for grandeur, and not too much for beauty. It
is all alive with a brisk navigation of boats and vessels
of different build and dimensions, and all of the most
picturesque forms and fashions. The present house is
what is called a bungalow or cottage, and was intended
only as a makeshift while the great house was erecting.
It is a cottage, indeed, but a very considerable building
compared with the European scale. The bungalow

was originally composed of three large rooms, which opened into a verandah surrounding the whole. Sir George Barlow, by converting each corner of the verandah into a small room, has greatly improved the comfort of the house. The verandah next the room is a charming apartment. It affords a long, shaded, airy walk with a most beautiful prospect, and we find it an excellent eating-room. It is within forty or fifty paces of the water's edge.

'Besides this principal bungalow there are a number of smaller ones like neat Swiss cottages scattered about the lawn. These afford accommodation for aide-de-camps, guests, &c., &c. A better and more regular house will certainly be proper. Such an one there was, but it was pulled down to make room for the projected palace, of which the ground-floor walls are finished. It would have been magnificent, I have no doubt, but in perfect contradiction with every purpose of the place. It would have been to come from Calcutta to Calcutta again; and you must have had the same multitude of troublesome attendants, and have lived the same full-dress, intolerable life at your country house as in town. I am extremely glad it has been stopped, and am selling off the materials which had been laid in, hoping there will be no change in my time. The road from Calcutta to Barrackpore is beautiful the whole way. The Danish town of Serampore, immediately opposite to these windows, is extremely ornamental, the river not appearing much wider than the Thames at Westminster, though it is considerably broader. But the clearness of the atmosphere and the strong light make all objects seem near. We have a cantonment of two or three thousand native troops close to us, and that, also, is very ornamental, though it may not sound so. But the officers' bungalows, ranged along the banks of the river, are extremely pretty, and the men's huts have the picturesque character of all the cottages of this country. The men themselves are still more ornamental. I never saw so handsome a race. They are much superior to the Madras people, whose forms I admired also. Those were slender; these are tall, muscular, athletic figures, perfectly shaped, and with the finest possible cast of countenance and features. Their features are of the most classical European models, with great variety at the same time; but the females seem still as hideous as at Madras, and one cannot conceive that they should be the mothers of such handsome sons.'

The first fleet that came out from England after Lord Minto's arrival at Calcutta brought the unexpected news of a change of Administration. Though it was known that Ministers had encountered considerable difficulty in proceeding with the Catholic Bill as it was called (a measure to enable Roman Catholics to serve in the Army and Navy with no other condition than that of taking an oath of allegiance[1]), the world was

[1] The bill, though intended chiefly for the benefit of the Catholics, extended the proposed concession to persons of every religious persuasion.

completely taken by surprise when it was announced that, in consequence of the irreconcilable nature of the views entertained by the King and his Ministers as to their constitutional duty on the matter in question, Lord Grenville and his colleagues had been dismissed. In the course of the Parliamentary debates which ensued it became known that the King, not content with the consent of Ministers to withdraw the objectionable Bill, had required from them a written pledge that they would never again propose further concessions to the Catholics. This pledge they refused to give, and immediately received their dismissal from the King, who desired the Duke of Portland and Mr. Perceval to form a new Administration.

The Duke was the nominal chief of the new Cabinet. Its chief members were Lord Camden, President of the Council; Lord Eldon, Chancellor; Lord Hawkesbury, Home Secretary; Mr. Canning, Foreign Secretary; Lord Castlereagh, War and Colonial Secretary; Mr. Perceval, Chancellor of the Exchequer; Mr. Robert Dundas, President of the Board of Control.

The new Ministers took their seats on April 8. On April 16 Lord Grenville addressed the following letter to Lord Minto:—

'Downing Street: April 16, 1807.

'You will hear from other quarters of the sudden revolution which has taken place in the political situation of your friends here. I have little doubt that you will entirely agree in the propriety of the conduct which they have held throughout the whole of a very difficult and delicate business, in which the most unfair advantages have been taken of them, and a spirit of low underhand intrigue employed against them, such as I am sure you had much rather see them the victims of, than think it possible for them to have counteracted by similar means.

'I remember nothing that I have thought more profligate than the attempt to excite in this country a spirit of religious dissent at a time when we have so much need of showing ourselves as an united people. Without giving to our opponents too much credit for talents which they certainly do not collectively possess, it is, however, difficult to think so meanly of their understandings as to believe that they really are themselves impressed with any belief of the dangers to the church establishment of this country from enacting the same laws here which have for fourteen years been in force in Ireland,[1] or from extending those laws in so far as was necessary to reconcile them to common sense. All this you will, I am sure, feel as strongly as I could express it, and I need not therefore dwell upon it. To a Government formed by a Court intrigue and resting for its support on an hypocritical attempt to

[1] By a law passed in the Parliament of Ireland in 1793, Catholics were allowed to hold commissions in the army in Ireland, and to attain to any rank save that of Commander-in-chief of the forces, Master-general of the Ordnance, or General on the Staff. The measure proposed by Lord Grenville's Ministry in 1807 extended to the Catholics of England the privileges already conceded to their Irish brethren and removed the restrictions enforced by the Act of 1793.

excite a popular clamour in favour of religious interests which no man of sense can believe in any danger, no sentiments can exist in my mind but those of decided hostility. Nor do I think your own feelings on this point can be at all different from mine. You will hear that the Directors have recalled Lord William Bentinck from Madras; a great disappointment as I believe to those who meant that he should have immediately superseded you in Bengal. With respect to your own conduct, I know you will allow me to speak to you with the utmost plainness and sincerity. I am far from feeling that I have any claim upon you in such a circumstance, nor, if I had, should I feel the slightest wish to use that claim for the purpose of influencing in the least degree the decision you may take about yourself. If you think on a deliberate review of the state of things at home and abroad that you can remain where you are with advantage to the public and with satisfaction to yourself, be assured that I speak quite sincerely when I say that I have no wish that you should act otherwise, and that on the contrary I shall feel sincere pleasure in thinking that one part at least, and that not the least important, of the interests of the country is in hands to which one can look with confidence and satisfaction; and that neither our private friendship nor the sentiments I entertain towards you as a public man will suffer the smallest diminution from your continuing to hold your office under the auspices of persons of whose conduct I think so ill. I hope therefore you will judge for yourself, and whatever your decision is, I beg you to be persuaded that I shall think it right, because it depends in part on circumstances of which you alone can judge—I mean the assurances of support which you may receive from the new Ministers, and the degree of credit which you may attach to their assurances. If your resolution should be to send a resignation, let me then suggest the propriety of your enclosing it to Elliot [1] with discretionary powers as to making use of it. This is not said because I believe much in the expectation which some entertain of another change taking place before long. I have seen enough of the politics of this country to know how very long a very weak and inefficient Government may maintain itself, if it has the Court favour with it, and is willing to make large sacrifices and compliances in order to retain that favour. And that this is the case in the present instance I believe no man doubts.'

In a letter of later date, Lord Grenville reiterated his earnest hope that Lord Minto would take no determination to resign except with the advice of his friends in England.

Neither of these letters reached him until he had adopted and acted upon a course similar to that indicated by Lord Grenville. He sent to his son a conditional resignation to be used or not, according to the judgment of his friends, and left it to the Ministry

[1] Right Hon. William Elliot of Wells.

and the Court of Directors to decide whether or no the appointment of Governor General of India should henceforth be considered as one of those dependent on the change of parties at home. In his letter to his son he said :—

'On public grounds I am sure that this distant Government ought not to change with every turn in domestic politics. The contrary principle would be productive of the greatest evil, and possibly danger, in India.

'When the political connexion of a Governor General with parties at home is found to divert him from the duties of his office it is time enough to remove him. On the question of adherence to political and personal connexion, I cannot think this office at all implicated in those considerations; but I hold that point as so sacred that, if there is a difference of opinion, or the slightest feeling on the subject among my friends at home, I hereby authorise you to resign for me. For I will not place myself or consent to stand upon doubtful ground in that respect. I received my office at the recommendation of Lord Grenville, in very peculiar circumstances, from the Court of Directors. It was not solicited; it was to me a real sacrifice of many things that are dear to me. It was a public accommodation at the time, and was generally gratifying to Government, to the Directors, and to the public. If I retain it, I shall not hold it of the favour or good will of the present Ministers; and, remaining subject to all its public duties just as before, I contract no new political obligations, form no new party engagement or connexion.'

The next fleet brought the confirmation of Lord Minto's powers from the new Ministers, coupled with expressions of an earnest desire that he should continue to administer the government of India, and a number of private letters from Windham and others urging him to remain in India. To Lord Grenville he replied :

'Calcutta: October 10, 1807.

'My dear Lord,—I feel most sensibly the kindness of your letter of April 16, which I have just received.

'My sentiments on the scene that was then passing in England are precisely the same as your own. . . . . The Ministry which has succeeded you has built not on sand but on dirt, which is a less stable foundation still. . . . . I need hardly say that I have thought much and deeply on the part which it becomes me to act on the present occasion. My first consideration was what political connexion, cemented by personal attachment, required or suggested. If I had entertained even a doubt upon that subject I should have considered that doubt as amounting to a decision, and I should have arrived in England by the ship which will carry this letter. But my judgment on that point was clear and immediate. To continue in the exercise of this office, distinguished as it is in so many essential points from any other in the Empire, holding my appointment by your express nomination and by the authority of the

Court of Directors, and deriving no new title from your successors that can either dissolve or weaken former connexion or create a new one, appears to me entirely free from any indication of separation from friends, and every profession of party connexion with those who are not so.

'I had determined, however, that there should be nothing questionable on that point, and accordingly I instructed my son to resign for me if there should be even a difference of opinion or of feeling upon it, amongst those to whom I am in heart as well as in opinion indissolubly attached. Your letter confirms my own judgment on this point, for I am persuaded you would not have contributed in any degree to the chance of subjecting me to a reproach so intolerable as that of preferring office to honour, if that delicate point had appeared to you involved in the question.

'My opinion, and I presume the universal opinion, is that frequent and light changes in the local Government of India are extremely hurtful to the interests of this country. . . . If the Ministers have the same sense of their public duties that I have of mine, the service will suffer no prejudice from the want of political connexion or even of personal cordiality between us.

. . . .

'If I find a want of support and confidence really detrimental to the interests I am charged with, and if I see reason to apprehend misconstruction of my conduct dangerous to my reputation, in either case the remedy is in my own hands. I shall not suffer it the meanwhile prudential considerations to weaken or cramp my exertions for the public service, but I may be a little more careful to preserve the means and documents of my own justification.'

This letter produced the following very hearty one from Lord Grenville:—

'Dropmore: May 24, 1808.

'My dear Lord,—I cannot express to you the satisfaction which I derived from your letter of October 10, the only one I have yet received from you since your arrival in Bengal. I had no doubt that your opinions would entirely coincide with those of your friends here, both as to the general question which has for the second time placed me at a distance from the public service of my country, and as to the particular measures which we adopted under the singular circumstances in which we were placed last year. The infatuation which still prevents the adoption of conciliatory measures towards the mass of the Irish nation, and keeps that island exposed to the double peril of civil war and foreign invasion, is indeed deeply to be lamented, nor is there any other quarter in which our prospects, alarming as they are on every side, are so gloomy as they are in respect to Ireland. But I should have still more deplored this calamity if it had indirectly led to depriving us in India of the advantage of your energy and abilities at a moment when they are likely to be so much wanted there. All my correspondence will, I trust, have shown you that, in taking the resolution of remaining there in the discharge of the duties of your most important station, you have done that which on every public and private ground is most agreeable to my wishes. But even if you had been led, from whatever motive, to have adopted in the first instance any different resolution, you would, I am confident, have altered your sentiments in that respect as soon as you learnt the danger to which it seems likely that our Indian Empire is soon to be exposed. As I have no means in my present situation to learn with any detail the information or opinions of Government on that subject (and indeed keep myself studiously at a distance from both), I speak only of what is publicly known. It is impossible to be without apprehension on a matter of such vital importance to the country, but I have great comfort in reflecting on the means of resistance which you possess, and on the decision and ability with which I am certain those means will be employed by you. I wish I could say or think the same of this country, but I verily believe I do not speak from party feelings when I declare that no nation was in my judgment ever governed by councils more deficient in every principle of true wisdom, or by men more bent on sacrificing to personal motives all those considerations by which the conduct of a Government ought to be directed. What the issue of the strange scenes now passing is ultimately to be no man can pretend to prophesy, but it is difficult even for the most sanguine mind (and mine is not a little so) to augur good from them to this country; and if evil is to come the best consolation that can attend it will be the reflection of not having contributed to it.

'With my best and most earnest wishes for your health and prosperity,

'Believe me ever, most sincerely and faithfully yours,

'GRENVILLE.'

In one of Lady Malmesbury's letters of this period, addressed to her sister at Minto, she advised her, 'to collect and arrange all her old letters, for there is nothing so curious. To consider letters as the true history of the times you should have them on both sides of the question, for we know how different is a story told by different people. Letters are more the account of prejudices and parties than the *truth*, but it is that very circumstance that makes them so amusing, as they give the *history of the passions* instead of passing judgment upon them.'

The contrast between her version of the circumstances that led to the dismissal of Ministers in 1807, and that given by Lord Grenville, forms a most apt illustration of her remark.

While his letters show a natural resentment of the unworthy methods by which his Administration had been undermined, she saw nothing but folly and obstinacy in an attempt to uphold principles against prejudices.

'Your surprise will be equal to our own,' she wrote

to Lord Minto, 'when you learn the great and wonderful events which have been happening at home. To account for (what I must call it) the infatuation of Lord Grenville, in bringing forward again a measure of which he could less than any man hope for the success after the experience he had had on the subject, is impossible. Both he and Lord Howick have admitted that, previous to this business, all went on smoothly between the King and them. But even admitting (what I do not at all believe) that he wished them away, how very strange to give him the only means that could not fail? It is truly what Sheridan said, "they built a wall against which they might run their heads, and took care to secure it by making it of the strongest materials."'

Only a few days before the Ministers went out, she had met most of their successors at Blackheath, at a dinner given by the Princess of Wales. The devotion of Lord Eldon and Mr. Perceval to her cause had long since obtained for them special favour in the eyes of Lady Malmesbury. On this occasion she described Lord Eldon as particularly agreeable, and he had assured her that ' he would not take office if he could.' *Le pauvre homme!* Within a week it was thrust upon him, and Lady Malmesbury wrote to her sister with some little bewilderment:—' The Prince, who was supposed to hate Lord Eldon and Mr. Perceval, as friends of his wife, appears to be very well pleased with the arrangement. He is all sweetness about it. This I think proves he is dying, but they do say that the Catholics in Ireland have been praying for Mrs. Fitzherbert. Nobody is pleased except Lady Grenville, who is delighted to escape from London politics to her garden at Dropmore.'

For a time a more than common bitterness was infused into the relations of politicians. The Whigs, whether Grenvillites or Foxites, were bound together by a principle and a prejudice. They believed in the justice of the Catholic claims, and they thoroughly mistrusted Canning; their opponents asserted that the safety of Protestantism depended on the King and Lord Eldon, and that the mantle of Pitt had fallen on the shoulders of Canning.

Even the correspondence interchanged between Spring Gardens and Minto assumed a sharper tone than was usual. 'You are outrageous,' wrote Lady Malmesbury to her sister, in reply to a letter brimming over with indignation at the treatment received by the dismissed Ministers, and at the loss of the cause they had espoused. 'You are almost as bad as Mrs. Neville, who called my friends "your fellows," to my face!'

Some of Lady Malmesbury's most intimate friends had come into power. Mr. Canning had taken the seals of the Foreign Office; her son, Lord Fitzharris, held the appointment of Under Secretary for Foreign Affairs; Lord Palmerston, whose footing in the Malmesbury family was almost that of a son, was in the Government; and Lady Malmesbury was not the woman to abstain from praise of her friends lest it should displease her opponents, nor did she condescend to the indifferentism which is content to say:

> Tel sera mon héros et tel sera le votre ;
> L'aigle d'une maison est un sot dans une autre.

'No Foreign Secretary,' she wrote to Lord Minto, 'has been equal to Canning—unless perhaps Fox. In these times when the fate of Europe depends on the Foreign Office in Downing Street, the labour is beyond belief; and when you add to this the House of Commons, and being up in that vile place till two or three o'clock every night, no constitution can stand it. Indeed Canning is quite knocked up, for to bodily fatigue anxiety of mind must be added, which you by experience will know how to appreciate; and Canning is naturally of a most anxious nature and not blessed with the *impassibilité* of a Grenville. Although in the opposite party, I am sure you have *la chose publique* too much at heart not to rejoice that, in the opinion of the very best judges, his talents and judgment have far surpassed even the expectation of his friends, and that all that can be done will be done; but certainly we never stood more alone. I think this an advantage, as we never yet have gained anything from our Continental alliances, and have lost a great deal often and many times. All our resources will now be applied to our own use, and as Ramsay said yesterday, "We can make war as well—and peace much better." I am glad to see they have left off their childish quarrels in the House of Commons. All the boys now think they have a right to speak and discuss and decide, and the two schoolmasters who fell upon them with their rods and chastised them well, being dead and gone, they run riot like any other schoolboys.'

Some natural rejoicing at Minto over the success of Lord Milton, the Whig candidate for the West Riding, brought down upon them the following cold water douche. 'You have heard of Milton's success against Lascelles. *I hear there is to be a petition.* All his adherents have flared about London in their orange colours. It is curious enough that this is the true Anti-Catholic colour; the old King-William badge against popery. Many of them, amongst the rest the Cavendishes, had the good taste to go to the Duke of Portland's ball all over their cockades, and somebody said they looked as if they had stopped at his stables and taken his horses' accoutrements. These are true English manners.'

We fear she must have thought Scotch principles even more objectionable than English manners, when in her next letter to Lord Minto, after congratulating him on the birth of his first grandson, she asserted that she had only consented to become his godmother on receiving a petition from the infant himself complaining of the hardship of his case. 'His mother a Presbyterian, his father he could not tell what, but he was always talking about Catholics with a tall thin gentleman supposed to be an Irish Jesuit— I consented to undertake the charge upon sole condition he was christened Martin Luther, which I think must secure him from all principles of emancipation. I trust I shall have the satisfaction of seeing him burn all his family in Smithfield some future day.'

The 'Irish Jesuit' was no other than her old friend Mr. Elliot of Wells—'Dominie' as she herself had named him—who after the recess had escaped from London to join his relations at Minto in 'making love to the rocks and glens, and preferring the notes of blackbirds, thrushes, and *cushat-doos*, to all the Catalanis and Billingtons in Europe;' and if he were a little tired of the House of Commons, 'was it wonderful for anybody who had outlived a Burke, a Pitt, and a Fox? . . . besides it has fallen into a sad snarling sort of style.'

[1] Wood-pigeons.

'And the deep mellow crush of the wood-pigeon's note
Made music that sweeten'd the calm.'—CAMPBELL.

CHAPTER III.

WHEN the new Governor General arrived in India he was to Indian politicians 'a dark horse.' Though he had taken part in all the great parliamentary questions of his time, his reputation as a public man rested mainly on his conduct of affairs while employed in the Mediterranean and at Vienna.

The few months during which he held the office of President of the Board of Control had given him a certain knowledge of current Indian business, but had hardly sufficed to make him known to Indian officials. It was generally understood that he had been in the front rank of those members of the Whig party who had been first to see that the principles endorsed by the French Jacobins were equally subversive of civil liberty and of national independence. There were disciples of the Wellesley school who augured well of a Governor General sent out by Lord Grenville, and trained under Pitt; and there were others who gladly remembered that he had sat at the feet of Burke before peace and retrenchment had been driven out of men's minds by dread of an impending dissolution of civil society.

While he was taking time as we have seen to gain

acquaintance with men and things, he himself was being subjected to the closest scrutiny, and very opposite interpretations were put on his most insignificant words and actions.

Early in November 1807, Colonel Malcolm [1] wrote to his friend Colonel Close [2] that he had lately learnt from a deep observer that Lord Minto's character appeared to be of a smooth and cautious rather than of a bold and enterprising cast. He therefore wished to know if there were any solid ground for a hint thrown out by Colonel Close himself, that the French intrigues in Persia had made a great impression on Lord Minto's mind. Whether in reply Colonel Close divulged his authority or not is unknown to us, but among Lord Minto's MSS. is the draft of a letter addressed to him (of whom Lord Minto in very early days formed a high opinion), dated a month earlier than Malcolm's enquiry, and strongly urging him to abandon a half-formed intention of leaving his post at Poonah to return to England, on grounds which proved the Governor General to be thoroughly alive to the dangers threatening India.

[1] Colonel Malcolm, afterwards General Sir John Malcolm. Well known as a soldier, diplomatist, and author of several valuable historical works on India and Persia.
[2] Colonel, afterwards Sir Barry Close, distinguished for eminent services in India as a soldier and diplomatist.

To Colonel Barry Close.

'October 11, 1807.

'The views which I entertain, not indeed of the actual state of India at the present time, but of prospects which events now in progress in Europe may possibly unfold, are such as to furnish a strong call on qualifications so tried and approved in the public service as yours.

'I do not allude at present to any expectation of an actual invasion of the British territories in India by a French army; but many circumstances denote very conclusively the extension of the enemy's views to this country.

'There is already a very active French diplomacy in Persia, which, after establishing an actual connexion with that kingdom on the subversion of our influence there, is seeking we know with great diligence the means of extending its intrigues to the Durbars of Hindostan.

'. . . One of the least doubtful consequences of any considerable success in the quarter to which the exertions of France are now directed, must be to unsettle the minds of the native princes of India—the counteraction of which must depend on the personal judgment and experience and the established weight and influence of those entrusted with British interests at the principal native courts.

'. . . I am happy to think there may as yet be a good deal of speculation in these anticipations of distant danger; but when so great an interest is depending, prudence will look beyond the scene immediately under our eye, and provide in the midst of apparent security against remote but possible danger.'

On the very day on which Malcolm had written to Close to discover the Governor General's political sentiments, the latter wrote to the President of the Board of Control a general sketch of 'foreign affairs,' including an account of the aid he had furnished to the Admiral, Sir Edward Pellew, towards an expedition intended for the capture of the Dutch squadron off Java, and the demolition of the fortifications of Crissy.

Whenever Bonaparte annexed some European State to his Empire of the West, Great Britain instantly took charge of that State's colonial possessions in the East. In 1807 Portugal and Holland had been conquered by France. Plans for the reduction of Macao, Goa, and Batavia were at once submitted to the Governor General. But for the execution of such considerable enterprises the hour had not yet struck.

Some of the considerations which decided the Indian Government to abstain from these are stated by Lord Minto in a private letter to Sir Edward Pellew:[1]

'The smallest relaxation in the economical system which is known to be *indispensable* both for the permanent restoration of our finances, and (which is more immediately in point at this moment) for avoiding

---

[1] Calcutta, November 1, 1807.

present distress or embarrassment at our treasury,—the smallest departure, I say, from that severe principle creates immediate speculation in the money market against us, and drives us back from eight to ten per cent. interest. This is one principal consideration, but far from the only one, which restrains us from engaging in plans which are attended with expense and with a great display of it, and which, although useful and desirable in themselves, are however not absolutely and obviously necessary. . . . . I certainly knew from verbal communications with the ministers whom I left in office that they thought very favourably of some designs which were under consideration for extirpating our European enemies from their military and commercial posts to the eastward of India, but we have under our eye the positive prohibition of the present ministers conveyed in their former administration against such plans. A positive prohibition of any expedition to Java and other places eastward of India was transmitted to the Indian Government when Lord Castlereagh, at present War Minister, was Secretary of State for the Colonial and War Department, and also President of the Board of Control.'

Notwithstanding these doubtful impressions of the ministerial views, the sketch of foreign affairs above mentioned contains a tolerably full outline of the policy which Lord Minto designed to adopt whenever the condition of the Company's finances admitted of such action.

'I confess that if economical considerations and

want of military force had not appeared to me conclusive against the measure' (a proposed enterprise against Batavia), 'I might not, on an occasion in my judgment so important, have permitted our *formal* incompetence to stand in the way of a great national service, but should have been disposed on forming the first provisional arrangements to exercise the best discretion I could on the several points I have alluded to, subject to the future consideration of government, and to embrace the responsibility which must often attach to the most useful public exertions.

'The main advantage that would result from such an enterprise would be the eradication of a hostile power and influence from every part of the East, and the necessity which that event would impose on our enemies and rivals, of conducting every enterprise against us immediately from Europe, without any established post of their own in this hemisphere for the various indispensable purposes of shelter, supplies, military dépôts, naval arsenal, or even political intrigue and combination.'[1]

Referring to rumours current in India of a project for the establishment of a French maritime post at the entrance of the Persian Gulf, he wrote:

'If a force adapted to the purpose (of invading India) could be collected there, gradually and in detail, either by sea or land, and the obstacles are not insurmountable either way, the trade of the Arabs and of the Persian Gulf in general is so considerable that

[1] To the President of the Board of Control.

tonnage would be found without difficulty to transport any number of troops, and the passage is short and easy to territories occupied by our professed enemies in India.

'We must not forget the nature of our tenure in this Empire, and that it would not require a great European army to disturb our security in India—20,000 French troops commanded by French officers, supplied with all the means which attend such armies, would not, I am firmly convinced, subdue us—but would create a struggle which must be attended with great present calamity, however successfully and honourably it might be overcome. For these reasons I should be sorry to see half the number of troops landed in India.

'An absolute ascendancy at the Porte or a positive conquest of Turkey, a confederacy with Russia in Oriental schemes, would tend to the furtherance, I do not say to the accomplishment, of Bonaparte's scheme against India.

'The mission of an able minister to the Court of Persia is one of the first measures that presents itself. On that point I would take the liberty of saying a few words.

'Whoever resides in Persia on the part of England should represent His Majesty and receive his instructions from his ministers. The interests of Persia are now so much connected with the politics of Europe, that no negotiation with that Court of a general nature could be carried on from hence. Yet India and the interests of England in Asia are so deeply concerned in the conduct of Persia, and so naturally implicated in its affairs, that I trust I shall be excused for suggesting two useful points in such a mission. First, that the English minister should have a close, confidential, and constant correspondence with the supreme Government in India, and should receive from that Government instructions in all matters of local concern which should not commit his Government at home on points of European policy.

'Next, that the *person* for that office should be selected here, or at least from the servants of the public in this country. None can, from their habits and from the peculiar case of their knowledge and experience, be so well qualified for the station. I confess I have one individual in my mind. I have never seen this gentleman in my life, but hazard the suggestion on a certain knowledge of Colonel Malcolm's superior qualifications.'

Of the financial prospect Lord Minto's auguries were more favourable than the Court of Directors had ventured to anticipate when he left England; 'but,' he said, 'in the event of war, estimates become wholly fallacious; and the only certain financial conclusion must be that, pending an invasion, no surplus, but on the contrary a great increase of debt, must be expected and provided for.

'If these regions ever come to be the scene of our contests with our European enemies, India will indeed be the apple in immediate view of the combatants, but Europe herself will be the real prize that is fought for. The struggle will be between two mighty Empires, and must assume a character and require an effort far beyond the scope of any contest which the E. I. Company can maintain, with resources calculated for a very different state of the world. For that occasion therefore, if it should ever arise, we shall receive our orders, and be supplied with proportionate means from England.

'Consistently, however, with this view of things, I think it right to apprise you that, if an attempt were actually made by France to occupy a post on the Coast of the Persian Gulf, or on any other point so situated as to facilitate any hostile enterprise against our Indian Empire, I should feel the occasion to be so important and so urgent as to require an immediate and powerful effort to dislodge the enemy, and to defeat his purpose, before so serious an evil had time to take root. I shall keep the possibility of such an event in mind, and shall endeavour both in my own arrangements and in my suggestions to the Admiral not to be found unprepared for it.'

In the meantime Lord Minto was able to open his official correspondence with the satisfactory assurance that he saw no reason to fear interruption to the system of public economy on which so much depended. No symptoms gave warning of any impending necessity for military intervention in the affairs of the native states. With all the more powerful princes of India the E. I. Company was in alliance; the others were not in a condition to cause uneasiness. The sole exception to the general tranquillity was a province within British territory which had been permitted to lapse into a condition of anarchy for want 'of good rule,' to borrow an expression once familiar on the Scotch Borders.

The province of Bundelcund[1] had been added to the dominions of the Company a few years before. Stretching from the Jumna to the great mountain chain that crosses India from the Ganges to the Gulf of Cambay, it includes both hill and plain—therefore also the human varieties which in unsettled times are as true to those respective localities as vultures and field-mice. On the crests of hills so high and steep that each hill is a natural fortress, stood, in the early part of this century, 150 forts more or less strong, held by as many chiefs, who rallied to their standards all the discontented spirits of the district, and the waifs and strays left behind by the ebbing tide of war. Safe in the inaccessibility of their fastnesses they spent their time much after the fashion of the Christian Knights of Europe, of whose exploits many a 'castled crag' remains to tell. They lived by plunder and rapine on their weaker neighbours—till at last a great cry went up from throughout the land which found a merciful hearing in the Council-room of Calcutta.

Lord Lake had assured the Government of Sir George Barlow that peace would never be restored to

[1] Bundelcund had been ceded in exchange for some districts in the South Mahratta country by the treaty of Bassein.

the district till the most important of these strongholds had surrendered, and Sir George had made answer that 'a certain extent of dominion, local power, and revenue would be cheaply sacrificed for tranquillity and security within a more contracted circle.'

Unhappily something more than this was likely to be sacrificed—viz. the character of the British Government for justice, and the very existence of the population it was bound to protect. When Lord Minto arrived in India Bundelcund was rapidly becoming a desert. One of his first measures, taken within a few weeks of his arrival at Calcutta, was the despatch of a military force into the disturbed districts. It was at the same time officially announced that 'the Government considered it essential, not only to the preservation of political influence over the chiefs of Bundelcund, but to the dignity and reputation of the British Government, to interfere for the suppression of internal disorder.' Writing to the Chairman [1] of the E. I. Company he said: 'These petty troubles have no very distinct object, certainly none in which the Company have any other interest than that which they must always feel in a punctual and easy collection of their revenues, and in the discharge of a duty which a Sovereign owes to its subjects, I mean that of preserving the public peace and protecting the weaker and more pacific part of the community against the oppression and violence of the stronger.

'The administration of Sir George Barlow has

[1] E. Parry, Esq.

hitherto employed on such occasions the usual and ordinary powers of legal government, aided by every effort of conciliation and persuasion to repress the insubordinate spirit of which I am speaking, and success has in general attended that just and prudent system. But in one or two instances these means have been exhausted without accomplishing the object, and an immediate necessity has arisen of resorting to military force, for the double purpose of suppressing a rebellious resistance to law, and of displaying both the power and the determination of Government to vindicate its just authority in the eyes of a people who would wait only for the assurance of an opposite character in Government, and of consequent impunity, to fall into general disobedience and anarchy.' The tone was new to ears accustomed to that of late assumed by the supreme Government, and produced an immediate and decisive effect. Many a petty Rajah rapidly discovered his interest to lie on the side of order, and long before the British force succeeded in quelling the fiercer spirits of the hills, cultivation and peace had returned to the plains.

The reduction of the most important of the mountain strongholds was not effected till after several campaigns, nor without considerable losses—'losses particularly in officers,' wrote Lord Minto, 'for which one feels inconsolable for such an object. That object, however, it had become indispensable to accomplish, and its necessity is strongly confirmed by the difficulty which has attended it.'

THE NATIVE RACES.

While the rumours of intended attacks upon our Eastern possessions acquired with every day greater consistency and probability, the attention of the Government was earnestly directed to the maintenance of such relations with their Indian subjects as would tend to obtain their loyal support.

Of the races subject to British rule, the most adverse to our power was necessarily the Mahommedan. To the Hindoos, though foreigners and conquerors, we were nevertheless the justest and gentlest who had ever held sway over them. To the Mahrattas we were a formidable danger indeed, but one the magnitude of which they did not as yet thoroughly appreciate. Among the Mussulmans alone, especially of the higher class, there existed an immense and weighty body of irreconcilable discontent, the natural result of the establishment of the Company's Government over a great portion of the Peninsula, to the extinction of the Mussulman power and the ruin of the individual influence, consideration, and fortunes of the race in which the principal native energies reside. 'In their minds had been planted all the hostile dispositions that are bred of despair.' Instruments therefore could not be wanting to foment real discontent, or to create artificial grievances. Some of this disaffection, it was hoped, would subside by the mere lapse of time, by the gradual extinction of old influences and the growth of new interests in the soil and prosperity of the country, originating in and dependent upon the British Government. Such had been the case in Bengal, where the same course was run from the demolition of the Mussulman power to the steady establishment of our exclusive authority, and the perfect identification of the mass of the people, their interests and feelings, with our government. 'If we avoid,' wrote Lord Minto to the Chairman of the East India Company,[1] 'as we shall with scrupulous attention, every measure that might furnish our enemies with even a pretence to work upon, —if we maintain discipline with a firm hand, and keep a watchful and observant eye on every attempt to practise on the prejudices of the native soldier—the danger will be confined to those general circumstances inherent in our situation, for which, as there is no remedy, it is neither profitable nor manly to make them the topics of fruitless dread and lamentation. . . . The only successful engine of sedition in any part of India must be that of persuading the people that our Government entertains hostile and systematic designs against their religion. This persuasion, if it could be established in Bengal, would be as fatal there as on the coast; but the difference is that nobody in Bengal is interested in propagating that falsehood, and to incur danger here we must ourselves furnish probable cause for sincere alarm.' The belief that 'this engine' could be successfully worked had been confirmed by recent events; for though the Vellore massacres were no doubt in part attributable to the general state of disaffection and humiliation of the Mahommedan population of the country, it was clearly proved that the sentiment on

[1] Lord Minto to E. Parry, Esq., September 1807.

which the agents traded was a universal though unfounded dread that the British Government was about to exact a forcible conversion of the Sepoys to Christianity. What to the natives could seem less incredible, or indeed more natural? Had not Hindoos seen their holy places defiled by Mahommedans? Why should Christians spare either the one or the other?

To calm such apprehensions, the Court of Directors had declared in a despatch,[1] dated May 1807, their firm resolve to uphold throughout their dominions the most perfect toleration of all creeds and rites; and at the same time they clearly stated the position of Government in respect to the missionaries.

'In the whole course of our administration of the Indian territories it has been our known and declared principle to maintain a perfect toleration of the various religious systems which prevailed in them; to protect the followers of each in the undisturbed enjoyment of their respective opinions and usages; neither to interfere with them ourselves, nor to suffer them to be molested by others. When we afforded our countenance and sanction to missionaries who have from time to time proceeded to India for the purpose of propagating the Christian religion, it was far from being in our contemplation to add the influence of our authority to any attempts they might make; for on the contrary we were perfectly aware that the progress of such conver-

---

[1] Instructions addressed to the Governor of Fort St. George, May 29, 1807.

sion will be slow and gradual, arising more from a conviction of the principles of our religion itself, and from the pious examples of its teachers, than from any undue influence or from the exertions of authority, which are never to be resorted to in such cases.'

In accordance with these instructions it became the duty of the Indian Government, not long after the Governor General's arrival in Calcutta, to take certain measures which had the result of embroiling him with the missionaries of Serampore, and with a party in Calcutta and in London of growing importance.

It is well known that Christian missionaries had long been familiar to the populations of Southern India. Roman Catholic missions had been established since the beginning of the seventeenth century in the Portuguese and French settlements on the west coast of the Peninsula. In comparatively recent times some Protestant missionaries, Danes and Germans, had established themselves at Madras, whence a few individuals made their way to Bengal. But it was not till the last decade of the eighteenth century that an Englishman was found to carry the Gospel to the natives of India. William Carey was the first English missionary to Bengal; and his life is a happy illustration of what may be done to overcome the most apparently insurmountable obstacles by a noble enthusiasm and an ardent character. Carey was the son of a shoemaker in Northamptonshire; a Baptist by creed. Alone and destitute of resources he arrived in Bengal, where without the licence of the Company no one was permitted to reside, but where, nevertheless, he remained on sufferance until, being joined by others who desired to assist in the good work, he and they removed together to the Danish settlement of Serampore. There they preached in the native languages, formed schools for the young, set up a printing-press, and a paper manufactory (this was the industry by which they lived), and devoted all their remaining time and energies to the translation of the Holy Scriptures and the dissemination of tracts in the various native dialects. Soon after Lord Minto's arrival, some of these publications attracted the attention of Government, and it being undeniable that they were calculated to offend the feelings of the native population, containing as they did offensive attacks on the Hindoo mythology and the Mussulman Prophet, the Secretary to Government received instructions to communicate to the Rev. Dr. Carey, the leading member of the mission at Serampore, a resolution arrived at by the Governor General in Council, to place their press under regulations, and to suspend the practice of public preaching by natives in the native dialects at the seat of government.

In an official letter addressed by Mr. Edmonstone to Dr. Carey it is stated, that 'the issue of publications and the public delivery of discourses of the nature above alluded to, are evidently calculated to produce consequences in the highest degree detrimental to the tranquillity of the British dominions in India, and it becomes the indispensable duty of the British Government to arrest the progress of any proceedings of that nature.

In the present instance this objection is enforced by the necessity of maintaining the public faith, which under the express injunctions of the Legislature has been repeatedly pledged to leave the native subjects of the Company in India to the full, free, and undisturbed exercise of their respective religions.' The letter concluded by expressing the Governor General's expectation 'that the press would be removed to the Presidency, where alone the same control that is established over presses sanctioned by the Government can be duly exercised.'[1]

Though the action of the Government was in strict accordance with the instructions issued by the Court of Directors, it raised a storm of angry feeling which temporarily obscured all sense of justice, and led to a remarkable oblivion of the Apostolical injunction, 'Be pitiful, be courteous.'

'This is the first instance,' says the author of a well-known biographical work,[2] 'in which the Government of India brought forward the plea of being bound by a *pledge* to grant the natives the undisturbed exercise of their "respective religions." No such pledge was ever exacted by the natives or granted by the Government. British rule was established in India by the sword and the sword alone, and at no period were the conquerors in a position which obliged them to give pledges to the conquered.'

Dean Milman, in the opening chapter of his 'History

---

[1] Letter to Rev. Dr. Carey, September 8, 1807.
[2] *Lives and Times of Carey, Marshman, and Ward.*

of Christianity,' remarks that the Romans conquered like savages, but ruled like philosophic statesmen. 'The kingdoms which were won by the most unjustifiable aggression were for the most part governed with a judicious union of firmness and conciliation, in which the conscious strength of irresistible power was tempered with the wisest respect for national usages.'

Some such rule as that under which Christianity found its appointed time appeared to Lord Minto not unworthy of a British Government though deriving its title from the sword.

When a public man is better liked than his measures, it is not uncommon to hear them ascribed to bad advisers. So it was in this case. But Lord Minto was not willing to accept a defence based on his ignorance of matters which he was bound to know; still less on his docility in accepting views inculcated by others. He had, he said, after deliberate investigation and reflection, thought it his duty to prohibit, for a time, public preaching by natives for the purpose of conversion, and also to prevent the dissemination of publications in the native languages, containing scurrilous abuse of persons and things holy in the estimation of our Indian subjects, whether Hindoo or Mahommedan. He had not, he confessed, been aware of the ruin which a removal of the mission press from Serampore would inflict on the missionaries, 'owing to the peculiar circumstances of their property' there. No sooner was this inevitable consequence of the intended measure seen than the order for it was rescinded. It was due to Dr. Leyden,

the eminent Orientalist, that at this juncture the
Governor General and the leading members of the
mission were brought face to face, and that the latter
were enabled to state their case personally to the
Governor General. Dr. Leyden stood high in the estimation of Lord Minto, by whom his learning and his
energy of character were fully appreciated. Moreover
there was a link between them of which both acknowledged the strength. Both came from 'Teviot-water,'
a fact held sacred even on the banks of the Ganges.
Dr. Leyden, as the personal friend of Mr. Marshman
and Dr. Carey, advised them to lose no time in crossing
the river to the pleasant park of Barrackpore; there to
seek an interview with the 'great chief,' for the osten-
sible purpose of offering him their translation of the
Ramayan. With knowledge of men, not always possessed by students of books, Dr. Leyden had seen that
sympathetic relations in one class of subjects would
indubitably lead to smoother ones in others. So it
proved. The conversation passed easily from literary
topics to those specially interesting to the missionaries,
and when the interview was over, both parties retained
impressions of mutual good-will. His visitors recognised in Lord Minto the candour and simplicity that
were natural to him; he found in them a sincerely
pious zeal, tempered with discretion, which won his
respect. The Governor General declared that nothing
was further from his intentions, or more foreign to the
views of Government, than to affect in the smallest
degree either the interests of the missionary body, or

the personal comfort and convenience of those worthy men, and he remained satisfied with their assurance that the works hereafter to be printed at Serampore should be previously submitted to the revision and sanction of Government. The press therefore remained at Serampore. It may be that he felt a little disappointment when, a few days after these events, an address was presented by the missionaries to the Government of Serampore, in which the concessions made to them were ascribed to the particular interposition of Divine Providence and the instrumentality of the Danish Governor. 'I confess,' Lord Minto good-humouredly remarked, 'that I thought it was to the Governor General in Council that gratitude was due, but I suppose I was wrong.'

Nevertheless his kindly sentiments towards the individuals belonging to the mission and his respect for their aims never altered. They are often mentioned in his correspondence as his 'very good friends,' and though a sense of public duty had imposed upon him the obligation of checking their over-zealous haste, his personal feelings ensured to their literary efforts his constant and warmest encouragement.

The whole question as between Calcutta and Serampore was disposed of in less than a month from the date of Mr. Edmonstone's despatch. In reply to the memorial of the missionaries—drawn up after the interview at Barrackpore—he was directed to state that 'the Governor General in Council was fully convinced of the rectitude of the intentions of the Society of Missionaries, and that the precautions which Government deemed it necessary to adopt against the unlimited employment of the press, proceed exclusively from the duty imposed on Government of reserving to itself the authority of determining what publications may, or may not, expose the public tranquillity to hazard, or involve a violation of public faith, instead of leaving the decision of such important questions to the judgment of others.'

But in the meanwhile 'the Battle of the Missions' was raging fiercely in London, where it occasioned the publication of more than twenty-five pamphlets; the charge, repeated again and again in them, against the Government of India being that of a proved desire to root up the Serampore mission and extirpate Christianity from India.

The Indian Government had distinctly stated that it had no desire to impede the circulation of the Scriptures in the native dialects, 'if unaccompanied by any comments on the religions of the country.' This was construed into a prohibition to carry the Gospel among the natives of India; though the missionaries were all the time very properly using the privilege accorded to them to print and circulate the Scriptures freely.

Lord Minto himself took great personal interest in the translations of the Scriptures proceeding from the Serampore press. In a public and published discourse, on the occasion of his annual visit to the College of Fort William, after warmly praising the efforts of the mission to cultivate the Chinese language, he said: ' I must not omit to recommend the learned and pious persons who have accomplished, for the future benefit, we may hope, of that immense and populous region, Chinese versions in the Chinese character of the Gospels of Matthew, Mark, and Luke, throwing open that precious mine with all its moral and religious treasures to the largest associated population in the world.'

Not long afterwards a specimen of printing in the Chinese characters by the natives employed on the Serampore press won Lord Minto's hearty admiration. He would gladly have headed the list of subscribers to the first work in the Chinese language to be published at Serampore—a translation of the Gospel of St. Matthew; but on finding that he could not ' step out of himself and separate his private from his public character,' and that objections were made to his appearing in the undertaking in his public capacity, he subscribed largely to a copy of Confucius about to emanate from that press, desiring that the profits derived from the sale of that book should be applied to the publication of the Scriptures. The idea was at once taken up, and the friendly spirit displayed by Lord Minto was cordially acknowledged. In a few days subscriptions to the amount of 2,000*l.* were obtained, intended to be applied collectively to the publication of the Scriptures; besides, we are told, direct contributions to the extent of 300*l.* Every gentleman in Calcutta was ready to add his name to the list, Lord Minto's example having ' served to stimulate the liberality of the community.'[1]

[1] *Lives and Times of Carey, Marshman, and Ward.*

At a later period of his administration, the Government subscribed a sum of 10,000 rupees towards defraying the expense of translating the Scriptures into the Malay language.

So much for the prohibition of the sacred Scriptures in British India.

The good understanding arrived at with Dr. Carey and Mr. Marshman was not sufficient to allay the irritation caused by the censorship instituted by the Government over the publications of the Serampore press. There were men in Calcutta whose views were of a more worldly nature, and who were by no means unwilling to cause trouble to the Government by assuming some of its functions to themselves. The Rev. Claudius Buchanan, one of the chaplains of the Presidency, was prominent among these. Though making use of the Serampore press, and in friendly relations with the missionaries, nothing could be less like the simplicity of their tenets than those held by him. In a memoir, 'on the expediency of introducing an ecclesiastical establishment into India for the benefit of our own countrymen, and as a foundation for the ultimate civilisation of the natives,' of which Mr. Buchanan was the author, he wrote: 'An archbishop is wanted for India—a sacred and exalted character, surrounded by his bishops, of ample revenue and extensive sway. . . . We want something royal in a spiritual and temporal sense for the abject subjects of this great Eastern empire to look up to.' Again: 'When once our national Church shall have been confirmed in India, the members of that Church will be the best qualified to advise the State as to the means by which from time to time the civilisation of the natives is to be effected.' The belief that the institution of a hierarchy would be efficacious in producing the conversion of the Hindoos was so firmly held by Mr. Buchanan that, as it was related at the time, while rejecting a suggestion that he might himself be the first archbishop of the East, he exclaimed, ' Place the mitre on any head. Never fear, it will do good among the Hindoos!' To Lord Minto, as a Scotchman, it may have been hard to perceive that the placing of a mitre on one head would inevitably infuse Christianity into another; but he fully recognised the meaning of the claim set up by Mr. Buchanan on behalf of his fellow-Churchmen to advise the State on the means to be adopted for the civilisation of the natives, and he did not therefore share the surprise of the simple-minded men of Serampore when they discovered, at a subsequent period, that Mr. Buchanan had never been entirely reconciled to the influence obtained by the press *for Dissenters.*

A memorial, drawn up by Mr. Buchanan for presentation to the Governor General in Council in reference to the measures lately adopted by Government with reference to the Serampore mission, was forwarded to the Court of Directors, with the comments and explanations of the Governor General and his colleagues. These appear to have satisfactorily disposed of the questions at issue. But it is remarkable that while the statements in this memorial were categorically refuted at the time, they have reappeared again and again with all the virulence peculiar to ecclesiastical censures. As late as June 1845, the 'Calcutta Review' contained an article entitled 'The early or exclusively Oriental period of Government Education in Bengal,' repeating the three leading charges in the paper of 1807;—that the Government had virtually suppressed the circulation of the Scriptures and the preaching of the Gospel;—that it only consented with extreme reluctance to abandon an intended removal of the missionary press from Serampore upon the remonstrances of the Danish Governor, who felt the honour and sovereignty of his nation to be involved in the issue;—that the consequence of the *imprimatur* imposed by Government was the submission of religious works to their native officers.

The charge of having suppressed the preaching of the Gospel Lord Minto disposed of as a misrepresentation of facts. 'I suspended the public preaching of natives to natives in the native languages at the seat of government, because, with the zeal of proselytes, they preached the same inflammatory matter and the same exhortations to civil dissensions as had been printed. The press is not suspended, but is kept under regulation. Preaching is suspended, but is not intended to be finally prohibited.'

The second charge, according to Lord Minto, 'did not contain a particle of truth.' Though the press was set up in Danish territory, the only market for its publications was British India; though the leading missionaries resided at Serampore, they were British subjects; Dr. Carey holding moreover an official appointment under Government, that of Professor of Sanscrit and Bengalee in the College of Fort William. Under such conditions it never occurred to anyone concerned that the honour of the Danish Government could be affected by the transactions that have been related, nor that the amicable relations between the Governor of Serampore and the Government of Calcutta were endangered because the former had made friendly representations to the latter concerning the peaceable demeanour and general good conduct of his neighbours, the British missionaries residing at Serampore.

To the third subject of complaint, that the *imprimatur* established by Government over the publications of the press necessitated the submission of works on the subject of our holy religion to the native agents of the Government, Lord Minto replied, that the intervention of a native was not necessary to enable members of Government to form their own opinions of writings produced in Persian and Bengalee; and that the regulation complained of already existed towards all the presses of Calcutta. If, therefore, the right of the Government to exercise an *imprimatur* over the press of Serampore were denied on the ground taken up by Mr. Buchanan that the civil power was incompetent to form a sound judgment of religious works, Lord Minto observed that the next step must be an ecclesiastical censorship of the press and a return to the dark ages. He disclaimed all desire to judge of the orthodoxy or the error involved in any theological propositions, but he asserted that it was in the capacity, and that it was the duty, of Government to decide whether or no the publication of certain propositions under the existing conditions could be continued with safety to the State. In illustration of his opinion that they could not be so, he quoted in a Government letter to the Secret Committee the following passage from a religious pamphlet published by Mr. Buchanan:—

'The Mahommedans profess a religion which has ever been characterised by political bigotry and intemperate zeal. In this country that religion still retains the character of its bloody origin, particularly among the higher classes. Whenever the Mahommedan feels his religion touched, he grasps his dagger. This spirit was seen in full operation under Tippoo's government, and it is not soon extinguished.'

It might well be asked whether such a passage as this should not reasonably induce the licenser to withdraw his *imprimatur* from a book, which, although containing no proposition that is not 'orthodox and true, and entitled on that account to a severely ecclesiastical *imprimatur*,' might nevertheless sharpen every Mahommedan dagger and plunge them into every Christian bosom in the country?[1]

[1] A somewhat amusing instance of the carelessness as to accuracy which distinguished the opposition to Lord Minto's measures is to be found in the accusation that he had manifested an intention to suppress the *Christian prophecies*. The fact was that an advertisement, sent by Mr. Buchanan to the Government *Gazette*, of the intended publication of a series of sermons on the Christian prophecies,

Lord Minto's correspondence from London left him no doubt as to the fierceness of the controversy that had arisen out of his policy towards the missionaries; it had extended to the Court of Directors; but he was confidentially informed that he had not only the entire approval, but the warm admiration, of four-fifths of the Court for the courage with which he had adopted a policy at once firm and moderate, though certain to provoke rancorous hostility to his government. It has been said that to some such hostility may be attributed the fact of Lord Minto's administration having failed to obtain the measure of public approbation which was its just due. But at the time not a few of those statesmen whose opinions he most highly valued considered that he was entitled to the warmest thanks of the public. Perhaps it was only to statesmen that the full extent of the danger to our empire in India was apparent, not alone from the immediate

delivered by himself in the Presidency churches, was suspended, according to the usual practice of that paper, until the MS. had been submitted to the superintendent of the Company's press.

The MS. never was so submitted, because Mr. Buchanan thought it his duty to protest against the civil revision of any theological work. He, however, represented his sermons to have been suppressed, and then, 'by a graceful negligence of style,' said Lord Minto, 'he made it appear that the prophecies themselves had been suppressed, and the Government was threatened with their accomplishment as a matter of great alarm and affliction to themselves.' What the contents of the sermons might be, Lord Minto would not undertake to say, as he had had no opportunity of perusing them. The Christian prophecies would certainly not have been objected to, and the so-called suppression of the sermons was due entirely to Mr. Buchanan's scruples of conscience which did not permit him to submit them to Government.

risk of collision with native sentiment, but from the pretensions of a section of the Anglo-Indian community to a dictatorial supremacy over the policy of the State. A private letter, addressed by Lord Minto to the Chairman of the East India Company, who was also a member of the Society for Missions to Africa and the East, and who was therefore naturally to be supposed well affected to their cause, shows that the Governor General was prepared uncompromisingly to assert the views on which his Government had acted.

'Let me recommend to your serious consideration the principal publications which have issued from the Serampore press, in the native languages, the sole effect of which was not to convert, but to alienate, the professors of both religions prevalent amongst the natives of this country. Pray read especially the miserable stuff addressed to the Gentoos, in which, without one word to convince or to satisfy the mind of the heathen reader, without proof or argument of any kind, the pages are filled with hell fire, and hell fire, and still hotter fire, denounced against a whole race of men for believing in the religion which they were taught by their fathers and mothers, and the truth of which it is simply impossible it should ever have entered into their minds to doubt. Is this the doctrine of our faith? In saying that it is not mine I am well assured that I express your sentiments as well as my own. If there are two opinions among Christians on this point, I can only say that I am of the sect which believes that a just God will condemn no being without individual guilt. But is this a judicious course to pursue for the purpose of conversion? The remainder of this tract seems to aim principally at a general massacre of the Brahmins of this country. A total abolition of caste is openly preached. A proposal to efface a mark of caste from the foreheads of soldiers on parade has had its share in a massacre of Christians. Is it possible that your Government should be required to countenance public exhortations addressed to a Gentoo nation to efface at once, not a little spot of yellow paste from the forehead, but the whole institution of caste itself, that is to say, their whole scheme of civil polity as well as their fondest and most rooted religious tenets? This is to be accomplished by coarse and scurrilous invective against the most revered order of Hindoo society and addressed to that order itself.

'I leave you to form your own judgment on these performances, which will be that of a Christian gentleman. . . . I am no enemy to the progress of Christianity in India. It is the way, I observe, of some who are personally engaged in the work of conversion to confound any little check in correction of their own errors with opposition or hostility to their purpose, and to call out Atheism, Deism, and above all persecution, whenever a slip in their own conduct has required to be rectified. . . . I do not think we should be justified in refusing the dispensation of the Christian revelation to this great country for our interest or security, but I am not equally ready to sacrifice the great interests which are confided to me to a blind principle of complaisance towards every indiscretion which zeal or negligence may commit.

'In my opinion the missionaries would advance better by mixing with the people, by habituating them individually to the more amiable points of their doctrine, and attracting to the latter by its beneficent influences, rather than by the mysteries and dogmas of their faith. I have some reason to think that the press and the pulpit have not worked well. In many instances I know that those who have not been made angry have been made merry by these engines of conversion. When the truth of his faith is questioned the Mahommedan frowns and the Hindoo smiles.'

A more formal document—namely, a general letter to the Secret Committee—ends thus : ' With regard to translations of the Scriptures into all the languages of the world, it is a work with which we warmly sympathise, and to which every countenance will be cordially afforded by us; but if the pupils of Mr. Buchanan should employ themselves in translating the wretched compositions which we have transmitted to your Honourable Company, we shall not think that they advance the cause either of religion or of letters, and they must expect no countenance from us either as Christians, as scholars, as statesmen, or as gentlemen.'

Serampore passed from Danish into British hands in January 1808, just a month after the date of Lord Minto's letter to Mr. Parry. Immediately on the receipt in India of the intelligence of a rupture between England and Denmark, the order to occupy

Serampore was given to the Company's forces. Writing of this event to Mr. Parry, Lord Minto said: 'Our worthy neighbours, the Serampore missionaries, have experienced no sort of inconvenience from our occupation of that factory. I flatter myself I am on the best possible footing with them, at least in temporal concerns. If they should be less satisfied on other points, I may hope, from the religion they and I profess, that charity will accompany zeal.'

Two years later he actively interfered to promote the extension of the ministrations of the missionary body to the great cities of Northern India.

In the course of 1810, permission was sought of the Government to establish missions in the N. W. Provinces. Two gentlemen in the Serampore mission desired to proceed to Agra and Delhi. The Governor General in Council stated that he saw no objection to allow them to do so, but desired them to make the application for leave to proceed there, *saying nothing of anything else.* This sentence was understood to mean that as their objects, more distinctly stated, might provoke a prohibition from the Court of Directors, Lord Minto took it on his own responsibility to give them the desired permission.

It seems strange that this act of grace, instead of being grateful to the missionaries, drew from the Rev. — Ward the comment: 'Now we are likely to get stations fixed with the public permission of Government, and we shall be tolerated like toads, and not hunted down like wild beasts.'

At that very time no one, however influential, was allowed to travel in India without a passport, or to reside there without a direct license from the Court of Directors. There are copies at Minto of several letters in which Lord Minto expresses regret that he cannot give the permission requested by residents at Pondicherry to travel in the Company's dominions; and in a letter addressed to one of his family he mentions the receipt of a somewhat harsh order for the immediate return of a gentleman to England, who had gone out in the same ship as himself, had lived eight months in his house, and had subsequently held some small appointment in Calcutta. That he had so done without license was no doubt an irregularity, and the orders of the Court had to be obeyed; but no evidence remains that the gentleman, who submitted to the undoubted authority of law, felt himself thereby to have had anything in common with a wild beast.

Yet when, in 1811, some missionaries who had arrived in India without license, though not without knowledge of the Company's regulations, were requested to depart, an outcry was raised against the persecution of the Government, and the irreconcilable enmity of its members to Christianity.

CHAPTER IV.

BEFORE the transactions described in the last chapter came to an end, Lord Minto had become familiar with Indian life. He had had experience of summer and winter, had found the cold weather delightful, save for the insatiable voracity of the mosquitoes that came in swarms from the cool air to the warmer house; and in the heat of summer had cooled and consoled himself 'by thinking of Minto and of those who were enjoying the green pleasures and calm comforts of that chosen spot. So pray be as happy there all of you as ever you can, for your enjoyments are my best punkahs, and your repose is my best recreation in this torrid zone of trouble and fatigue.'

One of the greatest trials of absence in those days consisted in the long interval which necessarily elapsed between the despatch of letters and their delivery in distant lands: it was sensibly enhanced by the uncertainty attending on their ever reaching their destination. The safest course was to entrust them to the Indian fleets, which only sailed twice or thrice a year, but which, being escorted by a convoy, generally arrived in safety. Next to the fleet, a King's ship was preferred; but chance ships or single merchantmen were deemed too liable to be captured, to be safe depositaries of letters. When these were of importance duplicates were generally sent by different vessels; but, in spite of all precautions, lamentations were perpetually recurring over the loss of letters, of many a gift of 'orient pearl and barbaric gold,' and, worse than all, of the ships that bore them, which found their way to the ports of our enemies and still more often to the bottom of the sea

Some smaller inconveniences there were in the slowness of communications that had occasionally a comic aspect, as when letter-writers in London, who had missed the May fleet, served up cold at Christmas the materials which six months before had been far more highly spiced; or when their correspondents in India congratulated them a year after date on events already repented of.

'*February* 8, 1808.'[1] Our last letters from home were still dated June, but we expect a fleet very soon. It will bring packets from you all, I trust. I may safely say that the single interesting occupation I have (bating my business, which is becoming interesting enough) is thinking of you and all your occupations. I am ravenous for all details and particulars, especially such as are agreeable to you, within doors and without.

'Nothing has come from England since the June fleet which sailed the 23rd of that month, and we are

[1] To Lady Minto.

wondering that some vessel or other has not been despatched to tell us of the events which have happened since that time. We have had no letters overland, the road being shut that way as you know, and all the news we live upon is rumour and surmise from such places as Aleppo, Bagdad, Bushire, Muscat, and other out-of-the-world regions. The war with Denmark came from Aleppo, where the Danish consul received it from Constantinople.'

It was not till April 14 that the long looked-for letters arrived. 'It is totally impossible to describe the excessive delight which they have bestowed upon us. In the first place I never received such a number of letters in my life; and I never received any more precious in every possible way. I have been reading and re-re-reading all yesterday and to-day. Thank God you were all well on September 8. I assure you it is a nervous thing to open letters after an interval of several months. . . .'

The tone of the family letters was especially jubilant, for they gave the news of the birth of Lord Minto's first grandchild—the son of his eldest son—and the answers from India were no less joyful.

To the young mother Lord Minto wrote: 'I have so many things to thank you for, I hardly know where to begin: first, for dancing with me at Kelso; secondly, for marrying graceless; thirdly, for making him so good a wife,—I really am much obliged to you for that; fourthly, for being such a good, dutiful, beautiful daughter to your good mother, God bless her! fifthly and sixthly, for two letters to me; and lastly, but indeed this is scarce worth mentioning, for being the mother of Gilbert's son.

'.... It is really hard upon me to have been away just when all this was about. I don't believe any of you could be more worthy of the occasion, or busier, or more frightened, or more nervous, or more delighted, or a more sincere admirer of the boy's fine figure. It certainly is very hard upon me; that you must allow. Still this most happy event has given me many a pleasant hour, and affords such a quiet dulcifying sort of satisfaction of mind as even the pains of absence cannot sour. I may live to toss him about and break his bones yet, though his father will have been beforehand with me. . . . One command that I lay upon you all is that he shall on no pretence whatever go to a Harlequin Farce till I return, and that then he shall sit between his two grandfathers; and three well-entertained babes we shall be. How we shall laugh—all three—except a few compassionate tears which I may shed at the cruel crosses of poor Columbine and at the parental distress of Pantaloon.

'Now, to be serious, I beg you to make the boy love grandpapa with all his little baby heart. . . .'

His letter to Lady Minto on the same occasion ends thus: 'The perfect happiness of the worthless pair, Gilbert and Mary, is really a sort of felicity to us all that makes me feel independent of fate and fortune. Whatever fall out, the family bark seems in harbour.

Gilbert himself is happy, and the rest can never want a home or friend.

> 'Guid angels keep young Minto's heir,
> And a' thae lads and lasses spare.
> I'll surely trust when I'm nae mair,
>   The bairns shall prove,
> In yon true fallow's bosom there,
>   A Parent's luve.'

A few extracts from his letters to his family will suffice to give us a glimpse of what may be called his private life—in all respects so different from any of the varied experiences of former years.

'April 1808.

'I continue to enjoy Barrackpore, and to find it a real consolation. My life would be very comfortless without it. I hardly ever go out at Calcutta. There is but one dusty drive, and I have hardly time for that . . . All that is to be done with *people* belongs to Calcutta. At Barrackpore I may read my despatches in peace and quiet the livelong day, and write what requires my own pen without interruption. Accordingly these are my employments from early in the morning till dinner at eight, excepting only a walk at sunset to catch the breeze along the river-side. My walks are generally, I may say next to always, alone; for John and all the young party are at that time hunting jackals, and very fit they should. The evenings as well as the mornings have been very delightful, and as the walk is the principal event of my Barrackpore day, it answers extremely well, though it would be improved, I confess, by a lady of my own age under my arm to tell how I like the breeze, and the moon, and the planets, and such pretty prattle . . .

'The principal defect in my comfort here is the total want of anything that can be called society to me. I am never alone, I mean when out of my shop; but there is seldom anybody who, either in age, tastes, or any other article, has anything in connexion with me; so that except on business there is a total and constant suspension of everything that is properly myself. This is nobody's fault but my own, for what business have I to grow old? . . .

'I have lately had a most agreeable visit from Mr. Smith, 'Bobus,'[1] the Advocate General. Though he is not exactly my contemporary, he has a great deal of excellent conversation that is a feast for all ages. We think alike too on European politics, which is rare here; and for that reason, as well as from a sense of propriety, I abstain entirely from that topic; but it is not unpleasant to be agreed with once in a way when one gets into good company.'

One of Lord Minto's most characteristic attributes was his sympathy with youth. He was adored by young people, and was equally the confidant of their

---

[1] Mr. Robert Smith, father of the late Lord Lyveden, and brother of the Rev. Sydney Smith. 'Bobus,' though he preferred a solitary to a social life, was well known to have no small measure of the same gifts for which Sydney was celebrated. One day when the Governor General complained of the torment he suffered from the mosquitoes at dinner, Bobus had a resource to suggest: 'You should always contrive to have some blooming youth fresh from England to sit next to you. They are sure to go to him.

pleasures and their troubles. If an imprudent marriage had to be condoned, it was his part to write a soothing letter to an angry parent, and to insinuate as gently as he could that, 'after all, a man marries to please himself, and not his father:' but when by vice and folly sons brought shame and ruin on their families, and cut themselves off from an honourable career, though his sympathy with the sufferers never failed, he was inflexible in the course he deemed due to the interests of the public service. The disclosure of some very grave irregularities in the conduct of the cadets at the military college of Barasut led to the ejection of some of the offenders and the removal of the governor. His successor met with a degree of resistance on his first appointment sufficient to daunt a keener reformer, whereupon Lord Minto wrote him the following letter, which inculcates on a public officer the system he always advocated in private education :—'As few rules and regulations as possible, but unswerving obedience to those that are necessary.' He was wont to say that good temper, more than any other virtue, is the result of habit, and that half the domestic unhappiness in the world is caused by a captious and irritating rule in early life.

To Captain Malcolm Macleod, Commanding at Barasut.

'Barrackpore: July 26, 1808.

'Dear Sir,—You will receive along with this a public letter, which will afford you sufficient support in carrying the proposed indispensable reforms into immediate effect. . . . I do not at all agree with you in thinking that your first arrival at Barasut is an unfavourable time for correcting these abuses; on the contrary, it was entirely expected that the change of the Commanding Officer was to be accompanied by a change of management; and the best policy is to *begin* with the same system which you are afterwards to pursue.

'I should wish, both for your own ease and for the benefit of the institution, that you may enjoy the goodwill and regard of the young men under your charge. But *essential* points must not be sacrificed to that object. Indeed, it is not the way to obtain it; the respect, and even the regard of boys is always lost by concession, and by any appearance of feeble conduct, which they are very quick at perceiving. Great command of temper is necessary; they should be dealt with as *men*, and as *gentlemen*. But perfect *steadiness* in material things is the quality most sure of obtaining not only their submission, but their respect and affection. I would not trouble and harass them much about trifles, but be inflexible in matters of importance. . . . . It will not be enough to *prohibit* private entertainments by an order; you will have to *enforce* the prohibition by *seeing* that it is not infringed. Your adjutants must occasionally visit their quarters, and take every other means to know whether this abuse is still practised.

'I flatter myself that, with every proper attention to conciliation, you will not lose sight of that firmness without which such a republic as you have to govern is sure of running into anarchy.

'The want of that one quality was your predecessor's only defect; and that defect has brought this important institution into discredit, besides drawing ruin upon a number of young men, and a severe affliction upon a number of families.'

In another letter on the conduct of the cadets, he wrote: 'I hear with regret of cruel and oppressive conduct to the natives. This I consider as ungenerous and unworthy of gentlemen.'

Occasionally it was the unreasonable desires of parents on behalf of their sons which caused him matter of regret. In a letter to Lady Minto he says: 'There is nothing in this country that a young *King's* officer *can* hold except an appointment as aide-de-camp. It is no sort of advantage to him to get it; on the contrary, it takes a young man entirely out of his profession, makes him idle, luxurious, and expensive, the consequence of which, I observe, is debt and distress. No parent at a distance will see the thing in that light, and I have been obliged to place several young men in that situation, with the consciousness that I was doing them a real injury in the shape of a very great favour. . . .

'The young men here would be better off if there were neither horses nor dogs in the world. . . . A hundred pounds is no violent price here for a dog; and as for horses, I wanted a quiet pad for my own hack, only just to carry me safe to cover, and a horse was brought for trial the other day who was nearly blind, so as to start at every bush, and not over sure. However they *only* asked 300*l.* for him, and I should have been tempted by the bargain if John had not advised me against a blind pad. Yet a horse I must have at any price, for I ride at least twice a year. I have just performed on a *charger*, having presented honorary colours to the 15th regiment of native infantry at Barrackpore, mounted on a war-horse decorated with gold embroidered housings, besides the ornaments which shone on my own head and heels. Prince Esterhazy, at the head of the Garde Noble, is a sloven to my resplendence. Then, as my respected friend, Mr. Merryman, would sometimes truly say, " The riding is nothing ; speaking is the thing." However, as one ought not to do two things at once, I thought it more prudent to dismount before I delivered a neat and appropriate speech. This part of the ceremony was at sunrise; the officers breakfasted with me, and I dined with them. Next day they gave a ball; but I was best entertained with a Nautch given by the Sepoys. This was much the prettiest Nautch I had ever attended, or rather approached nearer to pretty than any former specimens of that amusement which I had witnessed. It was performed in a large tent, and was extremely *scenick.* The lights, which were torches of hollow bamboo, with a thick wick on which oil was poured every now and then by way of snuffers, were held by men, black but handsome, and almost as naked as bronze figures which serve for candlesticks usually are. Chairs were set in a semicircle towards the bottom of the pavilion, on which we sat, and were plentifully sluiced with rose-water. A circle was formed of the Sepoys, in their own clothes (not in regimentals), all seated on their hams, and making a most picturesque amphitheatre. In front the dance was performed with the music, which was all national—instruments as well as airs and words —behind the dancers. The dancing was much in the same monotonous style as I have described in other letters, but the girls were Cashmerians, and accounted very superior to those of the Bengal provinces. They were handsomer than I had seen, and were better dressed; but beauty would be a strong word even for these paragons. The music was also Cashmerian, and some of the airs really were very pretty. They danced with something approaching oocasionally to grace, and managed their drapery very prettily, so as to remind one for a moment now and then of the Etruscan figures or those found at Pompeii. But they are over-clothed; nothing is seen but the head, arms, and toes—all of which are displayed for the sake of the ornaments—and there is such a quantity of clothing that it cannot well take the picturesque sort of folds which such flexible stuffs should take.'

'Barrackpore: May 24, 1808.

'I often wonder at my being able to labour all day and every day in this climate without ever flagging, much less having any notion of being ill. The weather seems a dull topic, but it concerns one so much here

that I must give it a place in my true and particular
history of our lives. This year has been uncommonly
favourable to beginners. The best weather generally
comes on about the middle of March, but our March
was the finest month in the year from beginning to
end. It was delightful. The heat increased about
the middle of April, but was quite endurable till the
end of the first week in May. By that time the hot
winds had set in, and their very name is sufficiently
descriptive of discomfort. However, at this period we
have relief a great part of the four-and-twenty hours,
for at sunset the wind cools, and, continuing to blow,
one draws it in luxuriously and revives. The heat does
not come on again till next forenoon. During the
first days of the very hot winds I bore it, and thought
that patience would carry me through; but it was too
oppressive at last, and I submitted to use the tatty.
That invention is quite effectual, and makes a temperate
zone between the tropics. I sat the livelong day behind the tatty, subject to no inconvenience but want of
light; however, with spectacles I could manage to read
my book and write my lesson. I began, nevertheless,
to count the days to the rains, which I had fixed for
June 10; when all at once, without any notice, as we
sat in Council on Friday, May 20, it became so dark
that we could not see our desks, and then came a deluge
with a tempest of east wind that would have made
Elliot shiver. From that hour the climate has been
quite heavenly, and not the less so in my estimation
for a good pouring shower almost every day. You must

not imagine that these are *the* rains. They are known by the name of the small rains; not that they are small while they are falling, for they come down in buckets; but they do not last long, and there is always an interval between these little gentlefolks and the grander rains that come in June. The whole surface of the country is already soaked, and the wind, therefore, is cool and pleasant. The thermometer was about 96° in the shade during the hot winds.

'28th—in continuation. I came to town yesterday to Council. I started at half after five in the morning which is early enough in this cool weather. An hour and fifty minutes is the time I generally pass on the road; the distance sixteen miles; but the road as smooth and level as the Mall; the carriage very light with four strong horses.

'29th.—I have been at church to-day, which is being a very good Christian, for it is close and warm, notwithstanding punkahs which are pulled by Mahommedans in turbans looking on their masters with the contempt which the faithful bestow upon infidels performing the impious rites of a false religion. There are few countries in which there is such a quantity of reciprocal contempt, from the mixture of so many different races professing different religions, and in general extremely bigoted each to his own. However, as a Christian, I am charitable enough to despise none of them, but only wish some of their superstitions were not so bloody and cruel. Human sacrifices are kept down with some difficulty, and particularly infanticide. Widow-burning is extremely prevalent, especially in this neighbourhood, I am sorry to say. The Brahmins have some profit from it, and it relieves the heir of the jointure or maintenance of the dowager; so that, to be sure, one ought not to wonder at Brahmins and heirs for encouraging the practice. The odd thing is that it prevails in the lowest condition of life. When a poor miserable peasant's wife happens to be of a good caste, which is often the case, nothing in the world will prevent her burning from pure gentility.'

CHAPTER V.

THE year 1808 was memorable in the annals of Europe as that of a supreme crisis in her fortunes. It found all the nations, save one, enthralled in the chains of the greatest military despotism recorded in history. It beheld the first link give way, when the spirit of national independence burst into vigorous life on the wild hills of Spain.

The position of England relatively to Europe after the Peace of Tilsit (June 1807) is thus commented on in a letter from a young Englishman in India to a friend. 'What an unexampled and surprising picture the state of Europe now presents; France, Russia, Austria, Prussia, Germany, Holland, Spain, Portugal, Denmark, Italy, Turkey—all Europe, save little Sweden—combined against our country. We may truly call ourselves "*divisos orbe* Britannos." Although this is a state of things which no one could ever have wished to see, I confess that I feel a pride in it. . . . I hope that we shall do as well as possible under such strange circumstances.

. . . .

'We have at different times paid Austria, Prussia,

France, and Germany; we preserved to Turkey a great portion of its empire, driving out its enemies, the French; we have constantly fought the battles of Europe against France; and all Powers are now ranged on the side of France against us. Hurrah for the tight little Island!'

We should hardly have ventured to quote so glaring a specimen of a spirit described in the slang of the present day as Jingoism—the English language having apparently no term of reprobation for it—had the writer borne a name less known and honoured than that of Metcalfe.

It was, however, the sort of spirit which, combined with conspicuous ability and strong character, had attracted the attention of Lord Wellesley, who, when Metcalfe was only nineteen, sent him in a political capacity to the camp of Lord Lake; and which in this year, 1808, marked him out in the judgment of Lord Minto for a still more important mission. To appreciate the policy of the Indian Government at this juncture it is necessary to revert for a moment to the events of the preceding year.

At the beginning of 1806 Persia, being engaged in hostilities with Russia, sent an Ambassador to Paris to desire the assistance of France. A cordial reception was given him, and it was announced that a splendid mission, having authority to make a treaty of alliance between France and Persia, would be despatched from Paris to Teheran.

In order to counteract the effect of these proceedings a similar course was adopted by England. An Envoy was appointed to Persia, and, with the object of lending greater dignity and importance to his credentials, it was suggested by the Court of Directors that, while remaining their own paid agent, he should be invested with the character of representative of the Crown. The proposal was acceded to by the Ministry of Lord Grenville. There could be little question that Persia was only important to France as a weapon of offence against Great Britain. Hence, those who knew most of Indian matters saw the necessity of selecting the most skilful of Indian diplomatists for the task of countermining the progress of France at the Persian Court; and the name of Colonel Malcolm, already known in connection with a successful mission to Persia in the time of Lord Wellesley, was pressed upon the Directors by Sir Arthur Wellesley,[1] by Lord Minto, then President of the Board of Control, and by other qualified judges:—' but,' wrote Sir Arthur from London to Malcolm himself, 'nobody here knows or cares anything about Indian matters, nor are those consulted who could give the information.' The Wellesley school of politicians was not in favour in Leadenhall Street; and thus it came about that the claims of Malcolm were ignored, and that Sir Harford Jones[2] was appointed to the Persian Mission, to represent the Crown while re-

---

[1] Afterwards Duke of Wellington.

[2] A baronetcy was granted to Mr. Harford Jones on his appointment to Persia, which was not made till after Lord Minto had left England.

ceiving instructions from the Company. Unfortunately, Sir Harford, though he had lived for many years in the East as a merchant, and latterly as consul at Bushire, was considered in India to be totally unfit to conduct so delicate a mission.

In January 1808, rumours reached India of the march of a French army under General Menou towards Persia on the way to India, while it became known that a great military embassy attended by four-and-twenty French officers and three hundred French soldiers had actually arrived there, giving it out that they were the advanced guard of an army. 'The first project is believed to be to take possession of a port on the coast of the Persian Gulf, by which they may communicate with the Mauritius, and receive supplies by sea, and from whence they may attempt an invasion of the western coast of India, and unsettle the minds of the native princes by promises, menaces, and intrigue.'[1]

Of the English envoy to Persia nothing was known at all. The last act of Lord Grenville's administration had been the appointment of Sir Harford Jones, who was directed to proceed in the first instance to St. Petersburg to offer to the Czar the mediation of Great Britain between Russia and Persia.

The peace and alliance between France and Russia had rendered the failure of this preliminary mission a certainty; while the fall of the Ministry that had en-

---

[1] Lord Minto to Lady Minto.

trusted it to him made it doubtful whether Sir Harford Jones would be confirmed in the more important appointment.

In the meanwhile the aspect of affairs was becoming daily graver, as the co-operation of France and Russia in the East grew more probable.

'As long as France,' wrote Lord Minto,[1] 'might be engaged in continental wars in Europe, the project of directing her arms towards this quarter must be considered impracticable; but if her armies have been liberated by a pacification with Russia and by the continued submission of the Powers of Europe, the advance of a considerable force of French troops into Persia under the acquiescence of the Turkish, Russian, and Persian powers, cannot be deemed an undertaking beyond the scope of that energy and perseverance which distinguish the present ruler of France.

'If one body of troops should succeed in penetrating as far as the Persian dominions, others may be expected to follow; and it may then be no longer at the option of the Government of Persia to prevent the complete establishment of the French power and ascendancy in Persia.

'The ascendancy of France being once established in the territories of Persia in the manner described, it may justly be expected that, from that centre of local power they may be enabled gradually to extend their influence by conciliation or by conquest towards the

---

[1] Secret and separate general letter, February 2, 1808, par. 24.

region of Hindostan, and ultimately open a passage for their troops into the dominion of the Company.

'Arduous as such an undertaking must necessarily be, we are not warranted in deeming it in the present situation of affairs to be altogether chimerical and impracticable under the guidance of a man whose energy and success appear almost commensurate with his ambition. We deem it our duty to act under a supposition of its practicability, and to adopt whatever measures are in our judgment calculated to counteract it, even at the hazard of injury to some local and immediate interests.'

In a private letter he wrote: 'What would have seemed impossible has become scarcely improbable, since we have seen one State after another in Europe, among them those we deemed most stable and secure, fall like a house of cards before the genius of one man.'

Before long, the vague rumours that had filled the world ever since the interview of Tilsit assumed more definite proportions. Though all that was possible had been done to secure secrecy, and though no written records have ever come to light of the personal communications interchanged without witnesses between the two sovereigns, it is now pretty well ascertained that the surmises hazarded from the first by those accustomed to watch the political skies, were nearly, if not absolutely, correct. Like those happy strokes of divination by which great discoveries have been made, what seemed to be the intuitions of statesmen were sagacious deductions from certified facts.

The indifference in England as to the dangers threatening India, of which Sir Arthur Wellesley complained two years before, now gave way to grave apprehensions. He himself wrote again to his former correspondent, Colonel Malcolm, that 'the state of affairs caused great anxiety, but it is of that nature which you have occasionally witnessed in timid and undecided men who fear something, they know not what, and are more afraid of the remedy than they are of the danger to which they are exposed.' This was in February 1808. In the course of the spring Lord Grenville, in a letter to Lord Minto already given, alluded to 'dangers to our Indian Empire, in presence of which Lord Minto could hardly have executed an intention, had it been formed, to resign his important functions there;' and the official correspondence from London showed that an invasion of India was looked upon by the ministers as a very serious danger.

It was believed, on what was considered to be good authority, that, in pursuance of an arrangement made at Tilsit, a Persian army of 30,000 men, with a body of Cossacks, was to assemble early in the spring of 1808 at Astrachan, to penetrate thence through the northern provinces of Persia, and support the operations of a French army, advancing simultaneously through the Turkish dominions, for which permission had been obtained from the Porte. To these projects seemingly pretty generally known, was added the 'secret information, to be, however, received with caution,' that advices from Paris described 'Bonaparte as considerably chagrined at learning that the Russians had entirely failed in their engagement to assemble a force at Astrachan, alleging the impossibility of providing supplies for an army in that country, and the unwillingness of the Cossacks to march (possibly in a direction where there was no plunder); that in consequence he had ordered Caulaincourt to remonstrate most strongly with the Emperor on the necessity of fulfilling his engagement. From the same source it is stated that Sebastiani has written from Constantinople that the Pasha of Bagdad (whom he accuses of being gained over to the English) has declared his resolution of opposing the entrance of any foreign forces into his territory, and that, the Porte having obtained information (possibly from Mr. Adair at Vienna) that by the secret articles of Tilsit [1] Moldavia and Wallachia were ceded to Russia, Servia and Bosnia to Austria, and Greece and the Islands of the Archipelago to France, the Turks must be considered as either secret or open enemies, and therefore he (Sebastiani) presses the immediate march of the French troops into Macedonia,

[1] If Turkey resisted, the two Powers were to divide her dominions. 'Si de son côté la Porte n'acceptait pas, on s'obligerait à soustraire au joug des Turcs toutes les provinces ottomanes, Constantinople et la Roumélie exceptées.' Lanfrey, from whose history of Napoleon the quotation is made, adds that the authenticity of these stipulations is 'indiscutable.'—*Histoire de Napoléon Ier*, tome iv.

as well as the throwing forces into the islands, whenever any opportunity of escaping the English fleet should occur.'

The sudden revolution in the Emperor Napoleon's policy towards the Turk, whom he had so lately called his best ally, was an essential element in the considerations upon which the policy of the Indian Government was shaped.

Lord Minto's view of the possible eventualities which might ensue is given in a private letter to Lord Caledon :[1] 'A partition of European Turkey is a step in the *regular* approach to India. It seems to facilitate in some points, though it may retard that enterprise.

'In other respects, I should think it reasonable to hope that the expulsion of the Turks from Europe may create obstacles in the way to India. It is impossible that the Ottoman Government and the whole Turkish race should not conceive the deepest and most bitter resentment against such an injury. One should look for a close communion between Great Britain and the Turk. And if that consequence were to follow the partition of Turkey, our opposition to the progress of a French army might begin on the banks of the Bosphorus instead of the Indus. The Turks may be terrified, it is true, and grant a passage to the French through their territories in Asia. But even in that case the French must be deeply committed in countries which will

---

[1] Governor of the Cape of Good Hope.

abhor them, and have conceived probably an affection for our cause.'

On a review of all the circumstances Lord Minto came to the conclusion that the Indian Government would be wanting in vigilance and prudence if they did not put themselves in a state of preparation to meet a possible if not probable struggle with France, or with France and Russia combined.

'Yet I am not sure,' he wrote in a letter on this subject to Lady Minto, 'that I shall not be blamed; for the attack, though we are strongly and positively warned of it, is not certain, and the most necessary preparations cannot be made without expense, which naturally comes more home to the feelings of my masters than remote dangers, however serious. However, in this as in everything else, I shall do what in my best judgment appears right, and not be led astray by the fear of the *Qu'en dira-t-on*? In the meanwhile the French are smoothing their way by magnificent embassies and numerous military retinues in Persia, and by swarms of agents of all ranks, qualities, and countries, all over the East; and they are beginning to be heard of at the Courts of our Indian princes and chieftains. But I think we shall overtake them in that race.'

To an enquiry concerning the disposition towards us of the native states he replied:[1] 'We have every reason to believe that all the states of India are satisfied of our disinclination to extend our dominions or to invade

---

[1] May 16, 1808. Secret and separate general letter.

their rights, and of our solicitude to maintain peace. But those states of which the power and dominion have been abridged, or of which the influence has been circumscribed, and against which the field of ambition and enterprise has been closed by the political position of the British power and ascendancy in India, cannot reasonably be supposed to entertain that sense of common interest with the British Government which should induce them to prefer the security of their actual condition to the alluring prospect of restored possessions, consequence, and authority. And demonstrations of the dangers to which their authority and independence would be exposed by the ambition of France would have little weight when opposed to the assurance of restoration to the dominion they have lost.

'With states of another description, engagements of co-operation might no doubt be formed, provided these engagements should involve obligations of defensive alliance against all enemies. Of such alliances there is too much reason to doubt the efficiency and the policy.'

A wise man will not allow an enemy to approach the gates behind which stand doubtful friends. 'I am strongly of opinion,' wrote Lord Minto to Sir George Barlow, 'that if this great conflict is to be maintained, we ought to meet it as early and as far beyond our own frontiers as possible. We ought to contest Persia itself with the enemy, and to dispute every step of their progress. The force which we can oppose to them in that stage of the contest is indeed much smaller than they would find assembled against them in our own territories; but in Persia we should have much less to contend with also, and we should meet an enemy much less prepared than he will be if we wait at home till he is ready to face us.

'This system, however, depends on the disposition of Persia herself to neutrality—that is, to let the French and us fight it out fairly between us. For if Persia is determined to support the French with all her power, I acknowledge that we cannot possibly *detach* such a force from our Indian Army as that state of things would require. At least we could not do so without finding some means to divide Persia and to have allies on our side as well as the French.'

For the elucidation of such problems as these the presence of an Envoy gifted with special powers of observation, as well as with diplomatic talents, was imperatively necessary. The state of affairs admitted of no further delay. And in absolute ignorance of Sir Harford Jones's movements, Lord Minto determined to send Colonel Malcolm on a mission to Persia.[1] 'By Colonel Malcolm, if by any man living, we may hope to detach Persia from her hostile alliance with our enemy; and, if that benefit is no longer attainable, we shall receive from Colonel Malcolm authentic information and judicious advice. If Sir H. Jones should have arrived in Persia, Colonel Malcolm will of course withhold his own credentials and diplomatic powers in Persia, and I do not see any necessary and unavoidable inconvenience from the character which he would in that

[1] To Rt. Hon. R. Dundas, President of the Board of Control.

case assume of Political Agent to the Governor General —the political (not diplomatic) representative of the E. I. Company, and of British affairs in India. He might furnish essential aid to the King's Envoy. If they clashed he could be recalled.'

To Malcolm himself he wrote [1] most confidentially upon the point of the military arrangements which certain contingencies might involve. 'Of these transactions our opposition to France in Persia is the anchor on which our hopes must rest; for if we permit that country to be the dépôt of her preparations against us, and wait at home till the enemy thinks himself that he is equal to the undertaking, we shall give him a great, and, as it appears to me, a most manifest advantage. My first anxiety, therefore, will be to know from you whether the disposition of the Persian Court or the state of that country admits of our meeting the enemy at the very moment of his arrival or approach to the Persian frontier. I am aware that this system will require a very considerable force. I shall learn from you what its amount must be, and shall in the meanwhile make every effort which the state of our resources admits of, to be prepared with an army, and the means of transporting it. In the meanwhile, I have imagined that a force of 20,000 or 25,000 men may be necessary. This will be a great exertion, and I don't think that we can go further. . . If 10,000 French troops were to come I conceive that

[1] This letter is printed in Kaye's *Correspondence of Sir J. Malcolm*, vol. i.

our force, which must consist of Sepoys in a great proportion, should be double; but if, instead of sending such an army, as has been announced, they should begin by collecting gradually a small force capable of establishing a French post on the coast, and endeavour to take root there before the grand design is entered upon, I think it of the utmost moment to disappoint this preparatory measure, and to expel the enemy with the least possible delay. We shall be prepared to push off 4,000 or 5,000 men on the first summons.'

The letter ends with the confession that 'Sir H. Jones is rather a *marplot* (I am writing confidentially) in our play.'

The instructions sent to Colonel Malcolm from Calcutta show that the policy he was desired to pursue was to be of a tentative character.

'First, to detach the Court of Persia from the French alliance; and to prevail on that Court to refuse the passage of French troops through the territories subject to Persia, or the admission of French troops into the country. If that cannot be obtained, to admit English troops with a view of opposing the French army in its progress to India, to prevent the cession of any maritime port, and the establishment of French factories on the coast of Persia.

'Second, to obtain authentic intelligence on all points interesting to the Government. It is scarcely necessary to particularise those points, which will necessarily suggest themselves to the mind of Colonel Malcolm. The principal of them are, the real nature and extent of the engagements entered into by France and Persia, and the real disposition of Persia respecting the execution of them. Colonel Malcolm's opinion and advice would also be required by the Government as to the policy to be adopted in either of two contingencies supposed—the active hostility of Persia, or her neutrality.'

With these instructions, Malcolm sailed for Persia; but before he left Bombay, though not in time for the most rapid express to communicate the intelligence to him, the news reached Calcutta of Sir Harford Jones's arrival at the Cape of Good Hope on his way to India, where he expected to receive the Governor General's instructions for the mission with which he had been entrusted to Persia.

Up to the arrival of Sir H. Jones's communication from the Cape, everyone in India had been in total ignorance of his movements. It was possible that Malcolm might find him in Persia, in which case, Lord Minto relied on his envoy's conciliatory qualities and magnanimity. 'For the first he would find exercise in his intercourse with Sir Harford Jones, and for the second in dealing with himself.' The contingency of Sir Harford's arrival at Bombay before the departure of Malcolm had also been foreseen. 'In that case,' wrote Lord Minto to Sir George Barlow, an old and cordial friend of Malcolm's, 'I have resolved to withdraw Malcolm's Persian mission altogether; but to beg Colonel Malcolm to accept a mission to Bagdad, and to take charge of our political interests and affairs in all the countries westward of Persia even to Constantinople. This is a wide and important field; it is entirely distinct from the province assigned to Sir H. Jones, and it requires judgment, ability, and activity which are not to be found there now. We should lose the advantage of Malcolm's talents and influence at the Court of Persia. But this loss we cannot avoid. We shall gain his exertions still nearer to the approaching danger . . . and his observation and judgment will not be confined to the spot on which he may reside, but will embrace the whole range of politics from the Indus to Constantinople.[1] This measure cannot but be attended with expense, which no man can wish to avoid more earnestly than I do; but to save the expense of an essential service, and to lose an advantage affecting so deeply the interests and even safety of the State, would be the greatest and worst of prodigalities.

'If India is invaded by a French and Russian army, that event cannot be ascribed to the character or counsels of the Indian Government. It is to the disasters of Europe, to battles in Poland, to the Peace of Tilsit, that the necessity of waging a burdensome war in India must be traced. This is a consideration very fit, in my opinion, to weigh in the councils of the British Empire, and one which constitutes a strong claim on the policy of the British nation for whatever support and cooperation the defence of India may be found to require.'[2]

This was written on April 21; on the following day

[1] To Sir George Barlow.
[2] To the Chairman of the East India Company, April 21, 1808.

came the letter of Sir Harford Jones, announcing his arrival at the Cape. On the 23rd Lord Minto wrote to inform Colonel Malcolm of this event.

'After perusing all that has been written to us from England on the subject of the mission, and after considering the authorities (the East India Company as well as Government) from which his powers are derived, I confess I feel that no authority in this country can be competent to delegate similar powers for precisely the same purpose to any other person. You know enough of my opinions on the whole of this important subject to make it unnecessary for me to describe the regret, public and private, which I experience in renouncing a measure on which I rested my chief hope of a successful issue to the struggle in which we are engaging; but there is no deceiving oneself on this point, and it is clear that your mission to Persia must be abandoned in the event of Sir Harford Jones's arrival in that country.' The letter concluded by offering Malcolm in the most urgent and flattering terms the commission to Bagdad, adding that his information and counsels would be required respecting all the territories from the Indus to Constantinople.

Of the success of his mission to Persia, or at all events of the diplomatic tact and skill which his measures would evince, none of Malcolm's Indian friends permitted themselves to doubt. Hence it was with equal surprise and consternation that his first despatches from Bushire were received. Lord Minto has told the story many times in despatches, letters, and minutes, but the most informal, and therefore the best version of it is that in the following letter to General Hewitt, the Commander-in-chief.

To Lieutenant General Hewitt.

'July 30, 1808.

'I am sorry to say in strict confidence that Malcolm has disappointed me exceedingly at the beginning of his mission. Instead of facilitating the commencement of his negotiation, he has begun by creating, I fear, insurmountable obstacles to his own progress.

'It is impossible to attempt in a letter even a summary of the proceedings to which I allude; but the general features are these. He charged Captain Pasley with a letter to the King, containing little more than the usual complimentary matter. But he charged him at the same time with a negotiation to be conducted by Captain Pasley with the principal Ministers of the King at Teheran,[1] the professed object of which was to obtain certain concessions, in the way of preliminaries to all negotiations, in consideration of which General Malcolm might be prevailed upon to advance. Failing such concessions, he threatened the immediate vengeance of the British Power, and declared his own determination to retire immediately from the Persian territory. You will be, I daresay, as much surprised as we have been to learn that the first condition required by Malcolm was the immediate expulsion from Persia of the French

---

[1] The King of Persia held his court at Teheran.

embassy with every man of that nation, and this Captain Pasley was authorised to modify only by admitting the temporary residence of a few French individuals who are engaged in works useful to Persia, but the whole mission was to be *peremptorily* dismissed. If Malcolm had obtained this object after a considerable residence in Persia, and after the utmost exertion of his own uncommon talents, I should have thought him eminently successful. But I am compelled to say that my confidence is entirely shaken by the injudicious course he has pursued, and the disadvantageous ground he has taken. Persia is in the hands of France, and was only to be weaned from that connection by good and convincing reasons urged in a conciliatory form. Intimidation, which Malcolm has chosen as the character of his negotiation, *cannot* succeed against the united force of the French and Russian empires, the vengeance of which Malcolm would induce Persia to provoke by menaces which she cannot think so formidable.

'Malcolm was received with every mark of distinction at Bushire by orders from Court, and Captain Pasley no less so at Shiraz, where the Prince's Court professes to be entirely English. The fact is that Persia is puzzled between the two great candidates for her favour, and while the French are well received at Teheran, the intention was that the English officers should be conducted with similar demonstrations of favour to Shiraz. A Russian Embassy has entered the Persian provinces from Georgia.'

'Malcolm's proceeding at Muscat,' wrote Lord Minto

to Mr. Edmonstone, 'has been affected with the original sin of his whole system.' What that was may be inferred from certain passages of a memorandum addressed by Lord Minto to General Malcolm, containing an explicit condemnation of the policy adopted towards Persia. This memorandum, docketed by himself as 'a rough draft of a minute to be forwarded immediately to General Malcolm, July 21, 1808,' begins by expressing the great concern caused him by the perusal of Malcolm's despatches from Bushire, setting forth the line of conduct which had resulted in his immediate departure from Persia. The difference between his own and General Malcolm's sentiments on the subject of the mission appeared so great, as to touch the general principles of the policy to be pursued at the present conjuncture. Lord Minto therefore felt that he must not from motives of personal delicacy shrink from the duties of his station, but must endeavour to provide for the public interests by recurring to methods more likely to lead to the important objects which he desired to attain. The grand and ultimate purpose of the mission to Persia was to withdraw that Court from its new and dangerous connection with France. Malcolm's peremptory demand for the expulsion of the French mission had left no room for consideration.

'The demand cannot be supported on any ground of justice. Persia, as an independent Government, has a right to receive accredited ministers from any other Court, and to enter into any negotiation she may think advisable. She may be indeed precluded by previous treaties with us from contracting engagements in contradiction to them; but if our claim to exclude the French mission were better supported on the point of right, it would still in the actual circumstances of the case be unreasonable to insist on it as a preliminary. Persia was and continues to be exposed to an invasion from Russia, which is to her a subject of great and reasonable alarm. She first applied to us for assistance. It was impossible for us, consistently with the relations in which we stood to Russia, to afford the aid she asked. She therefore gave us fair notice that, although she would have preferred our co-operation to every other, she was constrained to provide for her safety, by looking elsewhere for the aid which she could not obtain from us.

'Upon this ground her connection with France has been formed. France has promised on certain conditions to protect her against a Russian invasion; the promised service was to have been performed by military force. France is now in alliance with Russia, and is to employ her influence instead of her arms for the protection of Persia. If Persia in these circumstances suddenly and offensively breaks off the subsisting negotiations with France, instead of a contest with Russia alone, or instead of being protected by France against Russia, she must prepare for a conflict with the united force of those two Empires.

'It is therefore reasonable that, before she accedes to a demand involving her in such consequences, she should be informed of the means by which we propose to protect her against them. This is matter of negotiation, not for a preliminary, &c. &c.

'General Malcolm, knowing the political complexion of the Court, seems to have conceived that timidity was the quality on which he had the best chance of operating, and that the fear of France and Russia could only be combated by a still stronger apprehension of British power.

'Intimidation, therefore, was the engine he proposed to employ in the first stages of his mission. I confess that I should have thought it more advantageous to give an entirely different character to the negotiation. I can easily believe that the arrival of our Envoy in Persia in circumstances which would justify hostile measures on our part must have created solicitude concerning the intentions of this Government, and that the menace of some great measure of coercion or resentment on our part, to follow on General Malcolm's retreat from Persia, might operate favourably to his views in some of the minor points under discussion; but it cannot produce any substantial benefit, because in truth we find Persia herself under circumstances of extreme difficulty from which she cannot be driven violently, but from which she requires the hand of friendship to extricate her gradually. I regret that this expedient was resorted to; for not being founded in truth it savours more of artifice than I think suits the true dignity of this Government. If Persia is found to be decidedly hostile, it does not enter into our views to weaken our force and resources, in the fruitless endeavour to subdue that great country, whether supported or not by a great European army. I regret it also because, whether any short advantage is obtained by this species of intimidation or not, it must create irritation and disgust, and so far retard the desirable work of conciliation and of union which we have in hand.

'I should certainly not think it either becoming or politic to approach the Persian Court in a posture of supplication; on the contrary, we have ground for remonstrance against the more than unfriendly conduct of that Court. But we have not now to learn that a temporising compromising policy is the frequent refuge of weak governments, implicated in the disputes of more powerful States; and our intercourse with her should be tempered with indulgence for those obstacles to a cordial demeanour which we know exist.

'The dignity of our Sovereign and of our national character will not be impaired by forbearance, which is due from the strong towards the weak.

'In my opinion the most dignified basis on which we can treat with Persia is that of *common interest*. The measures we have to propose to Persia are those which I sincerely think can alone afford her any prospect of escaping from the pressing danger of being involved in the general scheme of French conquest. I would avow at the same time, without scruple or disguise, that we also have an interest in securing Persia against its occupation by French armies, and that the defence of Persia will be an additional means of security to ourselves.

. . . .

'From this avowal they will learn nothing that the French Ambassador has not long since taught them. But we shall obtain better credit in the advice we proffer to them for their own interests, when they know we have at least no hidden motive, and when we shall have given this pledge of our friendship and sincerity.'

The minute concludes with a hope that a door may still be left open to negotiation.

Malcolm meanwhile had convinced himself that the Persian Court was under the absolute control of the French Ambassador. It had issued the most positive orders, dictated jointly by the French Ambassador and by an Envoy lately arrived from the Russian camp on the frontiers, prohibiting the advance of Malcolm or of any individual of his mission towards the capital. It was suspected, and the fact was afterwards admitted, that designs were entertained of preventing the departure of the mission, or of retaining the chief members of it as hostages. Malcolm therefore took the resolution of leaving Bushire without awaiting orders, and of proceeding in all haste to Calcutta to make his explanations and to receive further instructions.

The mission from which so much had been expected had failed. It is possible, even probable, that a more conciliatory course than that adopted by the British Envoy might have enabled him to remain in Persia until a change of circumstances produced a change of sentiments on the part of the Persian Government, when his personal popularity and his conspicuous talents might have restored the prestige of the British name, and enabled him to conduct his negotiations with better effect than Sir Harford Jones; but the neglect with which the Indian Government had treated Persia during the years that had elapsed since Malcolm's first mission, had perhaps a greater share in producing the present disappointment than his somewhat ill-timed arrogance.[1]

The first intimation of Malcolm's return to India was given by the despatches which he brought himself, and forwarded to Calcutta from the north of the Hooghly.

It appears from his own journals that he was somewhat doubtful as to what his reception might be, and was proportionably relieved and gratified by its warmth.

---

[1] 'Malcolm,' says his biographer, 'found our enemies supreme at the Persian capital. Whilst we had been sleeping they had been striving. We had left the field of action clear for them, and they had occupied it with vigour and address.

'Malcolm had not estimated aright the extent of this occupation. He had relied too much on the influence we had established eight years before at the Persian Court, and had not sufficiently taken into account the alteration of circumstance and feeling resulting from the progress of Russian arms in that momentous interval. The Persians believed that we had deserted them. We had at all events looked unconcernedly on, or purposely turned our backs upon them, whilst they had been spoliated by the Northern conqueror.

'What, they asked, had we done for them? who were we that we should now expect a single word from us to dissolve a promising alliance, and to disperse a magnificent embassy, strong in all those external attributes best calculated to rivet the confidence of the Persians in the military strength and national greatness of their energetic allies?'—Kaye's *Life of Sir John Malcolm.*

Lord Minto rejoiced in his arrival as enabling them to discuss future measures by personal communication, and as an opportunity given to Malcolm 'to acquire a juster notion' of his sentiments.

'I confess I have not seen reason to recall the sentiments I entertained concerning the general policy adopted by him in Persia, but I note with satisfaction that what appears to have been the least prudent and judicious course has proved, as often happens in human affairs, the most useful and advantageous.

'Since success was impossible, it is satisfactory to have arrived at the knowledge of that fact as early as possible, and since moderation and forbearance could have made no difference in the result, it is well that his line of conduct has asserted the power of our country, and made manifest our knowledge of the influence under which Persia had adopted so hostile a course.'[1]

General Malcolm's information convinced the Indian Government that Persia was so entirely dependent on France and Russia as to give no mission from England a chance of success. This state of things was not occasioned by General Malcolm's conduct, as was proved by the plain avowal at Shiraz of orders issued in the most peremptory terms, before Malcolm's letters had been received, to prohibit his advance. The motive was no less clearly demonstrated—the *insistance* of the French and Russian Ambassadors, accompanied with menaces of an immediate rupture if the King's unwill-

[1] To General Hewitt, Commander-in-chief.

ingness to break altogether with England were not overcome.

Terror governed the conduct of Persia.

A French Ambassador could not but be absolute when France offered the only visible and imaginable protection against Russia.

All preparations for the despatch of military forces to Persia, on a large scale, and for the purposes detailed in the instructions carried with him by Malcolm, were now set aside; but Lord Minto did not think it advisable to renounce altogether 'that interesting quarter.' While refusing to entertain the whole scheme elaborated by Malcolm on his sea voyage, for the confusion of his enemies, Lord Minto, on the assumption that Persia was fairly entangled in the schemes of France and Russia, accepted the suggestion that a station on her coast might under the circumstances be usefully occupied by British troops. This station, 'to serve as a rendezvous, a dépôt, a point of departure and a point of retreat, as well as a centre of observation,' was to be the Island of Carrack, at the mouth of the Bassora river. It contained only twelve square miles, was healthy, and well supplied with water, and on it Malcolm had long cast covetous eyes.

'The primary inducement to the adoption of that plan (the occupation of Carrack) is that of placing ourselves in such a posture as might enable us to pursue whatever system of measures the progress of events and the many possible turns and changes in the conduct of the adjacent countries might render expedient.

'The separation of Persia from the cause of our enemy is obviously hopeless at present. . . . If Persia remains hostile to the last, and nothing is left but to impede and obstruct the joint operations of that Government and France, the post of Carrack can alone furnish the possibility of putting to profit such opportunities as may offer to make that attempt.

'To follow any other course would be to withdraw ourselves from the whole of that important scene, without divesting ourselves of the deep interest which attaches to it. It would be to throw up the game without withdrawing our stake, because the first deal has not been favourable to our wishes.

'Views of a similar nature, but applied to Bagdad, recommend the same measure of an independent footing in the Gulf. It must at present no doubt be considered as uncertain whether occasions will arise or not to call forth our exertions in the quarter now under consideration. The route of the French army may be very remote from the shores of the Gulf, and it may happen that no effort of ours, either in the southern provinces of Persia or in the territories of Bagdad, can have any influence on the actual defence of India.

'This may be true, and our position and preparations in the Gulf may not impossibly become the cause of their own apparent inutility, by diverting the enemy from the attempt in that direction. But in the first place this is not certain, and we should leave an important post unguarded if, on any such speculation, we should abandon that great means of our defence, and resign the whole of the southern route to fortune, or, to speak more justly, to the undisturbed progress of the enemy. In the next place, as I have already hinted, these measures may accomplish their purpose by impression alone, which, though its operation is less perceptible, may not be less efficient to its end, and the actual contest may be precluded by these demonstrations alone that we are prepared to maintain it.'[1]

'There are so many turns and chances in human affairs that I should think it highly imprudent to abandon all connexion with the countries bordering on the Gulf of Persia. If a partition of Turkey in Europe were to take place, it would become advisable that we should take some part in the affairs of Asiatic Turkey. I should not play the whole game in this great match if I neglected to provide a secure station for that purpose.'

General Malcolm appeared to Lord Minto singularly qualified for the execution of measures of this undefined but eventually active, enterprising, and complicated nature; and to him direction of them was therefore to be entrusted. 'Particular instructions cannot well be framed for cases which are only seen in anticipation, and may assume an almost infinite variety of forms and modifications; the defect must be supplied by the known talents, activity, and judgment of the man; and next by general principles laid down for his guidance which will embrace many particular points of conduct,

[1] To the Right Hon. R. Dundas.

and serve to regulate at least the general character of the system; the particulars of which will thus in its execution be more easily directed by himself.

'In the result, as I fear no want of energy in General Malcolm, so I am not apprehensive that those restrictive principles by which it ought to be regulated, and which have been fully inculcated both by written instructions and by frequent personal advice and admonition, will be in any degree forgotten.'

It is remarkable that, among the possible contingencies commanding the attention of Indian statesmen, the one never contemplated was that which actually occurred,—namely, a check to the power of France in Europe, decided enough to cause the abandoning of her views on the East, and the withdrawal of her troops from Persia. That France might do as she listed seemed to have become an axiom in the politics of the time.

We must now revert to Sir Harford Jones.

He had arrived at Bombay in April, following rapidly on his letter addressed from the Cape of Good Hope to the Governor General, yet not rapidly enough to arrest the departure of General Malcolm, which had taken place before his arrival. He therefore remained at Bombay to await the result of Malcolm's mission—a course warmly approved and encouraged by Sir James Mackintosh, then Recorder of Bombay, and a hearty admirer of General Malcolm.[1]

When intelligence reached Calcutta of the probable

---

[1] Colonel Malcolm received the rank of a Brigadier General before his departure for Persia.

failure of Malcolm's negotiation and of his withdrawal from Persia, the Governor General saw no further reason for detaining Sir Harford in India, and he, to whom everything relating to Persia had been unreservedly communicated, now received Lord Minto's authority to depart on the mission to which he had been appointed in England. This was on August 12. On the 22nd, Malcolm reached Calcutta, and on the same day, before the Governor General in Council had finished reading the despatches forwarded from the mouth of the Hooghly a few hours before Malcolm's arrival, orders were sent to Sir H. Jones to await further instructions at Bombay.

They appear to have had the effect of quickening his movements. He stood not on the order of his going, but went at once. On the 29th a still more urgent communication was addressed to him, after the decision to occupy Carrack had been arrived at; but, when it reached Bombay, Sir Harford was on the high seas. Letters at that period seem usually to have taken from eighteen to twenty days on the road between Calcutta and Bombay. On this occasion the rains caused a delay of five days in the arrival of the express. From Bombay it was despatched with great expedition after Sir Harford in a quick sailing vessel, and would have come up with him if she had not sprung a mast and been constrained to return to Bombay to repair.

Fortune at this juncture decidedly favoured Sir Harford. It was obvious that the measures in contemplation could not be proceeded with while an Envoy, representing His Majesty, was on his way to Persia. Some sanguine spirits entertained the belief that on the receipt of Lord Minto's despatches, Sir Harford's re-embarkation would immediately follow on his arrival. Lord Minto thought otherwise; and when, at the end of September, he acquired intelligence that Sir Harford's determination to proceed on his embassy had not been shaken by the first despatch from Calcutta, relating the circumstances under which Malcolm had withdrawn from Persia, Lord Minto did not hesitate to suspend the preparations which Malcolm had gone to Bombay to superintend. On September 30 the Governor General wrote to Malcolm that he had abandoned all hope of arresting Sir Harford's departure, and that in their ignorance of the reception he might meet with in Persia the expedition to Carrack must be *necessarily* suspended. 'We cannot commit hostilities in Persia while the King of England is negotiating with the King of Persia. . . . You will have to withdraw Captain Pasley and all your establishment from Bushire. There should be no possibility of *jostling* between anything that is yours and Sir Harford Jones's—I mean, no possibility of its being suspected or imputed by him.' The letter ends with the remark that he had great doubts of being able to control Sir Harford from Bengal, but that he had the right to do so, and should assert it.

It must be remembered that at this time the Government at Calcutta was convinced of the futility of any negotiation with Persia, and of the reality of the designs against India entertained by those who guided the counsels of the Persian Court. It followed that, in their judgment, Sir Harford's proceedings were simply obstructive, causing loss of precious time. But in the course of the winter a change came over the views of Indian statesmen. The apprehension of a French invasion had diminished, if it was not altogether removed, and in March 1809 Lord Minto was able to write to General Malcolm, with many expressions of regard and of regret at the inevitable disappointment the announcement he was about to make must cause him, that he had determined to abandon the expedition to the Persian Gulf; the last information from England having satisfied him that the affairs of Europe were sufficiently agitated to preclude for a time, on the part of the French, such difficult and distant projects as had called forth the late policy and measures of the Indian Government.

'He knew that a struggle was to be maintained for Spain, and had great hope, thank God, of that great and noble cause.'

With this letter the story of the Persian mission would have fitly ended, but the conduct pursued by Sir Harford Jones, on receiving in Persia the despatches forwarded to him after his hasty departure from Bombay, produced results which cannot be passed over in silence. All disputes are unpleasant to relate, more especially when in such a life as Lord Minto's they jar upon one like a false note in music; but as this episode has been frequently, and not always accurately related, it is necessary to treat of it in some detail.

It has been represented that the despatch of two missions to Persia had arisen from the jealousy entertained by the Indian Government of an Envoy from the Crown. This was not the case. The resolution to appoint an Envoy to represent both Crown and Company had been taken with Lord Minto's knowledge and participation, before he left England. He had doubtless strongly urged the propriety of selecting the individual to fill the office from the Indian service, which contained many eminent men well qualified for the post; but the advice related to the choice of the individual Envoy, not to the nature or source of his powers; concerning these there had been no discussion or difference of opinion. For nine months after his arrival in India Lord Minto heard no word of Sir Harford Jones, beyond the fact of his having been selected for the mission to Persia, to include a preliminary mission to St. Petersburg. In the meanwhile events were hurrying on: the circumstances under which the appointment had been made, and the Ministry who made it, had changed. The state of affairs in Persia was urgent. It caused, as we have seen, great anxiety in England as well as in India. Lord Minto consequently deemed it his duty to send a mission from India to Persia on the distinct understanding that Colonel Malcolm, to whom he entrusted it, was not to present his credentials if he found Sir Harford Jones there. In that case he was to subside into the agent of the Governor General. But even this secondary position originally assigned to him was cancelled immediately on the receipt of Sir Harford Jones's communication from the Cape.

Instructions were sent forthwith to Malcolm to abandon Persia, and undertake the mission to Bagdad. But in those days weeks were requisite for the transit of letters to Persia, and it does not appear that the orders of recall had reached Malcolm before his hurried departure from Bushire. When, at a subsequent period, Lord Minto sought to arrest Sir Harford's embarkation at Bombay, it was under the conviction that the time for profitable negotiation was past. His desire that there should be no *clashing* or jostling between Malcolm and Jones has been stated. What then was the cause of the bitter strife which reams of paper still exist to prove, if not the action of Sir H. Jones in repudiating the authority of the Government of India, in the higher character of representative of His Majesty? On his arrival in Persia he found that the aspect of things had entirely changed during the three months which had elapsed since Malcolm's departure. French promises had not been followed by performance; the Persian Court had cooled towards their new friends, and had grown alarmed at the prospect of a rupture with their powerful neighbour in India. On the receipt of the intelligence contained in the despatches to Sir Harford Jones from Calcutta, of the intended expedition against Carrack, anger was added to apprehension. Thereupon Sir Harford saw no better way of restoring the equanimity of the Persian Court, and of smoothing his own advance to Teheran, than to give them the assurance that a greater than the Governor General stood before them in his own person. Throwing off all allegiance to the Indian Government he proceeded to give a solemn pledge that no aggression should be committed on the dominions of the King of Persia as long as he displayed a wish to preserve amicable relations with the King of Great Britain.

How these pretensions were viewed at Calcutta will be best shown in the following extracts from the correspondence of the Governor General in Council with the Secret Committee. They distinctly state the nature of the powers with which Sir H. Jones had been invested, and also the responsibilities which attached to the Indian Government.[1]

'As we have already observed in our despatch to your Honourable Committee of January 20, we conceive that it was the express intention of Government in England in acceding to the request of the Honourable the Court of Directors, that Sir Harford Jones might be vested with diplomatic functions on the part of the Crown, to add weight and consequence to the authority of the local Government of India, and that it was the special duty of Sir H. Jones rather to combine than to separate the two authorities, and to employ the one as the means of adding dignity and efficiency to the other. We conceive that though Sir H. Jones was vested with a commission from the throne, he was bound by the

[1] Extract from secret and separate general letter, April 3, 1809.

spirit and letter of the orders which accompanied that commission to act exclusively under the instructions of your Honourable Committee and of the Honourable Company's Government in India.

'In Mr. Secretary Canning's instructions to Sir H. Jones of August 28, 1807, it is stated that " the Court of Directors of the E. I. Company, having represented to His Majesty's ministers, through the President of the Commissioners for the affairs of India, *that the mission with which Sir H. Jones was charged to the Court of Persia* would be likely to experience a more favourable reception at that Court if he were directly accredited from His Majesty, and enabled to bring forward in His Majesty's name the different propositions which he might be instructed to submit to the consideration of the Persian Government, Mr. Secretary Canning had received His Majesty's commands to authorise Sir H. Jones to assume the character of His Majesty's Envoy to the Court of Persia." It is further distinctly stated in the same letter, that the instructions by which Sir H. Jones's conduct in the execution of his mission was to be guided, he would receive from the Court of Directors of the E. I. Company, or the Secret Committee, or from their Government in India; and to those instructions Sir H. Jones was desired to conform. Sir H. Jones was at the same time authorised to sign in His Majesty's name any treaty which in pursuance of these instructions he might have occasion to negotiate with the ministers of the King of Persia, but was informed that, in the event of his being directed to hold out any promise of pecuniary or military assistance, such engagements were to be made only in reference to the forces actually in India, and to the funds of the E. I. Company, by whom all the expenses attending his mission were to be defrayed.

'Your Honourable Company did at the same time communicate to Sir H. Jones the general objects of his mission, and direct him as prescribed in Mr. Secretary Canning's letter to conform to such instructions as he might receive from their Company's Government in India for the accomplishment of these objects.

'It cannot be necessary to enter into any discussion for the purpose of demonstrating the inconsistency of our being charged with the defence and security of India against the dangers in which the mission to Persia originated, without possessing power to direct the negotiation with that Court, or to control the conduct of the minister deputed there; without being at liberty to determine the point of time at which negotiation should be undertaken; to judge whether or not the prosecution of it is compatible with the honour and interests of the Government committed to our charge, or to limit or extend the engagement for which we are exclusively responsible.

'A state of affairs may readily be supposed which would render the prosecution of a mission to Persia on the part of the British power, utterly subversive of the dearest interests of this country. In such a case it cannot be contended that the apppointment of a minister accredited to the Court of Persia by the authorities in England, under the contemplation of a different condition of affairs, should supersede a discretionary power, on the part of the local Government, to require him to suspend the exercise of his ministerial functions; or that a minister so appointed, proceeding without the authority of this Government, or in direct opposition to it, is empowered by his commission to pledge its faith to the adoption of a course of measures, not only unsanctioned by the Government on which the execution of those measures must depend, but expressly declared to be incompatible with its honour and interest. The assumption of such a power is the assumption of the government of this country, not the exercise of the ministerial powers delegated by the Crown to its accredited envoy. It is the assumption of power which the throne itself never claimed; and it is a direct opposition, not only to the spirit, but to the very letter of His Majesty's commands.'

Lord Minto, describing the grounds on which the supreme Government of India had hitherto carried on the connection with Persia, continues: ' By the laws which have been framed for the management of the honourable Company's affairs, the local Government of this country is vested with the power attached to sovereignty. It is empowered to administer civil and criminal justice, to levy war, and to conclude peace. It is equally essential to the preservation of this valuable branch of the British Empire that the States of Asia should consider the British establishment in India in the light of a sovereign State, as that the Government should actually exercise the powers annexed to it.

'In this character, the Company's Government has legitimately negotiated by means of ambassadors, and concluded treaties with the State of Persia on a footing of equality. In this character, the State of Persia has been accustomed to consider the British Government in India as vested with absolute authority to employ its resources in aid of the Persian monarch as an ally, or to direct its power against him as an enemy. It is in this character alone that we have been enabled to obtain those manifestations of respect, that regard to the claims of dignity, which, amongst all nations of the world, but in a special degree among Asiatic States, are essential to the maintenance of real power in the scale of political interest. This acknowledged character, as it constituted the basis, so it must form the cement of our external relations. To depreciate therefore that estimation of the power, and the dignity of the British Government in India, which, under a sense of its importance, we have successfully laboured to preserve amongst neighbouring States, is to fix upon the British Government the stigma of deceit, to affect the reputation of our public faith, and to expose us to much of the danger arising from a real loss of power and authority, by diminishing that awe and respect with which this Government has hitherto been contemplated, and on which the tranquillity and security of the British dominion in India mainly depend.'

In the meanwhile Sir Harford had succeeded in negotiating a preliminary treaty, and had prevailed on the King of Persia to send an Ambassador to England in company with Mr. Morier.[1]

The draft of this treaty was sent to the Indian Government for ratification, accompanied by a letter from the King of Persia to the Governor General, which was couched in language that the Indian authorities deemed to be intentionally disrespectful. Writing to Malcolm on June 27, 1809, Lord Minto said: 'Mr. Edmonstone tells me that in every circumstance and form of language it is wanting in the respect which has till now been rendered to the station of Governor General. It acquaints me with the arrival of an Envoy from the King of England, and the conclusion of a treaty of alliance between the two Crowns. It therefore requires me to give effect to the intentions of the two monarchies and of my Sovereign, by attending to the due and strong execution of all the conditions agreed on.'

This letter was looked upon as amounting to a

[1] In a letter of the following year Miss Elliot wrote to her father that 'the new Persian Ambassador who came home with Mr. Morier is very handsome and extremely admired by the ladies. Some people suspect he is "*no waiter, but a Knight Templar in disguise,*" or rather no Ambassador, but a renegade Jew. Some wise man asked him if he adored the sun in Persia; he said, "No, not in Persia, but he should adore it in England if he happened to see it." There is only one lady who can speak Persian to him, a Miss Metcalfe, who cracks Persian jokes to him, and laughs in Persian, just as if it was English. They say of course he is in love with her, but having two or three dozen wives already, there is no room for her, the more's the pity.'—This Persian Envoy is the hero of Mr. Morier's entertaining work, *The Adventures of Hajji Baba.*

deposition of the Government of India from the sovereign powers with which it had been invested.

Lord Minto did not hesitate to ratify the treaty, knowing that the public faith of England was thereby engaged, but he sent instructions to Persia disavowing the public character of the Ambassador, and desiring him to quit Persia immediately, on pain of having his bills dishonoured.[1]

This was in the summer of 1809, but so slow were the communications with England, that a twelvemonth elapsed before the final decision of the Home Government to assume the sole direction of diplomatic relations with Persia, reached India. While still believing the conduct of affairs in Persia to remain with the Government of India, Lord Minto thought it his duty to re-assert their claim to supreme authority over all their agents in the East.

'To despise is to weaken. Reputation is Power'— said an English writer well versed in the knowledge of courts and men. So thinking, Lord Minto asked

[1] The chief points of the treaty were, that any treaty made with other European powers should be considered void; that no force commanded by Europeans should be permitted to march through Persia towards India; and that, if any European army invaded Persian territory, the British Government should afford the aid of a military force or subsidy. 'The last point is the only one of importance,' wrote Lord Minto to Sir Gore Ouseley, 'and in my judgment it is fraught with mischievous consequences and may entail very grave ones.' This opinion was justified by the events of 1826-7, when, Russia and Persia being at war, these stipulations were not fulfilled by England; Mr. Canning being War Secretary at the time, Russia was allowed largely to extend her territories at the expense of the State which by the treaty of Teheran England was bound to defend.

Colonel Malcolm once more to undertake a mission to Persia, from whence it was believed that Sir H. Jones had retired in pursuance of the orders from Calcutta. He, however, had received orders from the Foreign Office in England to await the arrival of an Ambassador from His Majesty—Sir Gore Ouseley, who in pursuance of the new arrangement, was on his way to Persia. Thus it happened that Malcolm and Sir Harford Jones met at last in Persia. To Malcolm were given the honours of the situation by the King, who had a personal regard for him, and created for his special behoof a new order of knighthood, entitled that of the 'Lion and the Sun.'

But Sir Harford Jones carried away the more substantial satisfaction of having executed a treaty, which though it received much criticism from the Indian Government, was accepted and ratified.[1]

One of the disadvantages which could not but accrue to the diplomacy of the Company's Government by the withdrawal of Persia from the sphere of its operations, was seen when it appeared that, by an article of the treaty negotiated at Teheran by Sir Harford Jones, it was stipulated that, in case of war between Persia and Afghanistan, 'His Majesty the King of Great Britain should not take any part therein, unless at the desire of both parties;' while, in ignorance of the existence of any such agreement, Mr. Elphinstone had been authorised to form a defensive alliance with Afghanistan

[1] It was not finally executed till 1814, when the name of Russia was substituted for that of France.

against an attack from Persia, as was stated in the treaty signed at Calcutta on June 17, of the same year, 1809. Yet Persia and Cabul were both necessary members of the confederacy with which the Indian Government had proposed to resist an invasion of India.

CHAPTER VI.

LAHORE.

In order to obtain an uninterrupted view of all the circumstances connected with the Persian mission, they have been related without reference to other measures, which were simultaneously carried out and directed to the same object—namely, the formation of defensive alliances with the independent States on the North-Western frontier of India.

In a minute by the Governor General, September 15, 1808, it is remarked that even should France succeed in establishing an ascendancy in Persia, much would remain to be accomplished before India could be successfully invaded, and the hostility of the interjacent States, especially if seconded by the co-operation of the British power, might yet be expected to frustrate the design, or at least to reduce the invading army to a degree of debility which would give our troops a decided superiority in the field. The importance to our interests of previously establishing with these States a direct communication was obvious.

It was therefore proposed to send missions to the States lying on and beyond the Indus—Lahore, Cabul, and Scinde—for the purpose of organising a system of defensive alliances, based on a common interest in resisting the advance of an invading force.

The Home Government had been prepared by despatches of a previous date for the measures carried out in the summer of 1808. In a letter to the President of the Board of Control, February 10 of that year, Lord Minto had written:

'If the views of the enemy should extend to the direct invasion of India by an army proportioned to that undertaking, their march must probably be to the Indus, and must lead through the kingdom of Cabul and the territories of Lahore, as well as through the countries of several independent chiefs situated between Persia and the Company's possessions. It has appeared to be extremely desirable to push forward a British agency as far beyond our own frontiers, and as near the countries from which the enemy is to take his departure, as possible. We have not, till of late, had much inducement to frequent or to make much enquiry concerning the countries beyond the Indus; and there are difficulties attending the usual means of establishing an amicable intercourse with those governments or their subjects. We cannot safely rely on the fidelity or discernment of native agents, either for furnishing information or accomplishing any political objects our interests might require. I understand that the employment of Europeans in such services would be subject to great difficulties. Regular and avowed embassies, which would furnish occasion to the fixed residence, during periods like the present, of Europeans properly qualified in those countries, would undoubtedly be best calculated to fulfil my present views, which aim, first at obtaining early intelligence of the enemy's designs, and secondly at casting obstacles to his progress. The practicability of obtaining a reception for such embassies as I have alluded to, at any Court beyond the Indus, is still to be enquired into.'

The most formidable obstacle to any successful combination with the Western States was to be found in their mutual jealousies and conflicting interests. Between the Jumna—at that time the British frontier—and the Sutlege, the country was occupied by independent principalities belonging to the semi-religious, semi-military commonwealth of the Sikhs. Beyond the Sutlege, the territory known as the Punjaub, also occupied by Sikhs, was under the rule of Runjeet Singh, Rajah, or rather Maharajah, of Lahore—a prince distinguished for military capacity and ambition, whose dominions had rapidly increased since the downfall of the Mahratta power, and whose intention of extending them by further conquests over the Sikh chieftains eastward of the Sutlege had roused the watchfulness of the Indian Government. Beyond the Indus lay the kingdom of Cabul—the remains of a once splendid empire, which had extended from the Jumna to the Caspian Sea, from the Oxus to the Persian Gulf. Of this country scarcely anything was known before Lord Minto sent to it the embassy of Mr. Mountstuart Elphinstone. The States immediately surrounding it had been carved out of its ancient dominions, and Persia, Lahore, and Scinde were therefore equally the objects of its open or covert hostility. Among these rival potentates it became the duty of the Indian Government to decide whose alliance would be the most valuable, and to discover whether any of their conflicting interests were inveterately antagonistic to our own. Unluckily it proved that the Rajah of Lahore, whose territory lay in the track of every invader of India, was at once our most necessary ally and our most dangerous neighbour.

In the stringent instructions given to Lord Minto by the Company, to observe a policy of non-intervention in the affairs of States beyond our borders, it does not appear that any rules were laid down for the case of an urgent appeal by them for such intervention. A claim, based on the right of the weak powers to obtain protection from the stronger, had been made during the administration of Sir G. Barlow, by the Sikh principalities lying between the British frontiers and the Punjaub, which, after the overthrow of the Mahratta supremacy in those regions by the arms of Lord Wellesley, were unable to protect themselves against the encroachments of Runjeet Singh. The appeal had been met with a refusal; and what appears to be the inevitable result among populations in similar conditions, had ensued —the power and influence resigned by the Indian Government were transferred to another. The Rajah of Lahore, in his character of protector over his brother Sikhs, now threatened us with the establishment of a formidable military power on our frontier. 'Runjeet,' wrote Lord Minto, 'had alone been induced to meditate the extension of his dominions over the territories between the Sutlege and Jumna, by a manifestation of our intention not to exercise those rights of supremacy over the southern Sikhs which had been exercised by the Mahrattas. If we had not at an early period of time declared the Sikh chiefs to be entirely independent of our control; if at the time when the Rajah projected his first invasion of those territories we had declared a resolution to protect them; or even if we had attended to the united solicitations of the chiefs of those territories about the middle of last year to protect them against a second projected invasion, by announcing that resolution, no doubt can be entertained that the mere declaration of it would have been sufficient to deter Runjeet Singh from the execution of his design.'

To prevent him from carrying it out was an imperative duty on the part of the Government, which Lord Minto did not hesitate to acknowledge; but the immediate importance of securing his co-operation in a system of common resistance to an invading force made it unadvisable to proceed to extremities on behalf of the southern Sikhs, until all diplomatic methods had been exhausted to obtain his renunciation of further conquests in the direction of Hindostan.

'March 1 08.'[1]

'Although as a general principle we cordially recognise the wisdom and the justice of abstaining from all interference in the contests, disputes, and concerns of States with which we are unconnected by the obligations of alliance, and are fully convinced of the embarrassments and inconvenience of extending our protection to petty chieftains, who are unable to protect their territories from the aggressions of more powerful neighbours, yet we are disposed to think that cases may occur in which a temporary deviation from these general principles may be a measure of defensive policy, the neglect of which might be productive of much more danger and embarrassment than the prosecution of it, and that the certain resolution of the Rajah of Lahore to subjugate the States situated between the Sutlege and the frontier of our dominion would, under other circumstances than the present, constitute a case on which, on grounds of self-defence, the interposition of the British power, for the purpose of preventing the execution of such a project, would be equally just and prudent. Yet the accomplishment of the more important views already described seems evidently incompatible with a rupture with him.'

It was reasonable to suppose that the Courts of Lahore and Cabul would consider such missions as were in contemplation as a peculiar distinction calculated to give them consequence in the eyes of surrounding

[1] Despatch to the Secret Committee, par. 91.

powers;. nevertheless the Governor General did not
consider it either necessary or expedient to suffer the
prosecution of the measure to depend upon the result
of a previous reference to those Courts. He therefore
proposed to despatch envoys to both Courts without
delay.

The personal solicitude with which he watched over
the preparatory arrangements for the missions is shown
by a minute in his handwriting, stating the grounds
on which he deemed it his duty to disallow a measure
proposed by the Commander-in-chief, General Hewitt,
namely, the appointment of two officers of high rank
to accompany the missions for the purpose of making
a survey of the country for military purposes.

'June 1808.'

'It must always be with much concern that I find
myself under the necessity of objecting to any measure proposed by the Commander-in-chief, especially
on occasions of importance, and on points on which
his Excellency appears to have formed a decided
opinion. It is the importance of the proposition, however, recommended by his Excellency's minute, which
constrains me, after a full and anxious consideration of
the subject, to state the objections which in my mind
oppose its immediate adoption. . . . For a due consideration of this subject it is necessary to keep in
mind the proper object which is proposed by these

[1] Minute on proposal made by Commander-in-chief.

missions, and the particular circumstances under which they are undertaken.

'The object proposed is to conciliate the Princes who govern the States of Cabul and Lahore, to obtain their consent to the passage of our troops through their country, or their admission into their territories, for the purpose of opposing a French army in their projected invasion of Hindostan; and our hope also is to establish such defensive engagements with those Governments as may obtain their co-operation, or at least their friendly aid and assistance, to our military operations and to our cause generally.

. . . .

'I am persuaded that the Commander-in-chief will agree with me in considering it at least as questionable whether, in the event of Cabul and Lahore proving hostile or becoming so, it would be advisable to penetrate through their countries or to enter them at all.

'It is well known that the habitual and undistinguishing jealousy which is the personal character of Runjeet Singh, and is said to characterise also the regions in which his territories are situated, has been directed specifically against the British Government. He is aware that our interests and principles are unfavourable to some of the chief objects of his ambition; and, in addition to this particular cause of distrust, means have been found to create in his mind a still stronger jealousy—amounting almost to personal apprehension.

'It is certain that our endeavours to open a communication with Cabul, and to establish intimate relations with that State, will furnish abundant matter of uneasiness, and supply fresh food to the jealousy already entertained by Runjeet Singh, both of Cabul and of our Government.

'It is the business of the proposed mission of Mr. Metcalfe to remove these suspicions, and to plant in their room the seeds of confidence and union. This must be done in my opinion by a frank, open, and sincere avowal of our ultimate objects; and the best support which can be given to our negotiation must be a scrupulous and delicate conduct in every point of our intercourse with him. . . . The progress of two officers, especially of the distinguished rank and station proposed in his Excellency's minute, through the territories of Lahore, without permission or even any intimation of their intention, for the avowed purpose, or, if not avowed, for a purpose which cannot be otherwise than obvious, if the mission is to have any effect, would be an occurrence calculated to awaken the suspicion of less jealous governments than that of Runjeet Singh. I confess it appears to me highly improbable that these officers would be allowed to advance a step, after the intelligence of their operations should have reached the ears of Runjeet Singh; nor could anyone, in my opinion, answer for the personal safety of these gentlemen. If they should attempt to cover their proceedings under any connection with the political mission, it would only make the case worse; because it would give to the whole measure an air of artifice and deception which must preclude all hopes of conciliating the confidence of Runjeet Singh.

'With regard to Cabul the objection is precisely similar. With the King of that country we have never had any intercourse whatever. I hope that a sense of common danger, and a real identity of interests, may in the very able hands to which that mission is committed, become a foundation of solid union and of zealous and efficient co-operation. But here the work of confidence is to begin. All is yet to do, and I rely for success—here as at Lahore—only on the candid explanation of our true and real purpose, countenanced and supported by a general sincerity of demeanour and by the absence of all those traces of indirect and collateral design which, while they frequently fail in their own object, are very apt to frustrate and disappoint every other with which they are in any way connected.'

The minute ends thus:—'Speaking purely of military advantages, my opinion, I confess, is that the movement and operation of troops, as well as the success of a campaign, would be more facilitated and favoured by the friendship and assistance of the country which is the theatre of their operations without a previous topographical knowledge of the ground, or military report of its condition and resources, than by the possession of that knowledge in a hostile country.'

Mr. Metcalfe [1] was the envoy selected for the mission

---

[1] Afterwards Lord Metcalfe. Late Governor General of India, Governor of Jamaica, and Governor General of Canada.

to the Punjaub, and a more difficult task than that entrusted to him can hardly be conceived—to woo the great Rajah to an alliance, while refusing him the increase of territory on which he had set his heart. Charles Metcalfe was at this time twenty-three years of age; he was a lad of nineteen when Lord Wellesley sent him as political officer to the head-quarters of Lord Lake, where a combination of tact and spirit had established his reputation as one of the most promising of the younger civilians. On Lord Minto's arrival in India no name was brought before him with higher encomiums; and when selected for the most delicate of political missions, it was entrusted to his sole charge. He 'was to move' we are told 'without secretaries, assistants, or attachés; a military escort was to be provided, and a proper establishment of moonshees, writers, and servants was to be furnished. But the work of diplomacy was left entirely to his unaided counsels.'[1] He was to be the pioneer of the mission to Cabul. Besides collecting and communicating every information, political, geographical, and topographical, concerning the country he was despatched to, together with the real disposition of its ruler, the state of his government, troops, resources, &c., he was to push his *reconnaissances*, by means of secret news-writers, to Cabul, Cashmere, Peshawur, Candahar, Herat, and as far as possible into the interior of Persia.

[1] Kaye's *Correspondence of Lord Metcalfe*.

It was not the magnitude of an undertaking which would have daunted the men of those days.

Metcalfe left Delhi on August 12, during the monsoon of 1808; on September 12 he reached Runjeet's camp near the Sutlege, after a weary march over a country under water. Rains from above, quagmires below, had reduced the appearance of his escort to that with which Sir John Falstaff objected to march through Coventry, and Metcalfe was not without some similar sentiments. But when the Rajah contented himself with sending his Prime Minister and an escort of 2,000 men to meet him on his arrival, the young Envoy thought he might have come himself, and was careful to let it be understood that, whether in purple or in rags, he came to treat as the representative of British power; and Runjeet—who possibly experienced some such feeling as that expressed by Hyder Ali to General Malcolm, 'It is not what I see, but what I do not see, that I fear'—received him ever after as became his ambassadorial character.

Before the purpose of the mission was opened, its mere arrival had sufficed to awaken the jealousy and suspicions of Runjeet Singh. When its object appeared to be to gain his aid in counteracting the advance of hostile armies into India, the Rajah made it manifest that his co-operation, against a danger which produced no great impression on his mind, was only to be secured by the furtherance on the part of the Company of his own designs against the territories of the independent Sikhs. On finding that no promise of countenance to these designs formed part of Mr. Metcalfe's instructions, the Sikh Prince suddenly broke up his camp and proceeded to cross the river and attack the coveted territories. Then began a weary period of marching and counter-marching,—of fruitless negotiations and helpless acquiescence in the spoliation of those whom Metcalfe's employers proposed ultimately to protect ; while the Government at Calcutta looked on, not without anger, but with the determination to avoid a rupture while it was yet uncertain whether the big cloud in the distant horizon was to burst upon them or to disperse.

During this period of doubt and suspense Metcalfe's qualifications as a first-rate diplomatist were brought to the test. Nothing could exceed, we are told, the lucidity of his despatches, or the tact, skill, patience, and dignity with which he conducted these critical negotiations and finally carried all his points. It is impossible not to be struck by the respectful attention, the warm approbation, with which the practised statesmen of Calcutta received the reports and adopted the suggestions of a youth of twenty-three.

We have largely developed since then our systems of education, but it is questionable whether any system of mental training can equal that of early initiation into important and responsible business. As Goethe says :—

> Es bildet sich ein Talent in der Stille,
> Sich ein Character in dem Strom der Welt.

Had the Government at this juncture taken a more decided course, and prohibited the further acquisitions of Runjeet Singh, 'they must,' wrote Lord Minto,[1] 'have proceeded at once to employ a military force for the purpose of affording open and immediate protection to the Sikhs. For to declare that we do not consent to the proposed conquests, and at the same time to look on while they are achieved, is a contradiction calculated alike to alienate the Sikhs and to provoke the enmity of Runjeet Singh.' But though temporising, they were not idle. The Commander-in-chief received orders to prepare for an advance, and a private letter to him from Lord Minto shows that in the event of serious resistance from Runjeet, it was in the contemplation of Government to substitute a friendly for a hostile power between our frontier and the Indus. 'There is reason to believe that a considerable portion of the country usurped by Runjeet Singh is strongly disaffected, and should any grand effort be made, and be crowned with success, nothing would be more advantageous to our interests than the substitution of friends and dependants for hostile and rival powers throughout the country between our frontier and the Indus.'

These more extensive designs, depending on the contingency of a failure in the negotiations with Runjeet Singh, were not destined to be carried out. When from Europe came assurance that the arch-disturber of the world's peace had turned his mind from Asiatic conquests to others nearer home, the Indian Government prepared to withdraw from the more considerable undertakings which were required for the security of our Indian

[1] Calcutta, November 15, 1808.

frontier. But with the cessation of their apprehensions on the larger question, ceased also the necessity for an alliance with Runjeet Singh at the expense of those it was the desire and the interest of the Government to protect. Mr. Metcalfe was informed that the Government had come to the conclusion that the approximation of the Rajah of Lahore's military dominion to the Company's possessions, and the introduction of his power into Hindostan, would expose to imminent hazard the tranquillity and security of the British possessions. Upon principles purely defensive, the Government considered it incumbent upon them ' to oppose the extension on the Indian side of the Sutlege of an ambitious and military power, which would be substituted upon our frontier for a confederacy of friendly chiefs rendered grateful by our protection and interested in our cause.' He was desired to declare, and enforce, if necessary, the resolution of the Government to confine the dominions of Lahore within their ancient limits, and to inform the Rajah that it was the design of the Indian Government to establish a military post near the frontier of the Punjaub, not only for the security of the independent Sikhs, but, as our advanced post, to be connected with future defensive arrangements against the approach of an enemy from the quarter of Persia.

The sacrifices demanded of Runjeet were not to be wholly without compensation. It had long been his desire to form a treaty of general amity with the Government of Calcutta, by which the territories of each Power should be respected by the other. ' Although he mistrusted the sincerity of verbal professions of amity, he believed that implicit confidence might be reposed on the validity of our written engagements.' Lord Minto was not of those, who, according to the Eastern proverb, show nothing of the lion but his claws; Mr. Metcalfe was therefore instructed to conclude the desired treaty with the Rajah whenever the previously stated conditions were accepted.

When the final decision of the Council of Calcutta reached their Envoy, he was at Umritsur, where the Rajah had betaken himself to rest and recreation after the fatigues of war. Revellings and feastings had succeeded to military conflicts, and it became as difficult to find the Rajah sober as it had been to overtake him at all. When at last the communication of the Government was conveyed to him, the immediate effect upon him was that of 'a shock which sobered him at once.' Next day he took advantage of a disturbance between the Hindoos and Mussulmans of his holy city to remove to Lahore; but there too Metcalfe followed him, and at last the Rajah was brought to bay. The time for defiance as well as for conciliation was past. He must submit to retire to his ancient limits, to restore his late conquests, and to learn that a British force was advancing to see that the work was done. With praiseworthy self-restraint Runjeet received the decree in silence; then, turning on his heel, left the room. A few minutes more, and the astonished Envoy, looking from the window, saw him madly galloping his favourite horse round and round the courts of the palace. Metcalfe described the action as one of 'surpassing levity:' it was more probably the instinct of a proud and fierce nature aiming at self-mastery. But the struggle was not over; many weary months were still to pass, and many were the shiftings of purpose and of place, before, on April 25, 1809, the treaty was signed which advanced the frontier of British India from the Jumna to the Sutlege.

By it the contracting parties bound themselves to respect each other's territories, and the treaty was never infringed to the day of the Rajah's death.

This was perhaps the most decisive moment of Runjeet's career. The last great event of his life was the splendid reception given by him to the Governor General, Lord Auckland, when he, with his sisters, visited Lahore in 1838. They, the nephew and nieces of Lord Minto, were in the Upper Provinces when the old man died; and our last sight of the great Sikh is in Miss Eden's letters from 'Up the Country.'

Thirty years had brought about many changes. The tide of Runjeet's conquests, forcibly arrested in the east, had rolled back over the territories of many a chief whose palaces had been made desolate, whose holy places waste. Nor had those of the great King of Cabul been spared; from Peshawur to Mooltan all was the Sikh's. With the increase of dominion and dignity had increased the Oriental magnificence of his surroundings. Gold and gems were spread with lavish hands on all things pertaining to him—from the sacred temple of his holy city to the trappings of his steeds. But if there was less of martial simplicity than in his early habits and surroundings, there was far more of warlike pomp in the display in which his eye delighted; the English visitors were not left in doubt that the Sikhs and their Ruler were more even than of yore what their great teacher had proposed to make them—Lions of the Punjaub—'Lions of God like the lion-like men of Moab.'[1] But thirty years before, the facts would not have been recorded by an English lady after a morning spent in quietly sketching under the limes and the oranges of the Shalimar gardens.

Metcalfe's relations with Lord Minto during his mission to Lahore passed rapidly into those of mutual regard. On his return to the seat of Government he was added to the establishment as deputy to Mr. Edmonstone—'for' wrote Lord Minto to his wife, 'I have lately conceived a very high opinion of his talents and character, and particularly of his cool judgment and conciliatory disposition.' And a little later on, when Metcalfe had fallen into habits of intimacy in the society of Government House he wrote again—'he really is the ugliest and most agreeable clever person—except Lady Glenbervie—in Europe or Asia.'

Lord Minto's warm regard for him was shown in many a kindly letter, some of which are preserved in his biography; while the estimation in which he held the young diplomatist was evidenced by the high appointments in which he placed him; and we know from private sources that these cordial feelings were returned with an almost filial veneration.

[1] 2 Samuel, xxiii. 20

CHAPTER VII.

OF the three great missions sent out from British India in the course of 1808, the last—to the King of Cabul—was by no means the least interesting to the Governor General. Personally unacquainted with Mr. Mountstuart Elphinstone, Lord Minto had formed a very high opinion of his character and attainments. All men agreed that no better choice could have been made for an Envoy to what was still one of the most polished of Asiatic Courts, Mr. Elphinstone being as distinguished for his courteous and sympathetic bearing as for his wide acquaintance with Oriental languages and literature. By Lord Minto's request he was to correspond freely and fully with the Governor General; unluckily only a few out of a large number of his letters are preserved at Minto. The members of his mission were specially chosen for their fitness to acquire information concerning the nature of countries and populations almost unknown to us. In his delightful introduction to the 'History of Cabul' Mr. Elphinstone says: 'The countries under the King of Cabul had once extended sixteen degrees in longitude from Sirhind about 150 miles, from Delhi to Meshed about an equal distance from the Caspian Sea. In breadth they reached from the Oxus to the Persian Gulf, a space including thirteen degrees of latitude, or 920 miles.' This great kingdom had suffered considerable diminution before the days of our embassy to it, but there was a stamp of grandeur about it still. To the King of Cabul not only had the Mahommedan Sovereigns of India addressed their complaints, but the Mahratta princes had done the same. Runjeet Singh, though himself the chief despoiler of the Douranee power, manifested much jealousy of the British approach to the throne of the great King. To confront this potentate with due dignity the mission had been fitted out with considerable care and splendour.

The Envoy's staff, suite, and escort, were unusually numerous; nothing was neglected to ensure its success, or at all events to give a proper impression of the Power whence it came.

A very serious obstacle to the success of a scheme of co-operation between British India and the States on her north-western frontier lay in the difficulty of communication. The length of time required to move from point to point over unsettled districts, imperfectly known to the English, could not be calculated upon beforehand, and each Envoy had to carry on his negotiations in ignorance of the success of those simultaneously proceeding in countries which were to form part of a combined system.

The uncertainty of their relations with Persia and Lahore had obliged the Indian Government to give very indefinite instructions to Mr. Elphinstone when, in the month of October 1808, he set out from Delhi on his mission to the King of Cabul; and the same uncertainty as to the disposition of Runjeet Singh had led Lord Minto to advise the adoption of a route by the Cabul mission which, though longer than that through the Punjaub, would avoid the dominions of Runjeet, and would also give an opportunity of gaining information concerning a part of the country unknown to travellers.

The line of march adopted took them over part of the desert—at that time untrodden by Europeans—which lies between Delhi and the Indus, and led them by the great town of Bikaneer, where, before the vast circumference of the encircling walls, five besieging armies lay encamped. As the English caught sight of the high battlements and forts, the cupolas, domes, and spires, they were nigh believing that the delusions of the desert accompanied them still, and that the proud city, as big as Delhi, was no less the baseless fabric of a vision than the lovely lakes of seemingly clear and transparent water, reflecting in their pure depths every passing object, every tint of colour, with which the mirage had adorned the barren scene where no water was. From Bikaneer, where they were well received, though with great astonishment, they passed on through dependencies of the King of Cabul, till they reached Mooltan, five hundred miles from Delhi.

At this point of their journey they were detained for some time while communications were carried on by letter with the King of Cabul, then at Candahar. Without his consent, and the protection of a guard from His Majesty, 'it would be impossible,' wrote Mr. Elphinstone, 'to travel among the tribes beyond the Indus.' The answer to Mr. Elphinstone's application was long in coming, for, as they afterwards learned, the news of the approach of the mission was at first regarded with strong prejudice and distrust; the Afghan nobles disliked the idea of an alliance between the King and the British power, as likely to strengthen him to their detriment; and the King himself thought it 'very natural that the British should seek to profit by the internal dissensions of a neighbouring kingdom, and endeavour to annex it to their empire.' Curiosity is said to have had much to do with the final decision to receive the mission at Peshawur; but before it was made known to Mr. Elphinstone, he wrote a long letter to the Governor General, stating fully the reasons which appeared to him to necessitate an enlargement of his powers and authority to negotiate with the Afghan Court.

The dissensions, of which the King of Cabul had made mention, were many and serious. With Persia, with Lahore, with Scinde, with Cashmere, the King's relations were troubled; within his gates his rebellious brothers had raised the standard of a civil war. In the event of the British proposals being found acceptable to him, there could be little doubt that he would meet them with conditions which would secure assistance from the Company against his enemies, and that this assistance would be demanded in the shape of money, troops, and ordnance.

To send an army to Cabul Mr. Elphinstone thought would be impolitic, 'because it would be to meet the French on equal terms, and to waive the advantage of the strong frontier to the westward presented by the rivers of the Punjaub, the Indus, and the desert. In the present state of the intermediate country, I fear it will be found impossible to defend Cabul; it is, however, very much to be wished that it were practicable for us to contribute more directly to prevent that country falling into the hands of the French; for if they were once in possession of it, their invasion of our territories would no longer be a great and desperate enterprise, but an attempt which they might make without risk when they pleased, and repeat whenever the state of our affairs gave a prospect of success.[1] It is also very desirable that we should be able to hold out some advantage to the King of Cabul more attractive than that of mere safety from the French.

'If that specious people send an emissary to the King of Cabul, he will probably assume His Majesty's entire safety from the French, offer protection against the designs of the English, and promise in the course of the operations against India to reduce this Soubah, Bhawul Khan's country, and Scinde, entirely under the King's authority; perhaps he may also promise the

---

[1] We are informed that papers exist to prove that Bonaparte had fixed on the Gomul Pass, leading from Ghuznee to Dera Ismael Khan, as the line of his advance from Afghanistan into India.

Punjaub, Cutch, Guzerat, or some other country on this side of the Indus; or he may engage to procure a desirable settlement of the disputes about the Wharasan, getting over all difficulties by promised indemnities in India.

'Amidst all these dazzling prospects I fear an Eastern monarch might lose sight of the danger to which he exposes his crown by associating with such a nation of military adventurers, and would not give a very favourable hearing to a person who could only offer to destroy the illusion.

'The state of our affairs may hereafter admit of our holding out many attractions to the King of Cabul, but at present we can only display that of money. It might be expedient to instruct me how far to offer pecuniary aid, in case I found it necessary to counteract French promises, and what assistance we could give in ordnance, stores, and officers. It is desirable that I should be furnished with those materials to treat on as soon as possible, as some open negotiation will probably be required as a pretence for my remaining at Cabul. The Asiatics know nothing of the character of a resident minister, and so much are the Afghans impressed with the idea of an ambassador being always charged with some important communication, that their etiquette allows him only one audience to deliver his message, receive a reply, and take his leave. I have to beg your Lordship's forgiveness for obtruding the above questions on you, but great importance appears to me to attach to their early decision. I am afraid it will appear to your Lordship that my progress towards Cabul has hitherto been very slow ; but the delays which have occurred have been unavoidable, and they are of the less consequence, as I must remain at this place till I receive an answer to my letter to the King. It would be quite impossible to travel among the tribes beyond the Indus without a guard from His Majesty. I expect to receive an answer in course of a week, and if he continues at Candahar, where the last accounts left him, I shall be able to join him in a month from the time I leave Mooltan. Report states his intention to be to move to Peshore, in which case I should probably meet him within a fortnight after I leave this place.'[1]

Before this letter was received, the policy at Calcutta had undergone considerable modifications, and the reply informed Mr. Elphinstone that no thought of offensive operations against Persia was any longer entertained. He was, however, authorised to accede to engagements of a purely defensive character against her in the event of her aggression against the State of Cabul ; in this case military stores, arms, and ordnance would be furnished to the King on condition of his readiness to oppose the advance of a French army on India. 'It would probably,' said the despatch, 'be found impracticable to obtain the King's cordial attachment to our views and interests without some sacrifice to his.' These instructions were stated 'with a view to point out rather what is admissible than what

[1] Mr. Mountstuart Elphinstone to Lord Minto, Mooltan, December 14, 1808.

is desirable in the present situation of affairs, and under any circumstances the Government would approve of the Envoy endeavouring to limit the aid to be eventually afforded to the object of defensive engagements as much as possible, and consenting to afford assistance in arms, ordnance, and military stores rather than in troops.'[1]

The instructions from which the above extract is made, were not written when Mr. Elphinstone entered Peshawur, where the King had determined to receive him.

On leaving Mooltan the mission proceeded up the Indus, with much discourse of Alexander, whose exploits appear to have been singularly mixed up in the traditions of the people with those of Solomon and of Lord Lake. After crossing the great river they followed pretty closely the line of the late frontier at the foot of the Suleiman mountains. Encamping at the mouth of the Kurrum, where English troops now hold the ascending valley, they rested later on by the springs and the sycamores of Kohat,—a name grown familiar to us as a place of arms, of convoys, and of

---

[1] This passage of the despatch to Mr. Elphinstone is an adaptation of the suggestions made by himself in a paper addressed to Lord Minto some time before. 'The practicability of assisting the King with troops would be very doubtful. But a present of guns, stores, &c., and some instruction in the use of artillery might have the best effect. Such an arrrangement would strengthen the King of Cabul, and would give him confidence in us and remove any suspicions he may be persuaded to harbour that we have designs on his country, and would show him that we take a lively interest in his welfare.'

staff-officers, but to the Elphinstone mission suggesting gentler thoughts, for there their hearts were gladdened by an unexpected meeting with wanderers like themselves from English lanes and fields. The songs of thrushes and blackbirds were in the air; wild raspberry and blackberry bushes, 'all the better for being out of leaf, were putting forth new buds;' clover and chickweed, and golden disks of dandelions, peered up among the 'soft fresh verdure' of the early year; and, far more grateful to their eyes than the monotonous splendour of Indian vegetation, was last year's brown leaf, and the willow's soft and scented buds.

At Kohat to-day, the humble English flowers may grow by English graves, in the shadow of the church where are preserved the names of a long list of officers who have fallen since the frontier force was started about thirty years ago—'names scarcely heard of in England, but acknowledged out here to be those of first-rate leaders, first-rate soldiers, who have fallen like heroes, one after the other, in these frontier fights. The Englishmen we have on this frontier are a race to be proud of.'[1]

When the mission reached the fine old city of

---

[1] Lord Melgund to the Editor. Kohat, February 1879.

The frontier force is under the Government of the Punjaub, and has held, at a fearful cost of life, a frontier which it is hoped will now be exchanged for a better. This force is composed of native troops under a handful of British officers, and its duty has been to keep at bay all the wild tribes of the mountains, over a line extending many hundred miles.

Peshawur, crowned with its palace, shady with gardens and overflowing with population, the surrounding plain wore the first greenery of spring; and, in the glory of blossoming orchards and young leaves, Asia wore to them the hues of England. A remark to that effect having been repeated to the King, he courteously replied that where there was such affinity between countries there should be friendship between their peoples. It was no doubt politic to overlook some other features in the scene which suggested widely different thoughts; for, as unlike anything English as the barren hills that girded the plain, was a sight that gave the Envoy 'a strange notion of the system of manners in Cabul.'

Perched like birds of prey upon the rugged rocks sat 'a number of armed banditti, the fierce clan of the Khyberees,' appraising the worth and the strength of the approaching mission. Nor could it proceed in safety till terms had been made with the leaders of the band by the Afghan nobleman deputed to conduct the strangers into the town, who, in his rich dress and golden armour, ventured, almost unattended, into the midst of their matchlocks.

At this very time the Punjaub was quite safe for travellers. 'The Maharajah,' says one of Lord Minto's correspondents, 'has instituted a good police, and has made severe examples of the districts in which capital crimes and robberies have been committed, by putting to death all the inhabitants of the neighbouring towns and villages.'

The reception of the embassy by the king took

place on March 5. It is described as magnificent. After passing through courts filled with guards, and halls with courtiers, over rich carpets and under silken draperies, they reached the presence of the King, Shah Soojah, a handsome man of about thirty years of age, who received them seated on a throne covered with cloth of gold and pearls, himself a blaze of emeralds and diamonds, the famous Kohinoor being conspicuous above all.

On subsequent occasions the Envoy was admitted to more private interviews with the King, 'when it would scarcely be believed how much he had the manners of a gentleman, and how well he preserved his dignity, while he seemed only anxious to please.' The Afghan nobility struck Mr. Elphinstone as superior in refinement and tastes to the great men of India—their manners were more simple and their knowledge greater. It soon appeared that they were shrewd enough to perceive that dangers, against which the British sought their co-operation, must be of considerable magnitude, and that an advantageous bargain might therefore, not improbably, be struck between themselves and the Company. They remarked that, before making common cause with either of the European powers, they ought to hear what France as well as England had to say.

Some among them were by no means ill-informed as to the object of the mission, and even as to the events of recent history. Mr. Elphinstone having stated in conversation with the Khans that, since 1745, there had been no rebellion against the Government of

England, one of those gentlemen smilingly replied that Mr. Elphinstone had forgotten the American War; and then 'asked seriously why the insurance of ships should be raised so high by the French privateers when we had so manifest a superiority at sea.'[1]

A despatch[2] from Mr. Elphinstone, written some weeks after his arrival at Peshawur, gave every reason to hope that a treaty of alliance against the common enemy would be executed; but it was rapidly followed by a second containing far less favourable intelligence. In consequence of a renewal of insurrectionary movements, the King earnestly solicited pecuniary aid from the Company. The sum said to be required by him to ensure his success was not less than fifteen lacs of rupees. The Envoy, however, intimated that a much smaller sum would be of the most essential consequence to the King's affairs, and that, if he were at that moment authorised to offer two lacs of rupees, he had no doubt that, for the mere purpose of the alliance, he could obtain all the security that promises and treaties could give for the King's co-operation.

'The condition of the King's affairs as represented in these despatches, appeared pregnant with danger,

---

[1] The knowledge possessed by the Afghan nobleman sinks into insignificance before that of a Caffre chief as related to me by a correspondent. 'A friend of mine who fought in one of the early Caffre campaigns soon after 1840, I think, told me that, when after some internecine struggles they came to parley with their native foe, they were astonished to be addressed by the half-naked chief with the remark that he respected the British infantry, but that he had been looking into Napier's *Peninsular War*, and could not say that either then or now he thought so much of the British cavalry.'

[2] Secret and separate general letter, April 20, 1809.

and it seemed probable that before our instructions would reach the Envoy in reply, the crisis would be passed, and the King's dominion be either confirmed or subverted. We judged it proper, however, to decide, and communicate immediately our decision, on the case submitted to our consideration, and we observed that, under present circumstances, no advantages could be obtained from the state of Cabul, so important, solid, and permanent as would warrant a pecuniary sacrifice so large as that which our Envoy had represented that the King would require to ensure success; that the suspension of the projects of France, and the alienation from her alliance of the Persian Court, had removed the immediate importance of an alliance between the Indian Government and Cabul; but that, if the Envoy had reason to believe that a sum of money not exceeding three lacs of rupees would produce a disposition on the part of the King of Cabul to co-operate cordially at a future season in repelling a contemplated invasion—in other words, if morally assured of corresponding benefit to the British interests—the Envoy was authorised to advance that sum.

'We are aware, and have frequently advanced the principle as a rule of action in the prosecution of the late measures for the formation of defensive alliances against a European invasion, that a sense of common interest and common danger must form the basis of such alliances. At the same time, a rigid exclusion on our part of all acts of concession, and of all assistance to the views of the other party, though not directly tending to the main purposes of the alliance, is adverse to the successful cultivation of mutual harmony and good-will. Such acts of concession or assistance may influence a disposition balancing between the advantages and the hazard of accepting or rejecting the proposed connection; and a seasonable aid may afford to the other party that latitude of choice which is alone compatible with the power of action, by enabling it to maintain its independence and preserve the means of resistance against a foreign force, which, however dangerous as an ally, a conscious sense of weakness and the dictates of a temporising policy might compel it to conciliate.'

In the instructions forwarded to Mr. Elphinstone himself, of which the substance is embodied in the above despatch, it is stated that, 'although there is not now the same immediate exigency for forming a friendly connection with the Court of Cabul, yet that measure is of importance, and contains an object of sound policy, in the event, however remote, of either the French or any other European Power endeavouring to approach India by that route.'

Almost on the same day when these paragraphs were being written at Calcutta, Mr. Elphinstone was addressing the Governor General in a private letter as follows:[1]

'A very unfavourable turn has taken place in the King of Cabul's affairs. For some time past his prospects had appeared to be much improved. During

[1] April 26, 1809.

this period the negotiations continued, and the treaty was signed on the 19th inst. It merely binds your Lordship to assist the King of Cabul with money against a confederacy of French and Persians, and the King of Cabul to resist these Powers while their confederacy lasts, and to exclude all Frenchmen from his country for ever.

'A few days ago intelligence was received of the approach of Shah Mahommed's troops to Cabul, and of the entire failure of Ameer Ool Moolk's attack on Cashmere, and of the loss or defection of the greater part of his army.

'There are many contradictory accounts of this affair, but it seems certain that Ameer Ool Moolk had advanced very far into the passes when his supplies were cut off by one of the Rajahs on the hills on the way to Cashmere, who had afforded a passage to his army, but whom the Minister had afterwards disobliged. The army which had before been discontented for want of pay, being now reduced to much distress, and the most liberal promises being held out to deserters, a considerable number of the troops went over to the enemy.

'Shah Ool Moolk is making what preparations he can to oppose his enemies, but he is almost destitute of money; and though several of his ministers are rich, the habitual covetousness of the Douranees prevents their giving him any assistance. Ameer Ool Moolk, who is said to be possessed of a crore of rupees, has never assisted the King in any of his distresses, and is not expected to do so in this extremity. The King's forces, it is said, will be sent out immediately, and I suppose he will march as soon as Ameer Ool Moolk arrives on the way to Cabul.

'He is reported to have sent off some of his jewels to a fort of Akran Khan's among the Eusafzyes. The Khybers, in whose hills he formerly took refuge, are now divided, and part of them have refused him an asylum in case he is defeated. The tribes in this neighbourhood are all arming and assembling, to be ready to act as the times may require: some of them are connected with Mahommed, but the greater part of them are indifferent to both parties. This city and the country round it continue in perfect tranquillity.

'As the battle between the two Kings will probably be fought at no great distance from this, I shall, for the reasons I have formerly stated, desire to have my audience of leave, which it was always understood I should have when the King marched towards Cabul. I shall then repair to Attock, and wait the event of the struggle. If Mahommed is victorious, I shall wait the orders of Government, unless I find a speedy acknowledgment of the new King necessary. I do not conceive that it will be difficult to prevail on Shah Mahommed to agree to the same terms as those settled with Shah Soojah, but it appears to me that to do so will require an extra expense of about three lacs of rupees. For this reason in particular I am anxious to receive the orders of Government before I enter on any negotiation with him.'

On June 14 the mission retired from Peshawur, leaving its cool and shady gardens and sparkling fountains with regret. On June 17 the treaty mentioned in Mr. Elphinstone's letter was signed at Calcutta. Before the month had expired Shah Soojah had been completely defeated and had fled from his dominions.

With his successor the Envoy was not authorised to treat. The changed aspect of affairs in Europe, and the friendly relations established by Mr. Metcalfe's diplomacy with Runjeet Singh, had brought the Indian Government to the determination not to risk considerable expenditure upon uncertain and unprofitable alliances.

The most important result of the policy adopted by the Indian Government towards the frontier States during Lord Minto's administration, was the treaty with Runjeet Singh, which for thirty years maintained peace between the British power and the most energetic and powerful of native rulers.

The treaty with Persia, in so far as it pledged Great Britain to subsidise Persia in the event of her being engaged in 'an unprovoked war with any European State,' was, in Lord Minto's opinion, calculated to produce grave complications in the future.

The treaty with Cabul was rendered nugatory by the fall from power of one of the contracting parties who signed it.[1]

[1] An original copy of the treaty drawn up by Mr. Mountstuart Elphinstone and signed at Calcutta in 1809, is still in existence, and

It may nevertheless remain an open question whether the friendly relations established between the Company's Government and Afghanistan might not have been cultivated with better success if the far-sighted policy inaugurated by Lord Minto had been pursued and developed, and due importance attached to the movements of European States in that quarter: in such a course there might have been more of statesmanship and less of saltpetre.

One undeniable and important result of the scheme for the defence of India was the greater knowledge obtained by the missions of the countries and populations to which they were sent, and Mr. Elphinstone's 'History of Cabul,' Colonel Malcolm's 'Persian History' and 'Sketches of Persia,' and Sir Henry Pottinger's work on Beloochistan were conceived during the embassies sent out by Lord Minto. The first two works were compiled and published at the expense of, or with the assistance of ample and liberal aid from, the Indian Government, at the instigation of the Governor General.

is in the possession of Mir Hasham Khan, native officer in the 12th Bengal Cavalry, and grandson of the Vizier of Shah Soojah. The fact became accidentally known to Lord Melgund, the great-grandson of Lord Minto, while with the column of General Roberts in the Kurrum valley in the spring of 1879. He did not see the treaty, but he was informed that the original signature of Lord Minto was attached to it. Mir Hasham Khan is described as a very smart officer in one of our best cavalry regiments. This *rapprochement* between the descendant of the Governor General and of the Afghan statesman, was related in a letter from India while the foregoing pages were being written.

NOTE.

The State of Scinde had come within the scope of the defensive arrangements proposed by the British Government, but the indiscretion of their agent, Captain Seton, led to the annulling of the treaty concluded by him with the Ameer of Scinde.

It was found that Persian agents were negotiating with the Government of Scinde at the same time as the Envoy of the Indian Government; that they had authority to act for both France and Persia, and that the bait held out to the Government of Scinde was military aid to throw off the yoke of the King of Cabul, to whom they owed a nominal allegiance, and the possession of the Afghan fortress of Candahar. 'The chief ruler of Scinde informed Captain Seton distinctly that, despairing of the good-will of the British Government, he had intended to close with the offers of the French and Persians, but preferred the British alliance on the same terms.' These terms, agreed to by Captain Seton, were not consistent with the endeavours making to secure the friendship of the King of Cabul; hence the Indian Government repudiated the engagements made by Captain Seton, and sent another Envoy (Mr. H. Smith) to Scinde, to renew the negotiations with that Government, on the footing on which alone Captain Seton had been empowered to treat—namely, the admission, as a preliminary step to all further transactions, of a resident agent of the British Government (the commercial resident having been expelled in 1802).

'This measure is necessarily preliminary to the accomplishment of our ultimate purpose, that of withholding or detaching the Government of Scinde from connections with our enemies, as well as the more proximate purpose of securing an authentic channel of information and intelligence on points of the utmost importance to our interests.' 'No specific engagement could be entered into with that Government without the establishment of direct intercourse on a permanent footing,' 'the attainment of which will afford the means of watching its proceedings and of obtaining authentic intelligence concerning the designs of our enemies.'[1]

The conditions proposed by the British Government were ultimately accepted as the basis of a treaty of general amity between the Company's Government and that of the Ameer.

[1] Secret and separate general letter.

CHAPTER VIII.

THE news from Europe which exercised so decisive an influence over the course of events in India was that of the determined resistance of Spain to the French invasion, and the first successes of the British army in Portugal under Sir Arthur Wellesley.

The Battle of Vimiero [1] was hailed as the 'trumpet of a prophecy.' So unbroken had been the tide of Napoleon's prosperity that the defeat of one of his lieutenants, Junot, by Sir Arthur Wellesley, was magical in its effect on the temper of the nation. 'All the Whigs, as well as Tories, down to democrats and Methodists, are eager to send English troops and money to the assistance of that oppressed nation. . . . The Princess of Wales gave a dinner to the Spanish patriots. It was a mixed party, but none the worse for that, as all parties there were united in the grand cause.' [2]

---

[1] August 1808.

[2] Lady Crewe to Lord Minto, December 1808. She goes on à propos of the Princess's dinner-party: 'You would have smiled if you had heard the Pindaric jokes which flew across the table from our Royal hostess to Mr. Windham across Mr. Frere, and then across other people to Sir William Scott, for she spared no one of the party. There is nothing more propitious to mental coquetry than a disunion among statesmen.'

The rejoicing was not less in India. 'Great news is come to town,' wrote Lord Minto on February 2, 1809. 'A ship has just arrived from England which she left on September 17. She has brought us the triumphs of Sir A. Wellesley in Portugal. What a sunshine has broken upon the world! I feel now as if Gilbert the Sixth[1] might have a chance to cut the trees which you are planting, which, let me tell you, is a comfortable reflection.' The tidings of Wellesley's victory swept over India to Metcalfe's little camp on the distant Sutlege, and were sounded again from every gun, great and small, as they poured forth a Royal salute. On learning its cause, Runjeet desired his guns to take up the tale, and a second salute from the Sikh batteries proclaimed the participation of the Rajah in the British rejoicing—an act of courtesy which was much appreciated at the time.

'The news continues good from Spain,' wrote Lord Minto, 'yet I hope the rest of the world will not let this occasion slip once more; for, if they give him leisure, the monster will collect his rage, and it may go hard with the beautiful Spanish cause yet. Oh! that the

---

In his reply to this letter, Lord Minto says of the Princess: 'She has been badly treated, for the stones cast at her do not come from hands entitled to throw them. One bad thing, however, she is guilty of—ingratitude to Windham. I say nothing of myself, though she entertained me the day I took leave of her not only with the wish that Windham might be turned out of Norfolk with some great personal disgrace, but with the hope that Lord Melville would disturb me in India. However, I continue to lament her discomforts and to wish for her welfare.'

[1] His infant grandson.

fable of the bundle of sticks had ever been translated into any of the modern languages, for want of which, alas! it has become sad sober history instead of fable.' The first fleet that arrived in India after these lines were written told that the pride and rejoicing called forth by the brilliant campaign of Talavera had been severely checked by the retreat of our armies from Spain, and the Convention of Cintra. 'I grieve,' wrote Mr. Windham, 'over the circumstances that prevented the complete defeat of Junot's army, which I believe would have happened if Wellesley had been left to himself; though no doubt the insolence of the Ministers, founded on merits not their own, would not less have excited in one's mind great impatience.'

'It has been a disastrous month,' wrote Lady Malmesbury in February 1809; 'but after all the French have had a practical lesson as to our fighting, and the world has seen they are not invincible.' Lord Minto's correspondents in general betook themselves to the usual consolation of Englishmen in disaster, and abused the leaders of parties all round.

'There is not a statesman endowed with superior talents. The deaths of Pitt and Fox have produced the same effect on the public as that of Garrick did on the stage. Stars will not do when we are used to the light of the sun.'

'The Hollands are in Spain,' wrote Lady Crewe; 'but Miss Fox wrote to me some months ago that her brother was very angry with his Spanish friends for their absurdity in supposing that they shall be able to restore their present King, and that they ought to feel gratitude to Bonaparte for having rid them of so weak a prince. "Is it possible," she said, "that we are to fight in so bad a cause?" When I read this, I could not help thinking that we should always have something to dread of the *republican hobby-horse* in the part of opposition! I am sorry to say that I see this tendency prevail much more since the last defeats than it did before. Mr. Whitbread, however, met with no encouragement at the time he published a pamphlet to advise peace with Bonaparte in the summer, and Heaven grant that Mr. Canning may have influence enough over the present Parliament to prevent that experiment for a year.'

To these letters Lord Minto replied: 'Spain is indeed a lamentable tale. As to the invasion of India, I presume if Europe is entirely subdued, the King of Men may carry his views to the eastward, but I am strongly inclined to believe that they would be limited to disturbing us by inciting some of the Asiatic States to make incursions into Hindostan, supported and directed by partial aid in small bodies of French and perhaps Russian troops, and good European officers. The difficulties in the way of an advance by a large European army are scarcely surmountable. However, we should always have ample notice; for rapidity is practicable in the invasion of Spain or Italy, but is simply impossible in transporting a French army to the Indus, with all its artillery, stores, and apparatus, the whole of which must attend it, for the most indispensable equipments of a great European force do not exist on this side of Vienna, and can neither be kept up nor, if lost or wasted, can be renewed in Asia, excepting only in our own provinces, where all the resources of war abound, and are to us at hand.'

It must have been grateful to him to learn from Lady Minto that his Indian administration had won the warmest approbation of Lord Wellesley. 'He highly approves of all you have been doing in your kingdom. We are now enjoying Minto,' she goes on, 'in its greatest beauty. Everything looks fresh and delightful: you know I enjoy this season (May), and this year it affords me double pleasure, for I have learnt to look with composure from Minto to India, and without the misery which made even green leaves look dusky and the clear streams troubled. I believe you all to be well and happy, and I hear from every quarter, and in every account of India, nothing but praise of you and your government. If Burke could look down and see you at the head of that oppressed people, it would increase even the happiness of heaven.'

May in India wore a very different aspect from that with which it smiled on Minto.

'I do remember a time,' wrote Lord Minto,[1] 'when May was a season of tempered pleasures. Here it brings rains so perpetual and heavy, that if in June greater rains come, I don't know how we shall get our

[1] May 15, 1809.

house repaired, which is already leaking at every pore. The country is one sheet of water. Here and there you see a little island about the size of half an acre, which happens to stand a few feet higher than the rest. It is no exaggeration to say that persons now pass in boats across the country which they were ploughing two or three days back; but the crops will be improved by this operation, for paddy rejoices in water. The native children, I mean the young ones, are all stark naked, and, most of the habitations being on the edge of ponds, are not very unlike tadpoles; they are uncommonly lively merry monkeys, and I am not at all annoyed by their black skins. You never saw a country so swarming with population. . . . Business here appears to me to breed in the boxes, as Lady Palmerston used to say of keys in a lady's pocket. However, the business is pleasant now, consisting principally of orders to countermand military operations and preparations, and to save Johnny Company's cash.'

The two years 1808 and 1809 were, perhaps, the busiest of Lord Minto's administration. India was supposed to be at peace; but that word must be taken in a relative sense, for in India the public peace was kept by armies. If certain feudal chiefs rejected the authority of their lord paramount, their relations with whom had been recognised by the Government of Bengal, British troops brought them to reason. If an ambitious Rajah cast a covetous glance on his neighbour's territory, a British detachment gave him an unmistakable reading of the *dictum*, 'Cursed is he who removeth his neighbour's landmark.' If the free lances of the hills showed too great a fondness for the mango groves and rice fields of the plain, English colonels and their soldiers appeared rapidly on the scene, and the depredators were chased up the high hills and expelled from their strongholds on their summits. From such operations as these there was no rest.[1]

The internal safety of Bengal, however, remained intact from open enemies, and it was with equal dismay and surprise that it was found necessary, in the course of 1809, to employ the regular forces to extirpate the gangs of banditti or dacoits who had penetrated into the heart of the Presidency, and with whom the native police were accused of being in league.

'They have of late come within thirty miles of Barrackpore.[2] The crime of gang robbery has at all times, though in different degrees, obtained a footing in Bengal. The prevalence of the offence occasioned by its success and impunity, has been much greater in this civilised and flourishing part of India, than in the wilder territories adjoining, which have not enjoyed so long the advantages of a regular and legal government ; and it appears at first sight mortifying to the English administration of these provinces, that our oldest

---

[1] In 1812-13 several Rajahs and Chiefs, such as the Prince of Rewa and the Rajah of Machery, were punished for high-handed dealings with their neighbours. In reference to such operations, Malcolm in his *History of India* remarks : 'All these acts of consideration and vigour kept the smaller dependencies of the State in good humour.'

[2] Lord Minto to Lady Minto.

possessions should be the worst protected against the evils of lawless violence.

'It has been said that the prosperity and undisturbed tranquillity of these lower provinces, which have never seen war within their limits during the present generation of their inhabitants, that is to say, for half a century, have afforded two inducements to the desperate associations which have so constantly harassed them under the name of dacoits. First, the riches of the country have presented the temptation of good plunder. Second, the long security which the country has enjoyed from foreign enemies, and the consequent loss of martial habits and character, have made the people of Bengal so timid and enervated, that no resistance is to be apprehended in the act, nor punishment afterwards. There have, however, certainly been other more specific causes for the extraordinary prevalence of the crime at particular times or in particular quarters. Among these has been the nature of our judicial and police establishments. The judge and magistrate is an English gentleman; but all his subordinate officers and instruments are necessarily *native*. The probity and good intentions of the English magistrate may in general be relied upon; but his vigilance, personal activity, intelligence, or talents, are not equal in all cases to his integrity. The consequence often is, that the practical and efficient part of the police is cast upon the black subaltern officers, amongst whom it is hardly too much to say, although it sounds like an uncharitable partiality to my own fair complexion, that there is scarcely an example of fidelity to any trust, and scarcely an exception to universal venality and corruption. The magistrate derives his information of the crimes committed in his zillah from this corrupt source, and trusts for the detection, apprehension, and punishment of the criminals to these venal agents. The consequence has in many instances been, as it has been lately ascertained by the most minute and authentic investigations, that the magistrate has remained entirely ignorant of a very large proportion of the offences committed within his jurisdiction, and has congratulated himself on the good order and exact police of a country in which the inhabitants could not sleep securely in their houses, and in which great bodies of armed banditti have been robbing and burning the villages, and murdering and torturing the people all round him. The native officers of police have very generally been connected with the gangs, and I may say universally silenced either by bribes or intimidation. Another peculiarity in India is the total absence of a local gentry to whom the charge of the local police and other local interests may, as in England, be at least in part committed. So far from aid in these objects, Government has often to contend with the counteraction of the landed interest. The zemindars, or gentlemen of landed property, have very commonly no other idea of an estate than as a field to plunder in, nor of the influence which property gives, than as a power to extort and pillage amongst the people subject to them. The leaders of the dacoits find it their interest to conciliate this class of people, and by a participation in the plunder, or by other inducements, obtain a secure refuge and protection in their estates. The best security of all, however, enjoyed by the dacoits, has been the intimidation of the unhappy people who are the objects of their rapine and cruelty. It is impossible to imagine, without seeing it, the horrid ascendancy they had obtained over the inhabitants at large of the countries which have been the principal scene of their atrocities. They had established a terrorism as perfect as that which was the foundation of the French republican power, and in truth the *sirdars*, or captains of the band, were esteemed and even called the *hakim* or ruling power, while the real Government did not possess either authority or influence enough to obtain from the people the smallest aid towards their own protection. If a whole village was destroyed, not a man was found to complain. If a family was half murdered, and half tortured, the tortured survivors could not be prevailed upon to appear against the criminals. Men have been found with their limbs and half the flesh of their bodies consumed by slow fire, who persisted in saying that they had fallen into their own fire, or otherwise denying all knowledge of the event that could tend to the conviction or detection of the offenders. They knew, if they spoke, they would either themselves or the remaining members of their families be dispatched the same evening. By these measures such a vigorous efficient government was erected by the banditti in these districts, that they could send a single messenger through the villages with regular lists of requisitions from the different houses and families,—some to furnish grain, some forage, some horses, some two sons to join the gangs, some labourers to carry the plunder, or to bear torches, or to act as scouts; some were to send a wife or daughter to attend the gangs.

'I was not a little shocked, and could not help feeling some shame, when I became fully apprised of the dreadful disorders which afflicted countries under the very eye of Government; and for many months past it has been one of the principal objects to put this monstrous evil down. Partly by a new selection of magistrates, who appeared peculiarly qualified for that species of service, by new regulations and additional penalties, and by the employment of the most active efforts, supported by regular force, to seize the *sirdars* and make some signal examples, I am happy to say that hitherto the success has even exceeded my expectations. In Nuddeah, which was the principal seat of this evil, there has not been a single dacoity during the last months; and it is in that one district that the computed average of persons put to death in torture was seventy a month. Nine sirdars have been executed at one spot, and the impression of that example was remarkable. The people had come to think it impossible that the leader of an established gang should be punished, or at least capitally punished, and they looked on with fully as much awe as satisfaction on this proof of the supreme power of Government. The consequence of these examples, and of the determination Government has evinced to subdue these villains, has been the breaking up of the gangs, the flight or seizure of the captains, and a sufficient return of courage and of confidence in the protection of Government amongst the people to procure both prosecutors and witnesses for the detection and punishment of these and all other crimes. It will require a continuous exertion, however, with such improvements in the general system as events and reflection may suggest, to enable us to triumph finally and permanently over this deep-rooted mischief.'

The dacoits unhappily still ply their trade in certain parts of India, under much the same circumstances as those in which flourish their congeners, the banditti of Europe; but, unlike them, they follow peaceful occupations by day, and their own peculiar industry by night. Both dacoit and brigand are at the lowest depth of their respective civilisations, the essential distinction between them being that the dacoit begins his campaign by a propitiatory sacrifice, and the brigand ends his with an expiatory offering.

About the same time, the early part of 1809, troubles suddenly broke out beyond the British frontier, which brought the Indian Government face to face with the problem how to reconcile the interests of India with the peremptory instructions issued by their chiefs at home on the subject of non-interference with the internal affairs of States so situated.

One of the consequences which had followed on the

defeat of the great native States of the peninsula,
before the British power was far-stretching enough to
assume their lost authority, was an increase of audacity
on the part of the semi-civilised tribes whose home was
in the wild recesses of the Ghauts, or on the table-lands
of the Deccan. The Pathans, Pindaries, and others,
with more or less countenance from the Mahrattas,
became exceedingly dangerous to their weaker neighbours.

In the early part of 1809, Ameer Khan,[1] a Pathan
chief, at the head of a numerous army invaded the
territories of the Rajah of Berar—who, though not an
ally of the British, was in close contiguity with their
frontier—and threatened the whole country of Nagpore. Here was a case in which the instructions of the
Court of Directors as to the duty of non-intervention
could only be observed to the detriment of British power.

'The question was not,' observed Lord Minto,

---

[1] This adventurer made himself hateful throughout India when in the following year he instigated a murder which would have seemed less unnatural in the annals of antiquity than in those of the nineteenth century. The most ancient of the Rajpoot Princes, the Rajah of Oodypore, had a daughter so young and fair that, like a second Helen, she set the world on fire. Rajpootana was distracted by the wars of her suitors, till one fatal day it was suggested to her father by Ameer Khan that peace could only be restored to his distracted country by her death. Ameer Khan's power lent weight to his words; the counsel was listened to, and finally accepted. The elder sister of the ill-fated princess was deputed to present her with a poisoned bowl, desiring her to save her country by the sacrifice of her own life. She, a young and lovely girl of sixteen, is said to have accepted the decree in all meekness, and to have drunk off the fatal potion, exclaiming, 'This is the marriage to which I was foredoomed.'

'whether it was just and expedient to aid the Rajah in the defence and recovery of his dominions; although in point of policy the essential change in the political state of India which would be occasioned by the extinction of one of the substantive Powers of the Deccan, might warrant our interference; but whether an enterprising and ambitious Mussulman chief, at the head of a numerous army, irresistible by any power except that of the Company, should be permitted to establish his authority on the ruins of the Rajah's dominions, over territories contiguous to those of our ally, the Nizam, with whom community of religion, combined with local power and resources, might lead to the formation of projects for the subversion of the British alliance: of such a question there can be but one solution.' That solution was the immediate expulsion by the Company's troops of the invader from Berar, whose Rajah must have been agreeably surprised to find that the assistance of the British, being designed for the preservation of their own interests, was to be gratuitously given. Colonel Close, who commanded the troops employed in the operation, not only carried it out successfully, but proceeded to occupy the capital and territory of Ameer Khan, who retired rapidly before the British advance. Its arrest, by order of the Government, at the moment when the annihilation of Ameer Khan's power, and the dispersion if not destruction of his army, were seemingly within the grasp of the English commander, has been criticised as an error of policy on the part of

Lord Minto's Government. He himself said of it that 'the extent of the political arrangements, as well as of the military operations, to which the prosecution of these views would lead, together with the great increase of expenditure which must ensue,' had determined him to content himself with the immediate object of arresting the invasion which threatened the integrity of our own dominions.

In Bundelcund, where the military operations, begun two years before, were not yet completed ; in Hariana, a territory which more lately the Indian Government was forced to annex in the interests of civilisation and humanity, 'because nobody else would have it,' he had had occasion to experience the truth of a leading principle in the government of semi-civilised populations—that where one rule is destroyed, another must be substituted.

He was not prepared to pursue the defeat of Ameer Khan to the point of assuming new and permanent responsibilities ; but in a minute dated December 1, 1809, he observed that 'it has not perhaps been sufficiently considered that every native State in India is a military despotism ; that war and conquest are avowed as the first and legitimate pursuit of every sovereign or chief, and the sole source of glory and renown ; it is not therefore a mere conjecture deduced from the natural bias of the human mind, and the test of general experience, but a certain conviction founded on avowed principles of action and systematic views, that among the military states and chiefs of India the pursuits of ambition can alone be bounded by the inability to prosecute them. It was for the Government of England to decide whether it was expedient to observe a strict neutrality amidst these scenes of disorder and outrage which were passing under our eyes in the north of Hindostan, or whether we should listen to the calls of suffering humanity, and interfere for the protection of those weak and defenceless States who implore our assistance, to deliver them from the violence and oppression of an ambitious and lawless upstart.' When these observations were answered, it was found that a considerable change had come over the policy of the Court of Directors. They stated that 'they did not conceive that measures of defensive policy could be construed into acts of unnecessary interference in the affairs of foreign States,' and they expressed themselves 'not satisfied with the expediency of abstaining from disabling any Power against whom we have been compelled to take up arms, from renewing its aggression' (September 1811).

A more complete exoneration of the Wellesley policy, so violently assailed a few years before, could hardly be required; nor a more instructive commentary on Talleyrand's celebrated reply to one who asked him the meaning of the term 'non-intervention': 'C'est un mot politique et metaphysique qui veut dire à peu près la même chose qu' intervention.'

Lord Minto was in Java when this despatch was addressed to him: after his return to India questions of a more pressing nature occupied his attention, but almost his last letter to the Secret Committee related to the increasing importance of the Pindaries.

The last and not least important measure of this year (1809) consisted in a naval expedition against a formidable horde of pirates on the Persian Gulf. Their settlements extended for a stretch of 400 miles along the coast, whence these sea brigands scoured the Indian seas, their small fleets carrying off the inhabitants of the villages of the shore, destroying the coasting trade, and capturing, not only small vessels, but any stray merchantmen that came in their way. One such capture, accompanied with circumstances of great barbarity, was an exploit which drew upon them the signal vengeance of the Indian Government. A formidable expedition consisting of two frigates, six armed vessels, 900 European troops, and 500 Sepoys, was sent to their coasts, and, after a desperate resistance, their settlements and fleets were captured and destroyed, and the commerce of the Persian Gulf was rescued from their depredations.

Thus, by land and sea, the Company's dominions were preserved intact, and its power upheld. And every despatch to England contained well-deserved encomiums of the skill and valour and discipline of the forces employed in defending the frontiers, or in protecting the subjects of the Empire. And yet, while the events described were in progress, a cloud had appeared on the horizon of more portentous dimensions than any of its predecessors in those stormy regions. 'I have determined to go to Madras as soon as possible,' wrote Lord Minto in June 1809. 'The differences between the Madras army and Sir George Barlow's Government have risen to a most violent height, and more suddenly than I imagined.'

CHAPTER IX.

The troubles in the coast army require to be dealt with in some detail, because Lord Minto's share in their final reduction has been scarcely appreciated, while he himself considered it second to no other part of his administration in the importance of its results. When he arrived in India in 1807, he found Madras still simmering in the dregs of the agitation produced by the mutiny and massacre of Vellore. The danger from the native soldiery was past, but there remained a state of excited feeling and of bitter antagonism among the higher officials of the Presidency that boded future mischief.

Their controversies produced a general spirit of cabal and combination, and violent attacks made by high functionaries on each other diminished the respect due to them in their public capacity. While the question of the recall of Lord William Bentinck was still pending, Lord Minto gave his opinion as opposed to that measure. He thought that the conduct of individuals on that occasion (the Vellore mutiny) had been blamed with too little attention to the different points of conduct under consideration in connection with the precise circumstances of the time when they took place. 'I am apprehensive also that these occurrences may not be favourable to the restoration either of civil or military authority. The mutiny was completely subdued, opinions were settled, and men's minds were composed on these questions. Those who had suffered the sentence of the law were regarded as criminals justly punished for atrocious offences. Now that a Governor and Commander-in-chief are publicly condemned and punished, on the other hand, in the view of the very mutineers and their adherents, the public mind may perhaps be unhinged again, and those who were hanged and shot by the subordinate local authorities for mutiny and murder, may seem to have been justified by still higher tribunals, and may start up under our sanction into saints and martyrs. I do not say this reasoning would be just, but worse reasoning has often satisfied men's passions in their own cause.'[1]

These representations were disregarded, and some of the consequences foreseen by the Governor General took place. The native soldiery, indeed, do not appear to have been affected as he had conceived it possible they might be; but the dissensions in the European society were aggravated, and the Government of Fort St. George necessarily suffered in the estimation of the Presidency.

In the same despatch of November 26, 1807, Lord Minto answered in the following terms a question that had been addressed to him by the Court of Directors con-

[1] To the Right Hon. R. Dundas, President of the Board of Control, November 26, 1807.

cerning the expediency of excluding the Commanders-in-chief of the two minor Presidencies from seats in Council.

'The point is so entirely new that I cannot, on the sudden, offer any opinion worthy of attention. I presume that measure may have been suggested to the Court of Directors by the experience they have so frequently had, especially at Fort St. George, of long controversial and often warm and intemperate discussions in Council between the civil and military authorities. It has happened also in late instances that notions concerning military ascendancy have been entertained and asserted which are wholly incompatible with the received and established principles of a government by law.

'The introduction, for example, of the judicial system, that is to say, the administration of civil justice between man and man, and the suppression of public disorder and crime by a regular magistracy, has been objected to and resented as a degradation of the military character, and an unjust diminution of its influence and authority in India, where it once stood in the place of law, and was more suited, as it is contended, to the habits and tastes of the people than civil justice administered judicially by magistrates. This doctrine will sound so strange in English ears that the fact of its being maintained will scarcely meet with credit. These sentiments, however, have been distinctly recorded in the enclosed pamphlet which Sir John Cradock left behind him, and, I am sorry to learn, are not less warmly professed by General McDowell . . . The inconveniences which have been in some instances felt from the Commander-in-chief holding officially a seat in Council, have I believe been very real, but I confess I doubt the expediency of adopting the particular remedy proposed. I am disinclined to it as a very considerable *change*, and as one calculated to separate still more from the general government of the country, and not only to alienate but to irritate in a high degree, the mind of the army, a great and powerful body in India, whose cordiality and co-operation in the views of Government is extremely essential.

'There is little doubt that the measure in question would produce this effect. It appears to me that other remedies, not liable to the same objection, might be applied in most instances to the inconvenience complained of. The first is a careful and fit choice of the man for the office of Commander-in-chief. Military endowments he ought certainly to have. He should possess also a sound judgment and a conciliatory disposition. He should come out penetrated with, and well instructed in, the indispensable subordination of the military power to the superintending superiority of the civil Government.'

The Court of Directors nevertheless decided on excluding the Commanders-in-chief of the minor Presidencies from Council, and appointed General McDowell to the post of Commander-in-chief vacated by the recall of Sir J. Cradock.

Thus early in his Indian career did Lord Minto

impress on the Court of Directors the necessity of an unfaltering insistance on the supremacy of the civil over the military power. His own experience in Corsica had shown him the inconveniences arising from excessive military pretensions. He had learnt at Vienna to attribute the misfortunes which had befallen Austria to 'a military faction which substituted party spirit in the room of all the duties of soldiers or citizens —that party spirit spread through the Empire.'

He found in India a state of affairs peculiarly favourable to the development of strife between the civil and military authorities. A recently conquered and imperfectly settled country had been brought under the influence of the civil Government within the memory of the senior officers of the army, leaving some chagrin and jealousy with those who had been used to wield both political and military authority. Since 1765, when Clive put down a mutiny of the officers of the Bengal army, scarce a decade had passed without an open struggle between the military and the civil power;[1] and only ten years before Lord Minto's arrival in India a mutiny of the Bengal officers, which had lasted upwards of two years, had ended in complete victory. Sir John Shore, afterwards Lord Teignmouth, the Go-

[1] In an able article on the mutiny of 1809 which appeared in the *Quarterly Review* for May 1811 (vol. v.), the following summary of the various mutinies of the Company's officers, from 1765 to 1796, is quoted from a published paper entitled, 'Reply to the publication of William Petrie, Esq., regarding the late transactions at Madras.'

'A mutiny of the officers took place in the year 1765; which was only suppressed by the firmness of Lord Clive.

vernor General at the time, had no doubt been recalled; but the fact that open resistance to regular authority had successfully wrung from a weak Government more than it had contended for, justified the belief that representations made by numbers and supported by clamour would not fail to obtain their ends. Lord Wellesley's commanding character and his brilliant military achievements had suppressed any open expression during his government of military discontent, but there still remained the fact that India had been won by the sword and was held by the sword. Lord

'At an earlier period, in Bombay, the military rose upon the civil power, and assumed the government which they held and retained in their hands for two years. In or about the year 1776, Major-General Stuart at the head of the army seized on the then Governor of Madras, Lord Pigot, confined his person and subverted his government. In the year 1783 the army of Madras compelled the Governor, Lord Macartney, to revoke his orders, and to re-establish some allowances which he had found it necessary to discontinue. Actual violence was not indeed resorted to, but the receipt of three addresses on the same day on the subject from the three principal stations of the army convinced his lordship of the necessity of giving up the point. At a more recent period in Bengal, in or about the year 1796, the countenance which the army assumed must be fresh in the recollection of everyone.

'It appears further, from the Parliamentary papers before us, that even at the commencement of the late mutiny, 1809, the notion of the *rights of the army*, and that of forming associations to plead these rights, were familiar to the Madras officers. In notions of this kind the officers of the Indian army, in general, seem to have been encouraged by the British Government. . . . Persons avowedly acting in the capacity of agents of the Indian army have been admitted to a formal audience by Her Majesty's ministers in England. On what principle men of the highest ability, political knowledge, and patriotism, for such these ministers were, could consent thus to recognise in the army an independent and substantive power, we are at a loss to imagine.'

Minto was resolved that India should not be governed by the sword.

In the course of 1808 when an expedition to Persia was under consideration, the supreme Government announced to that of Bombay an intention of raising a cavalry regiment on the Bombay establishment; it was subsequently found that this might be done with greater facility at Madras, and the first plan was therefore abandoned; but not without exciting the resentment of the officers of the Bombay army. They considered their honour and dignity to be wounded by the course the Government had adopted. How Lord Minto received their complaints, his letter in reply to Jonathan Duncan, Esq., Governor of Bombay, will show.

'I enter, I assure you, warmly into every feeling which belongs to the disappointment of expectations reasonably entertained, and necessarily near the hearts of those concerned, although I cannot with the same truth and sincerity consent to their aggravation by pressing into their alliance imaginary, or, at best, gratuitous sentiments of offended honour which have no room in the case.

. . . .

'Our option lay between the course which was evidently the best for the public advantage and security, and that by which we might desire to gratify a few officers of the Bombay army by a deliberate sacrifice of higher interests. We made the choice which our duty required, and which must obtain, I have no doubt, when clearly explained, the suffrages of the Bombay army itself; a body as much distinguished for genuine public spirit as for military excellence.

'I consider the interests of all the servants of the public, and more especially of that honourable class which provides for the safety and prosperity of the country by their own dangers and privations.

'But the interest and security of the public are the first and highest care of those to whom that public has committed the trust of exercising authority in its name, and that great charge constitutes the primary duty of governments,—a duty, indeed, in which all those participate to whom their country has in any rank or condition confided any portion of its power, whether civil or military. These are indeed, very trite and general principles, but they are none the less those which must govern my conduct.

'In the application of them, therefore, if a regiment is to be added to the Company's establishment, the first point to be considered in the mode of its formation must be the public interest; next, but subordinate to that consideration, the interest and pretensions of individuals or bodies connected with the measure. . . . Our military arrangements in all circumstances must be determined by the exigencies of the State.

. . . .

'As to menace, or any attempt at intimidation, the case is not to be supposed; the supposition alone would constitute an injury and insult to the honourable men who compose the Bombay army. But if in any quarter of the world, where I might happen to be the depositary of public authority, such a case should arise, my mind is settled on the only principle adapted in any circumstances to that exigency,—to admit of no compromise with an evil far greater than any that can be incurred, even by a defeat, in resisting it; but to maintain the full and unqualified sovereignty which is in reality the safety of the State, by combating either the seditious combinations and cabals, or the criminal violence, of its servants, to the last and utmost extremity. I am clear that if such an event could be imagined, it would be better for the public interest to be fairly subdued than to yield. The former would be a single, local, and very transient evil, quickly and certainly repaired. The latter never happens without operating a general and permanent relaxation of authority and diminution of all the public energies throughout the empire in which it occurs.

'I take the two great pillars of every human government to be—first, that all its measures be directed to the public good; next, that its authority, thus exercised, be maintained with unshaken firmness and resolution.'

This warning note had a graver significance when, in the following year of 1809, the mutiny of the officers of the Madras army broke out. It was no doubt attributable to a variety of causes, among which must be acknowledged certain real grievances on the part of the army, and certain serious mistakes on the part of Sir George Barlow, Governor of Madras. A consideration of these lies beyond our province, which is simply to relate the position assumed by Lord Minto with regard to the powers in conflict—always bearing in mind that his active interference, by written and personal advice and support, only began after the discontent of the officers had taken the form of insubordinate opposition to the Government. The immediate cause of the disturbances at Madras is stated in Marshman's 'History of India' as follows:[1] 'After the Mahratta War the Court of Directors had been fierce for retrenchment, and had threatened to take the pruning knife into their own hands,' if the Madras Government hesitated to use it. 'Among the plans suggested for reducing the military charges was the abolition of the tent contract, which furnished the officers in command of regiments with a fixed monthly allowance to provide the men with camp equipage whether they were in the field or in cantonments. The system was essentially vicious, . . . the Quartermaster General, Colonel Munro, had been requested to draw up a report, and both Sir John Cradock and Lord William Bentinck had come to the determination to abolish the contract, when they were suddenly recalled. It fell to the unhappy lot of Sir George Barlow, already sufficiently unpopular, to carry this resolution into effect. This retrenchment increased the resent-

[1] Vol. ii. p. 240.

ment of the officers, and they determined to wreak their vengeance on the Quartermaster General, who had stated in his report that the result of granting the same allowance in peace and in war for the tentage of the native regiments, while the expenses incidental to it varied with circumstances, had been found by experience to place the interest and the duty of commanding officers in opposition to each other. . . . The officers called on the Commander-in-chief to bring Colonel Munro to a court martial for aspersions on their character as officers and gentlemen. The Judge Advocate General to whom the question was fully referred, considered that the officers had neither right nor reason on their side; but General McDowell, then on the eve of retiring from the service, yielded to their wishes, and at once placed him under arrest. He appealed to the Governor in Council, under whose authority he had acted, and the Commander-in-chief was ordered to release him.'

'The battle was then joined,' wrote Lord Minto in a private letter to the Chairman of the East India Company.[1] 'The Commander-in-chief committed open sedition, and sent forth an inflammatory appeal from the acts of Government,' the effect of which, as described by Colonel Malcolm, was that of 'waving a torch over a powder magazine.' To General McDowell's unwearied efforts 'to establish a confederacy between his own resentment at his exclusion from Council, and the

[1] April 25, 1809.

imaginary grievances of the army,' Lord Minto ascribed the state of feeling that displayed itself in the absurd attempt to try Colonel Munro for his report on the tent contract. The arrest of Colonel Munro on those scandalous charges was a gross abuse of his authority. ' I consider the standard to have been set up against the Government by that act, the scope of which was to bring a military regulation solemnly adopted by the Government of Fort St. George and by the supreme Government, under the cognisance of a band of officers to be tried as a base and scandalous crime.

'The attempt was to wrest the regulation of the army, and the control of military arrangements and economy, out of the hands of Government, in which the constitution of these Provinces and of every other country in the world, and, above all the rest, of Great Britain, has anxiously and jealously placed it, and commit it to the officers of the army themselves.'

Up to this point there seems to have been no difference of opinion among calm men as to which party in the conflict had right on its side ; but a change became apparent when the violent order of the Commander-in-chief was immediately followed by a counter order no less intemperate from the Government, coupled with the dismissal of two officers of high rank who had countersigned and published the order of their superior. Lord Minto, true to his principle that the specific questions in the controversy were of very minor importance compared with the fundamental and most important consideration of the permanent relations between the civil and military powers, publicly and steadily supported the Government of Fort St. George. That he did not do so in a spirit of blind partiality to the proceedings of Sir George Barlow, is proved by a confidential letter to his son, in which he confessed his real sentiments and the reasons for their suppression.

'This measure—the removal of the Adjutant and the Deputy Adjutant General for giving circulation to General McDowell's general order of January 28—started a question likely to unite military opinions against the Government of Fort St. George. It became the immediate ground of the general combination of the army, and furnished the first *questionable* matter in the struggle Sir George had to maintain against a military faction already determined to carry their personal opposition against him to extremity. It was made the *hinge* of these dissensions.

'You will see that I have given unqualified support to the Government of Fort St. George on this delicate point. I was not and could not be consulted when the measure was adopted. If my judgment had been to be given in that stage I should certainly have dissuaded it; and in truth both I and my colleagues in Bengal learnt the occurrence with the greatest possible regret. We felt distinctly all the consequences that were to follow; a general bond of union among the disaffected, and a plausible pretext, which had not before existed, for discontent and clamour, was now furnished by this most unfortunate and impolitic measure. I am making this confession most confidentially to you and my very few confidants. In India it is a secret to everybody but Mr. Lumsden, Mr. Colebroke, and General Hewitt.

'I had to consider, however, not whether the measure was to be taken, but, being already taken, whether it should be reversed. To put Sir George in the wrong on *any* point, but especially on the main point, was to overthrow his Government and give a complete triumph to military combination for all time to come: for it must not be forgotten that the successful combination of the Bengal officers in 1796, when Government at home took fright, is the real root of the late insubordination in the army of the Madras Presidency.

'I had nevertheless to satisfy myself upon the abstract merits of the question: for, although the public safety might require that I should support an impolitic measure, nothing could have induced me to strain the point of justice; and if these officers had appeared to me unjustly removed, or if military principles had in my judgment been really violated on this occasion, I must have restored the officers, and disavowed the principle, without regard to consequences.'

The letter goes on to state at considerable length the incontrovertible grounds or arguments by which Lord Minto satisfied himself that the action of the Adjutant and Deputy Adjutant General, in publishing and disseminating the general order of the Commander-in-chief, in defiance of the regulation that all orders should be in the first instance submitted to the Government, was a dereliction of duty that justified their dismissal by Sir George Barlow from a legal, though not from a politic, point of view. Having reached which conclusion he did not hesitate to give his unqualified support to the Government of Fort St. George. In a letter to the Secret Committee he urged upon them the adoption of a similar course.

'In these circumstances the safety of India must depend upon the support given to the local Government by the authorities in England. I can have no right to dictate any judgment to those to whom I am myself subordinate, but my duty requires that I should state my opinion.

'An army, that is not subordinate to the Government of the country in which it serves, is its master; and, while this inverted order of things continues, no Government can be responsible for the conduct of affairs of which they are in reality divested. The present is a fair trial of strength between legal government and its most formidable rival. Feeble measures will not decide the contest, and a mere negative to the pretensions of the factions will not prevent the frequent repetition of the experiment which is now making. That can be effected only, not by demonstrating the vanity, but by showing the dangers, of such transgressions. The two leading points, therefore, in the measures which I recommend at home are,—first, a clear and distinct support of the Government of Fort St. George; second, the signal punishment of the principal offenders

'One essential point is to take care that the present factions be not enabled to claim the slightest degree of success in any of their real or professed objects. Whatever may be thought of the question concerning the restoration of the Commander-in-chief to Council, it could not, I think, be adopted at the present moment without great and important mischief.'[1]

When Lord Minto wrote these lines he evidently thought the crisis over. Nothing was further from the truth. Within two days, on May 11, an order, issued by Sir George Barlow, for the removal of four officers from their commands, and the suspension of eight others, caused the scarcely smothered flames of disaffection to burst out with renewed fierceness. The grounds of this summary proceeding were stated to be the discovery by the Governor of the existence of combinations and cabals among the officers; in proof of this a memorial was produced, confessedly drawn up by the officers and for private circulation among them, stating their grievances and demands, and appealing from the Government of Fort St. George to the Governor General to whom it was addressed. This memorial, having been obtained by the Government of Madras from sources not divulged, was forwarded to Calcutta. There appears to have been no question as to its authenticity, and though it had not reached him by the channel intended by the memorialists, the Governor General answered it point by point in a letter to Sir George Barlow, who was directed to publish it to the Madras army.

This paper in its entirety is too long to be inserted

[1] April 25, 1809.

here; it is too good to be mutilated. It is, in fact, an exhaustive statement of the questions at issue between the officers and the Madras Government, and likewise of the general principles which necessitated the subordination of the army to the State. When in due time it reached England, Lord Malmesbury described it as the finest and ablest State paper he had ever read. Lord Minto himself thought it far too long; but he desired, he said, 'to convince the reason of the younger officers as well as to enforce their obedience, and to lay a statement before the army of principles he thought ill understood.' While Sir George Barlow was content to reiterate that the first attribute of the executive is strength, Lord Minto insisted also on what he considered to be the corollary of the same principle—that the strength of the executive lies in its being derived from the national will, whence its rightful claim on the obedience of all classes of men. The antagonism displayed to the executive at Madras arose in its seeming to be the will of Sir George Barlow.

It was a habit of mind with Lord Minto to look for the causes of things below the surface. In this case he saw in the majority of the officers very young and half-instructed men ('and who so confident of himself as a half-instructed man?'). He saw them brought together in a distant corner of the Empire, removed from the influence of such public opinion as exists in all large and mixed societies, tempted by the circumstances of their case to exaggerate their own importance, till the interests of a few officers became in their eyes the cause of an army, and till the reciprocal duties of brother officers became more to them than the primary relations which knit together the citizens of a common State. He entertained, therefore, a sanguine hope that the promulgation of sounder principles would check the progress of error. From the letter to Sir George Barlow we propose to quote only one passage, from which the general tone and spirit of the argument may be inferred.

'We are accustomed in England, without distinction of profession or degree, to speak with pride and reverence of that nice and scrupulous solicitude which pervades the constitutional policy of Great Britain on every point that affects, however remotely, the great and primary concerns of civil liberty and domestic security,—blessings which it is natural to value most highly in a country where they are best known and experienced. It is this great national sentiment which requires, as the main and most indispensable provision for civil security, the absolute unqualified subordination of the army to the State, or in other words to the Government of the country. Out of the same principle springs the necessity of peculiar restraints on the military body, and the abridgment in their case of some privileges and practices which are permitted, because they are not deemed hazardous, in other parts of life.

'Among the chief of these restraints are to be placed the strict prohibition of military combination for the furtherance of professional views or wishes, and of open and concerted opposition by military men in their military character to the Government or the persons who administer it. . . .

'It were to be lamented, and little to the credit of military men, if, on points which touch so nearly all that is most dear to their country, they should cease to think and feel as Englishmen when they become soldiers, and should suffer the partial spirit of a profession to wean them from those sentiments and sympathies which, like their brethren in civil life, they imbibed with their milk, and which distinguish and illustrate their nation.'

Though this paper, dated Fort William, May 27, 1809, purported to emanate from the Governor General in Council, and was therefore signed by the members of Council generally, he himself said of it: 'Whether it is thought good or bad, prosy or otherwise, it is certainly my own, for I wrote every word of it myself.'

Several of the suspended officers went to Calcutta and laid their grievances before Lord Minto. From them, and by letter from Colonels Malcolm and Close and Sir George Barlow, he was kept aware of the progress of events. Malcolm wrote that Barlow's blindness to the increasing dangers amounted to a disease of mind: Barlow, that Malcolm's love of popularity prompted him to recommend concessions which the honour of the Government forbad it to grant. Colonel Close agreed with Lord Minto that submission must precede concession. But of the former there was no sign. A regular organisation of revolt was framed. The open revolt of Masulipatam (where the officers seized the fortress and put their commanding officer under arrest) left no doubt as to the lengths to which they were prepared to go. It was quickly followed by the mutiny of Seringapatam. From Masulipatam, where he had been sent by Sir George Barlow on a mission, Malcolm wrote 'that there was not a Company's corps from Cape Comorin to Ganjam that was not implicated in the general guilt—that is not pledged to rise against Government unless what they call their grievances are redressed.' Colonel Close, who, on account of his great popularity with the army, had been sent to Hyderabad to take command of the subsidiary force, was met at the camp by the whole of the troops under arms and prepared for action. Plans were formed for concentrating the rebel force; all concealment was thrown off, and menaces were heard that 30,000 men would march upon Madras. The Jaulna detachment actually quitted their station in the execution of that plan. Public treasure was seized, correspondence interrupted—in a word, civil war had commenced. At this juncture the cool courage and energy of Sir George Barlow saved the Empire from what at best must have been a disastrous struggle.' 'He determined,' says Marshman in his

---

[1] 'There are men now living,' writes Sir J. Kaye, in the *Correspondence of Sir J. Malcolm*, 'who look back with astonishment, almost with incredulity, to that period of mutinous excitement. At many of the large army stations the officers of the Company's regiments avowed themselves ready for any act of daring revolt. They encouraged one another in treason; they talked of fighting against a tyrannical Government in defence of their rights to the last drop

'History of India,'[1] 'if necessary, to march the loyal portion of the army against the disaffected. The fidelity of the King's troops could be relied on. To test the loyalty of the officers he demanded the signature of all, without distinction, to a pledge to obey the orders and support the authority of the Government in Council at Fort St. George on pain of removal from their stations on the coast, though without forfeiture of rank or pay. This measure, however, did not produce the intended effect, as not a tenth of the whole body of officers consented to affix their signatures; lastly, he directed the commanders of native regiments to assemble the Sepoys and assure them that the discontent of the officers was a personal affair, and that the Government had no intention to diminish the advantages which they had enjoyed, but were rather anxious to improve them. The Sepoys and native officers remained faithful to their salt.'

In Lord Minto's opinion this measure was as wise and bold as it proved to be decisive. Without their instruments the officers were powerless; they had not doubted the readiness of their soldiers to adhere to them; inability to proceed in their criminal designs was the real

of their blood. Seditious toasts were given at the mess tables, and drunk with uproarious applause. From day to day tidings went forth from one excited station to another—tidings of progressive insubordination which fortified with assurances of sympathy and support the insane resolves of the scattered mutineers. The arrival of every post raised a fever of expectancy. Letters from the disaffected cantonments were eagerly read and instantly circulated. The moral intoxication pervaded all ranks from the colonel to the ensign.'

[1] Vol. ii. p. 243.

ground of the collapse which ensued. Sir James Mackintosh took a different view. Writing of these events to Colonel Malcolm he 'confessed that were he asked whether the deposition of a Governor by military force or an appeal to private soldiers against their officers be the greater evil, I am compelled to own that I must hesitate.'[1] Lord Minto did not hesitate to declare his conviction that the power which entrusts to the soldier his sword has a supreme claim to his fidelity.[2]

'If,' he wrote in a despatch to the Secret Committee, 'they had in truth, as their officers appear never to have allowed themselves to doubt, adhered to their cause, and had been thereby betrayed to their ruin in the pursuit of criminal designs totally foreign to their own interests and concerns, it is impossible to foresee the dreadful extremities to which they might have been impelled against those who would have been justly responsible for these disasters.'

Lord Minto had intended to go to Madras in July; but the confident assurance of Sir G. Barlow that matters were quieting down, added to his own wish to

[1] Sir J. Mackintosh to Colonel Malcolm. Bombay, August 20, 1809, published in *Correspondence of Sir J. Malcolm.*

[2] In the article on the Madras mutiny, already quoted (*Quarterly Review*, May 1811), the following passage occurs: 'The policy of detaching the Sepoys from their rebellious officers had been adopted by Lord Clive, the father of our Indian dominion, on the mutiny of the Bengal officers in the year 1765. In truth, he in 1765 carried his policy to a much further extent than Sir George Barlow in 1809; for the former, finding that the refractory officers whom he had discarded, showed some disposition to continue embodied in his neighbourhood, actually dispatched a corps of Sepoys to disperse these officers or to bring them prisoners into the camp.'

let the minor Government do its own work if it could, caused him to delay his departure, until the news of the revolt at Masulipatam reached him, when he at once embarked for Madras on August 5. Before leaving Bengal he wrote to General Hewitt, who was at Agra, to prepare himself for civil war. The monsoon delayed his passage, and when he arrived he found to his sincere satisfaction that the crisis was at an end.

Sir J. Mackintosh was not disappointed in the expectation he expressed in a letter to Colonel Malcolm that Lord Minto's great abilities and humane character would dispose him to conciliation. On his arrival at Madras he was informed that the officers had made their submission, and addressed on August 11 'a penitential letter' to himself. His own letter, nominally addressed to Sir George Barlow, but substantially to the army, had been published by order of the Madras Government at every military station in the Presidency; and though too late to stay the seditious proceedings then on the point of breaking out, it seems, nevertheless, not to have failed altogether of effect; for it was remarked at the time that their general confidence in Lord Minto's justice and moderation caused the news of his approach to be welcomed even by those who knew how unflinching had been his support of Sir George Barlow. Lord Minto desired to weaken as little as possible the Government of Fort St. George; he therefore, on arriving at Madras, announced his determination to interfere in no degree in the government of the Presidency, which was in all respects to be carried on as if

Calcutta were still the seat of the supreme authority; but he felt that he should discharge imperfectly the extraordinary powers entrusted to him if he contented himself with professing a blind concurrence in counsels over which he had come to preside. He determined therefore 'to pursue a personal investigation of the facts, followed by a mature deliberation on their results, before committing himself to any of the principal points depending.'

An order, dated September 25, 1809, conveyed the judgment at which he arrived after the most searching enquiry and anxious consideration. It stated in clear but most moderate terms the offence against the just authority of Government, of which the coast army had been guilty, and then proceeded to make a selection of the offenders for punishment.

'The selection,' says the order, 'is to consist of the officers in command of stations, or bodies of troops; commandants of corps; and persons peculiarly distinguished for a forward and violent part in the most criminal acts or proceedings of the army. Officers included in the two first categories would be sent for trial to courts martial, the number not exceeding twenty-one.' Those in the last were permitted to take their choice of trial or dismissal from the service. To the rest of the army a general and unqualified amnesty was granted. The language of this general order admirably reflected the spirit of its author. It was at once firm and generous. It demonstrated the Governor General's determination to do no more than was neces-

sary for the vindication of justice. It firmly reasserted
the principles of military subordination to legal authority,
which the proceedings of the army had set
at defiance, and it did not shrink from a tribute to
Sir George Barlow, to whose firmness and energy it was
due that a monstrous conflict had been avoided between
the coast army and their country. The order ended
by an earnest exhortation to the officers to think less
lightly than they had been accustomed to do of violating
the first, the most sacred, and the most characteristic
duty of a soldier, fidelity to the power he serves. 'I
entreat them to be persuaded that no man of honour
at the head of a Government will ever compromise with
revolt, and that in every case the conflict must be
carried to the last extremity. My sentiments on that
subject are not equivocal, and are not assumed for the
occasion. They have been pronounced long since, and
previous to any indication of troubles on the coast. My
fixed and firm principle is, that the utmost evils that can
flow from a contest with revolt, and even from defeat, are
much inferior to the greater, more permanent, and more
extensive mischief of concession. In such cases the
revolted party may recede, and will always do so with
honour, sacrificing nothing but passions and crimes.
The Government against which the revolt is made, has
no option but to maintain the contest or abandon its
trust and fly from its duty.'

In the letter he addressed from Madras to the
Secret Committee, congratulating them on the termination
of the dangerous troubles which had agitated

the Presidency since the month of January, he says:—

'Greater perils have, perhaps, never threatened the possessions of the Honourable Company, or the British empire in India; and so great an alarm has seldom subsided so suddenly, so entirely, and with so fair a prospect not only of the permanent restoration of former security and tranquillity, but of the improvement of these blessings. . . . When I embarked at Fort William on August 5, the most recent events were the mutiny and revolt at Masulipatam. I received also with considerable uneasiness casual accounts of an engagement between the King's and the Company's troops at Seringapatam.

. . . .

'The only certain and infallible issue of a contest so unnatural and so lamentable as that which we might have had to maintain was the total and irretrievable ruin of thirteen hundred English gentlemen, who were engaged in an enterprise equally criminal and hopeless.

'In a case of such general participation by a numerous body in the offence which is to be punished, it is obvious that the penalty cannot be extended to all, and that some must be selected for examples; . . . that these examples need not be numerous is my opinion.'

In a later letter, describing his final measures, he wrote:

'I considered that the mass of the offending officers

were to be necessarily replaced in stations of trust; that our native armies were still to be commanded by them, and that, whether the penalty should fall on few or comparatively on many, our army was still to be composed of associates in the common offence.

'Policy, therefore, if not a more generous principle, points to conciliation as the most expedient as well as, in other points of view, the most commendable foundation of our measures. The change in events has changed the principle.

'While revolt was on foot, conciliation which would have been mistaken, or perhaps justly taken for weakness, must have impaired both dignity and power. After submission, a conciliatory course becomes a point not merely of prudence but of magnanimity.'

It had been Lord Minto's anxious wish that a Commander-in-chief should arrive at Madras from England before his own departure took place; when that was found impracticable, he invited General Hewitt to Madras. 'The fit moment had arrived for the important work of reviving discipline. The power of Government and of the Commander-in-chief cannot at present be disputed or opposed. Futurity is so impenetrable that the favourable moment ought not to be lost. The task will not, I think, be difficult, but it requires prudence and judgment as well as firmness and power, for the disease is pretty much fixed in the habit. It is one of those undertakings which precipitation has a tendency to retard. The art of government consists in distinguishing between the course which is suited to extraordinary conjunctures, and the permanent policy by which men are to be governed.'[1]

'Revolt must first be subdued; the next care is to prevent a return of that evil. No doubt the strong and successful repression of the late seditions would tend to discourage similar dispositions in the future; but other means yet more efficacious should be combined with these, for the actions of men being prompted as much by their passions and tempers as by their reason, a sense of danger will not always restrain them. That real grievances must be redressed will not be disputed; but it appears to me that a Government should study even the passions, the temper, the prejudices, and the errors of those who are subject to their rule. It would follow from this principle that if any peculiar circumstances in the late events should appear to have promoted them, or to have increased the difficulty of restraining them, and that these circumstances should be capable of alteration, it should be done.

'If there be reason to think that any obstacle to the restoration not merely of discipline, but of temper and harmony, now stands in the way, that obstacle, although it should be connected with the most unreasonable and most unjustifiable passions and prejudices of the time, had better be removed, provided the measures taken for that purpose can be ascribed to a spirit of wise conciliation, and cannot by any possibility be set down to motives of intimidation—and this advantage does

---

[1] Lord Minto to the Secret Committee.

belong to the stronger party after victory—with a view to promote future harmony with a subdued adversary.'[1]

'Madras: February 3, 1810.[2]

'It is quite uncertain when I shall get home (to Bengal). I intended to go about the middle of this month. But although the army is in a perfectly *safe* state, it is not like any other army or any other set of people that ever was. There is a good deal of irritation kept up by the courts martial; and different incidents in the late troubles are still fresh enough to make bad blood between one corps and another. Wherever there is any agitation at all, the Company's officers cut the King's, who make them very welcome and hold them mighty cheap, as well they may, being in the right and the others in the wrong. This is not like discipline, nor like an entire return to tranquillity, but it is not quite out of nature; and I think myself that all will get right, provided there is a little temper and patience with this temporary evil. Regular and steady discipline must certainly be restored, or rather created, for it never existed here; but these wild steeds must be handled and bitted, and not backed in a moment by a rough-rider. Everything is so perfectly secure on material points, that a quiet process may be tried, without danger from new mischief. As discipline *must* be enforced, however, quicker or slower,

---

[1] The letter ends with some practical suggestions for improving the condition of the higher ranks of the army.

[2] To Lady Minto.

that undertaking cannot be left to Sir George and General Gowdie.

'One is hated, indeed execrated, though unjustly, yet heartily. The other does not inspire much awe. I propose, therefore, to invite General Hewitt here immediately. He has all the qualities that suit the occasion. His authority, which is the highest military authority in India, will be respected. He has excellent military principles, abhors a departure from the soundest military character, is firm, temperate, and judicious. We are on a most cordial footing, and I shall wait for him here, and leave him in charge without anxiety when we have thoroughly compared our ideas. *Coventry* is the order of the day. Indeed there is no other deviation from discipline, or none to speak of. This is closely connected with the recent violence, and if no new *exciting cause*, as Wilson calls it, be created, the old impressions will gradually wear themselves out, and the effect will disappear with the cause.'

The disappearance could not be counted upon so long as the courts martial continued in session, nor until, by the arrival of the Commander-in-chief, a military authority should have been established superior to that of the very well-intentioned, but not able officer who commanded the coast army in the meantime; and thus Lord Minto remained at Madras for fourteen months.

The sentences in several instances were not approved by the Government, and were suspended during re-consideration; and in England, as in India, a violent controversy arose upon the general policy which had been observed towards the rebellious army. Some blamed it as too severe, some as having unduly slackened the reins of authority. It was no doubt due to the dissensions on the subject in the Court of Directors that Lord Minto was left without any official statement of their opinions on these weighty matters for more than *two years* after they took place.

CHAPTER X.

Lord Minto's pre-occupations at Madras were not wholly of an unpleasant kind; for, during his residence there, a marriage took place between his youngest son, John, and Amelia Casamaijor,[1] a young lady whose family had long been in friendly relations with that of Lord Minto. He told his correspondents at home in a very amusing style of the series of emotions which possessed his whole being, and dispossessed each other during the space of one quarter of an hour; from the incredulous horror with which he had learnt that 'the boy' contemplated matrimony, through various phases of fury and amusement, till all culminated in a sudden but profound conviction, that it was the very best thing that could have happened; and he found himself blessing and kissing everybody all round, thinking in his heart all the time that it would have been more natural to fall in love with her mother, a very handsome woman, than with a chit of eighteen. The marriage took place at Madras, in December 1809, and, besides being a very happy arrangement for the principals, greatly con-

---

[1] Third daughter of James Henry Casamaijor, Esq., of Madras.

tributed to the cheerfulness and comfort of Lord Minto's life in India.

After describing the wedding, he wrote to his wife.

'December 20, 1809.

'My domestic longings are becoming every month more importunate and unreasonable. I first determined not to reckon for many years to come, well knowing that the hours of expectation would not be made fewer by any sort of computation I could contrive, but that they would be much increased in length and retarded in velocity. Then I compromised for quarters of a year. Then it came to months, and now I grieve to say that I am actually counting days, with all the exactness of a clock. The days are innumerable indeed, yet, being a good arithmetician, I actually know their number. It is a long line of march in which one rank seems to stop another, and the whole column seems to stand still. It would be a great joy to skip a day, but that *never* happens. I reckon this diurnal reckoning one of the most improvident acts of my life, and I must go on counting and longing to the end of the chapter. One of my common vigils is performing the voyage home, and then the journey from one well-known sign-post to another, from the Red Lion, Barnet, to Minto. As I have a perfectly fair wind, and plenty of it all the way to Portsmouth, and good roads and horses to Minto, I meet with no let or hindrance till I come to the Lower Lodge, and from thence to the Lilly Law is a tedious distressing job. I always go the Cornhill Road, for the sake of touching at Lennel,[1] and sometimes I meet a Mintonian there, looking out for me.'

'March 29, 1810.

'I shall be happy, I confess, to find myself at Barrackpore once more. I think I have the business in as favourable a state here as it is reasonable to expect. The ways of thinking of this army are radically bad; but there is not a shadow of danger left, and I feel great confidence in the efficacy of all that has been done, in preventing any return of the confederating, that is to say, in truth, mutinous practices, which have been witnessed on so many other occasions. There is still, however, a great deal more petty indiscipline, such as *Coventry* and insults to obnoxious individuals, than can be accounted military or suffered to continue. But these irregular habits are naturally cultivated in times of trouble, and they have been kept in more than their usual or natural activity by the irritation of the courts martial sitting on the comrades, associates, and only the other day accomplices, of those who witnessed their proceedings. The trials are now all concluded; and that exciting cause being removed, a steady and temperate course of alterative remedies, that is to say, a gradual but uniform introduction of regular discipline, and inculcation of sound military principles, of which I have not been sparing, may in my opinion accomplish the object. The courts martial have been very

[1] The residence of Mr. and Mrs. Brydone.

soft, which, besides depriving the cause of discipline of salutary examples, has laid Government under the necessity of doing ungracious things and incurring odium which ought not to have been thrown upon it, by censuring and refusing to confirm sentences of too much lenity. The courts martial have found all those who have been tried, *guilty*, except one who is *honourably acquitted*, directly contrary to evidence; and those who have been convicted have only been cashiered for the most flagrant and dangerous mutiny. But I cannot afford to write another despatch on this subject.'

Soon after Lord Minto's return from Madras to Calcutta, his second son, George Elliot,[1] following the example of his younger brother, married a young lady of great personal attractions, who was much admired in the society of Calcutta. Like her sister-in-law she was immediately installed in apartments at the Government House, which 'was much improved thereby in cheerfulness and comfort.' 'My reigning theme is my daughters-in-law. I cannot repeat too often that E. is really lovely in face, person, and character. There never was a more sweet and gentle disposition; and A. is my grand favourite, with mirth, good temper, good sense, and good character. I have occasion for all the comforts I can snatch; for my work is hard and fatigues both body and spirit, not by bodily exercise but by the effect of mental labour on a body entirely at rest. I am as entirely done up by ten o'clock as if I had been all day

[1] Captain George Elliot, afterwards Admiral and K.C.B., married in 1810 Eliza, daughter of James Ness, Esq.

on the moors, and I am in general too much over-worked to be *frosty-mornish*. However, I have a good quiet sort of contentedness, and spectator-like enjoyment of all the happiness about me, which serves my turn. A few gulps of caller air down our strath will make me too young and oppressive for the best nerves among you.'

A present from his eldest daughter of Scott's last poem, 'The Lady of the Lake,' gave him great delight. ' I wish,' she wrote to him from Edinburgh, where the family were spending the winter of 1809-10,—' I wish that the *Edinburgh Review* was to be out before the ships go, but it will not. Mr. Jeffrey will certainly review it himself, and I cannot help thinking he will be a little puzzled; for he does not like to be scolded by Mrs. Scott or to hurt *Walter*, though he pretends not to care; and yet he is very likely to bully himself into being more severe than he would naturally be, to prove to himself he really does not care. It is impossible for anybody that does not know this odd little man to enter into the merits of his character; but it is the most amusing thing to watch when you do understand it, and to observe all the odd contradictions, or seeming contradictions, produced by the same causes. It seems a paradox to say that he is not in the least ill-natured; and yet I never knew an acquaintance of his that did not say the same thing, and though he wonders how anybody can be so silly as to mind the tone of ridicule he assumes and the severe things he says in his Reviews, he really is sorry when they do. He is very proud of himself because he has bullied us all (Lord Webb,[1] and I can't tell you who) about Crabbe; who has just published a new volume, full of horrors of all kinds which he chooses to admire; and we expect a very favourable review of it in the next number. I have not much objection to this; but if he is not more respectful in his review of ' The Lady ' than he was in that of ' Marmion,' I shall vow vengeance on his little head. How to execute it will be the most difficult job; for he cares for nothing that anybody can say or do, unless perhaps one was to gag him; but then death would soon put an end to his torments, and he would die of a repletion of words.'

The winter of 1809–10 was a very pleasant one in Edinburgh. Dugald Stewart had not yet quitted the chair of Moral Philosophy; and the influence of his character, manners, and taste, gave a tone to the College which was said to be of even greater advantage to the students than that they derived from attendance at his lectures. Playfair still occupied the chair of Natural Philosophy, and found time to fall into the chains of the lively Mrs. Apreece, better known in after years as Lady Davy, but who in 1810 made the world of Edinburgh stare when introduced to it under the auspices of the Duchess of Gordon as the true Corinne. Where Playfair was, generally came Lord Webb Seymour, the gentle and the wise, the two friends being so inseparable as to be dubbed husband and wife. These were intimate friends of the Minto family, as were also ' John Murray

[1] Lord Webb Seymour.

and Henry Cockburn, as full of fun and sense as an egg is full of meat,' Thomas Thomson, 'the oldest, the gravest, and the most learned of all,' and the Clerks of Eldin, 'a family of geniuses' revolving round their aged father, irreverently nicknamed 'old Tactics.'[1] On this foundation Lady Minto and her cousin, Lady Carnegie, had in a former year instituted a côterie, dignified by the name of the 'Brown Toast Club,' in allusion to one of its fundamental laws—that the members should trust to 'the cup which cheers and not inebriates' for their exhilaration, and to buttered toast for their support. So popular were these meetings that hard-worked lawyers sat up all night to prepare their work in Court next day rather than lose the evening hours with the Brown Toasters. 'Jeffrey is most entertaining with his miseries of writing reviews with his head full of bad law, and his law with his head full of reviews, and passing his nights scribbling and being abused for his pains. He is so smitten just now with M.'s beauty that his friends say she must cover her face if he is to write any more reviews. Many people would in that case bid her show it for humanity's sake.'[2] To one of these 'small parties' came Madame Catalani. 'She sang one song delightfully,' wrote Lady Minto; 'then, having a cold, would not sing again, but consented to show attitudes,—as Lady Hamilton did in her days of beauty,—and we were all in ecstasies. I think her beau-

[1] John Clerk of Eldin, 'inventor of the modern system of naval tactics.'

[2] Hon. A. M. Elliot to her father.

tiful, the finest eyes I ever saw; and her manner so gay and natural as well as graceful that I rejoiced I was not a man to become her slave. The evil-minded accuse her and her family of being spies employed by Bonaparte: certain it is that the husband's sister is established here as a person of very considerable fortune, and says Bonaparte gave her permission to come to England for no given time; but I do not see what they can spy, for in England nothing is a secret, or ever will be. They may tell him all the Ministers are at variance, and the country with the Ministers; but, as to anything they intend to do, I suspect it is more than they know themselves.'

To these cheerful letters Lord Minto replied:

'You were Brown Toasts at the date of your last letter from Edinburgh, and I think this must be about the pleasantest part of your lives; inasmuch as wit, and learning, and good sense, and good humour, and good character withal, which are the portion, I believe, of every member of your Club, make excellent *four hours*. I shall be delighted to be admitted to your Thé, though not legally qualified; but the black kettle and brown toast would make my outlawed mouth water if it were only for the base corporeal gluttony of the thing. So, Molly, put the kettle on, and I'll be with you in a trice. You will find me an old carle; I really am tired—I mean weary; and it is full time I was out of harness, and without my shoes in one of your mother's best improved grass-parks. It would be a vain attempt to tell you how I long for the goal of my seven years' race. I have been at full speed the whole way, and a round or two more would break me down, I do believe.'

The last fleet of 1810 brought to India the distressing news of the death of Mr. Windham. To Lord Minto it was an irreparable loss, for their friendship had begun in early life and been faithful through long years. No important step had been taken by the one without previous consultation with the other; and, with considerable difference of character, there had been singular harmony in their sentiments.

'Windham expired at between eleven and twelve o'clock on Monday,' wrote Lady Malmesbury on June 6. 'He had taken the opinion of eleven medical persons before he consented to the operation, and only one was against it. He is universally regretted by all parties and persons. He was of that valuable description of men, whom Burke so finely described, that become daily more valuable as the race becomes extinct, for such it will be soon—the high-minded, honourable, true-born gentleman; and yet he was an illegitimate son, and his mother of the lowest description. As Fitzharris said to me, he was one under whom, if bad times came, one might have fought without fear of disgrace. My Dominie never left his bedside nor rested the three last nights.' Another correspondent wrote: 'I am assured by the physicians that the solicitude and enquiries have been double what were expressed for Mr. Pitt and Mr. Fox.'

The operation mentioned by Lady Malmesbury, which appears to have been very doubtfully necessary, was occasioned by the results of an accident met with by Mr. Windham in the preceding year.

'One night,' wrote another correspondent, 'in the beginning of July 1809, as he was returning home alone and on foot from the Miss Berrys', where he was spending the evening, he perceived a fire; and after tracing it found it next door to the house of his friend, Mr. North. The exertions he made to save different articles of value showed all his characteristic energy. In carrying a load of books he fell, and received a contusion on the hip. A tumour was the consequence, and an operation the conclusion. His constitution did not rally. He saw the approach of dissolution without the least unmanly repining, though he owned he had many reasons for wishing the prolongation of life, particularly in so far as affected Mrs. Windham. On the evening before he died he signed a codicil to his will, and, having done so, shook hands with the witnesses with a smile on his face, and in half an hour fell asleep never to awake again in this world. As a statesman, an orator, a man of literature and science, a man of purity and integrity in public and private life, of various accomplishments and social qualities, he has not left his equal behind him.

'Previous to the operation he wrote to his friend, Dr. Fisher, and told him what he was about to undergo; that he understood there was much hazard in his case either way, and he very earnestly wished to receive the Sacrament, which was accordingly administered to him, and he expressed much satisfaction in having performed this duty, as if he expected that this might be his last opportunity.

'By an observation in his diary, the day you took leave of him, he seems to have had a presentiment that you would never meet again.

'Though he reached the age of sixty, I wonder how he could accomplish half the manuscripts he has left behind him. 1st, a complete translation of De Thou's history; 2nd, an immense body of mathematics; and lastly, an uninterrupted journal from January 1782 to within four days of the operation that proved fatal to him. Nothing, however, is likely to prove fit for publication except the mathematical works, which he desired, only two days previous to his death, to be submitted to the inspection of Dr. King, Bishop of Rochester.'

CHAPTER XI.

THE most brilliant chapter in Lord Minto's Indian government is that of his foreign policy. When Mr. Canning declared that he would call the new world into existence to redress the balance of the old, he expressed in an effective phrase the spirit of the policy carried out by Lord Minto in the East. The conquests of England in one hemisphere redressed the balance of power in the other. Every fresh gain by France in Europe was followed by a corresponding loss in Asia. It was the glory of Lord Minto's administration that, whereas at its commencement dread of a French invasion of India haunted the imagination of statesmen, at its close France had lost all her acquisitions eastward of the Cape. The isles of Bourbon and of France, the Moluccas, and Java, had been added to the colonial possessions of Great Britain, the fleets of France were swept from the Indian seas, and England was without a rival in the Eastern hemisphere.

The first step in this great scheme was not the most successful. On the conquest of Portugal by the French, the Indian Government received orders to occupy the Portuguese settlements in the East. Goa was already protected by British troops, though the civil administration was still carried on by Portuguese. It was intimated that Macao should in similar manner be protected by a British occupation from annexation to France. A small expedition was sent from India to Macao in September 1809; but, though it effected a landing, it was met with such firm though courteous opposition by the Chinese authorities, that it was deemed expedient to re-embark the troops and to abstain from any further designs in that quarter, leaving the Chinese to guard their own coasts, which they appeared well prepared to do.

About the same time, three ships of the line, carrying troops, took possession of Amboyna, the chief of the Dutch Spice Islands, or Moluccas, and early in the spring of 1810 the whole of the group was annexed to the British crown. These small expeditions were despatched from India while Lord Minto was at Madras. Immediately on his return to Calcutta preparations were commenced for more important enterprises.

It will be remembered that within a few weeks after Lord Minto's assumption of the reins of government in 1807, plans were submitted to him for the reduction of the islands of Bourbon and Mauritius, and of Java, which the fortune of war had transferred, along with the Moluccas and other settlements eastward of India, from the possession of the Dutch to that of the French.

These plans had been laid aside on the ground that the time for their execution was not come; first, because of the financial difficulties in which the Company's affairs were then involved; secondly, because of some uncertainty as to the approval of the Ministry which had lately taken office in England. The Whig Ministers, Lords Grenville and Grey, while yielding to none in their desire to promote a system of public economy, had entertained and discussed such 'plans' with Lord Minto before he left England; but the Ministers who succeeded them were believed to have other views. Lord Castlereagh, who had become War Secretary, had in 1800 forbidden any operations eastward of India, and expeditions against the French islands had been positively interdicted to the Indian Government, in spite of the severe damage sustained by their merchant trade from French cruisers.

In one of his first letters from India to the Chairman of the East India Company, Lord Minto had pointed out the importance of a conquest of the Isle of France or Mauritius, and the Isle of Bourbon:—'The Mauritius affords a secure port for equipping and refitting ships of war and other cruisers against our trade, and a place of refuge and safety for them and their prizes. Every project of the enemy which requires a naval and military force, will find facilities in the possession of the Mauritius. Troops, stores, and shipping may be almost imperceptibly assembled there, separately and in detail, which could not without extreme hazard of failure, be dispatched in a body from France.' Twice during the administration of Lord Wellesley, had expeditions to the Coast of Malabar been sent out from the Mauritius, and the capture of British merchantmen even in the Bay of Bengal had grievously humiliated the Government of India, which would at once have resented the injury by a descent upon the islands, but for the refusal of the Admiral on the station to act under any orders unless issued through the Admiralty.[1]

In 1809 no fewer than six Indiamen were taken on their voyage. It was then felt to be high time to protect our maritime trade from further depredations, and early in 1810 an expedition sailed from India to the French islands under circumstances which Lord Minto's letters will best describe.

[1] On the first occasion, a frigate from the Mauritius landed a number of French troops and others at Mangalore on the coast of Malabar, who joined the standard of Sultan Tippoo, dignified him with the title of Citizen Tippoo, declared his dominions a republic, *une et indivisible*, and planted a tree of liberty. On the second occasion a large armament arrived off Pondicherry, consisting of two ships of the line, two frigates, and two corvettes, with a large staff of officers and 1,400 European troops, destined to re-occupy Pondicherry after the Peace of Amiens had restored that dependency to France. On the appearance of the French squadron in the roadstead of Pondicherry they were informed that the Governor General had resolved not to give up the French settlements (as he had nevertheless been ordered by Royal warrant to do) until he had had time to communicate with the English ministry. The fleet returned to Mauritius, and before a reply to Lord Wellesley was received, England and France had resumed hostilities. Lord Wellesley had designed an expedition against the French islands which was frustrated by the jealousy of the Admiral. The troops intended for the purpose were the contingent of 4,000 Europeans and 5,000 Sepoys afterwards sent to co-operate with Sir R. Abercromby in Egypt, and who encamped on the shores of the Mediterranean on August 27, 1800. This expedition —for the troops marched 120 miles over the desert to the Nile—was thought at the time a feat to be proud of, and greatly to illustrate the resources of the Empire.

'March 26, 1810.'

'I am just sending an expedition to make the conquest of the Isle of Bourbon. There is the fairest prospect of success. I propose to follow up the blow by attacking the Mauritius, generally called the Isle of France. These two acquisitions will be of extreme importance: they are the only French possessions east of the Cape, and furnish the only means our arch-enemy can command for annoying us in this quarter of the world, till an army can come here in its shoes. From the Isle of France all the cruisers have been sent out against our trade; against which a very large squadron have done little to protect us. The losses of the Company, as well as of the general trade, have been enormous. The Islands have been blockaded by a squadron under Admiral Bertie who commands at the Cape, and they have experienced some distress from that measure, but none sufficient to produce a chance, as it appears to me, of their surrender. In the meanwhile the small island of Rodriguez was, in consequence of orders from England, taken possession of by a detachment of European and native troops from Bombay. The intention was merely to secure water and send refreshments to the blockading squadron. The command of the troops was given to Lieutenant-Colonel Keating. Two captured Indiamen were taken by the French frigate Caroline into Port St. Paul on the Island of Bourbon. This tempted Commodore Rowley, who

¹ To Lady Minto.

commanded the blockading ships, and Lieutenant-Colonel Keating to attack Port St. Paul, an enterprise which was conducted and executed in a very masterly manner, and with entire success... The success of this operation induced them (these officers) to recommend that a reinforcement of about 2,000 men should be sent from India with which addition to the force at Rodriguez they had a confident expectation of being able to make the entire conquest of Bourbon; which they consider as an important step towards the reduction of the Isle of France. It is upon these grounds that I have fitted out the present expedition, which I have made somewhat stronger than was desired, in order to provide against the preparations for defence which may have been made since the attack on Port St. Paul.

'A second expedition must be sent against the Isle of France, and a much larger force: including those going now about 10,000 men. The first will sail from Madras about May 1; the second will probably depart from India in August.

'Calcutta: September 19, 1810.

'I have been forced to suspend, much longer than I like, my quotidian plan of correspondence by two reasons, hard work and constant attendance, required principally by the expedition to the Isle of France, which has been pushed forward through many difficulties, sometimes by absolute determination rather than by visible means. I have been pretty nearly alone at times in thinking it practicable to make the attempt before next April, a delay which might probably have been fatal to the ultimate success. If the troops do not rendezvous off the island in time to attack by the middle of November, it is not entirely prudent to attempt it later, for the violent hurricanes which seem to live in those islands and to come out, like swallows, at certain seasons, sometimes are experienced in the course of November, though seldom before the middle of December; and, indeed, they will be quiet in their caves sometimes the whole year, without taking the trouble of coming abroad at all. Although it would be hazardous to keep a large fleet of transports exposed to these birds of prey, or to land troops at a time when their ships and stores may be blown off or *worse*; yet single ships or more which have a port to come to, may run in and bring succours during the tempestuous season, without greater hazard than the object deserved. The French accordingly employ the hurricane months, when the blockading squadron is obliged to quit the ground, to throw in supplies, and we are informed that, in consequence of the apprehensions excited by our late measures, the most positive assurances have been given to the Governor of the Isle of France that troops, military stores, and all other means of defence shall be dispatched from Europe this very season. It is of great consequence therefore, that *we* should be at Port Louis to receive such supplies from France, rather than Monsieur De Cāen. This is one of several reasons and certainly the strongest, which has made me *damnatus obstinatus mulier* (*vide* Cowslip's translation), and determined me to push off the expedition now, whether it was possible or not. The weight of opinions was strong against me in all quarters, but when once the point was decided, all hands concurred lustily in the execution, and lo and behold! everything is actually afloat. Three divisions of troops from three Presidencies are now on their passage, with a very perfect equipment, having six weeks to perform a voyage which *may* be done in one month; five weeks is a fair allowance, so as to arrive at Rodriguez before November 1. And this reminds me of a Piedmontese gentleman, who said that he had watched the quarrels of *mules* with men for several years, but had never in any instance found the mules in the wrong. Our fleets may still be dispersed by bad weather on the passage; or some accident, not to be foreseen, may occasion delay; but we have done our part, and there is the most reasonable prospect of success. The force is quite equal to the service, according to the most prudent and scientific opinions; and all the information we possess, down to a very late date, would make the difficulties less than we are prepared to surmount. . . . . None of the officers who have served against Bourbon consider the event as in any degree doubtful. . . . We ought not therefore to fail, although War is a fine lady and too capricious to be entirely depended upon.'

A month after the expedition had sailed from India, instructions[1] were received from home, re-

---

[1] From the Right Hon. R. Dundas, dated June 13, 1810.

commending the measure which—wrote Lord Minto—
'a strong sense of duty to the public had induced him
to adopt under a heavy responsibility.' 'About the time
your letter reached Fort William,' he wrote to Mr.
Dundas,[1] 'you had probably received in London accounts of the surrender of the Island of Bourbon; and
the expedition against the Mauritius had been despatched from the three Presidencies a month before
I had the honour to receive your commands.

'The change which has taken place in the finances
of the Company in India since 1807 has removed all
the difficulties which then existed in the supply from
hence of pecuniary funds for the expedition. The
remarkable improvement which has happened in that
branch of our affairs, and the present flourishing state
of our finances, I believe unexampled, afford no motive
for undertaking chargeable and unnecessary operations;
but these circumstances do certainly remove from
measures which are expedient and important, the obstacles of pecuniary embarrassment; especially when
the Company is only required to make the advances,
without being ultimately charged with the burden, as
in the present instance.

'Let me here indulge the flattering hope that,
while the amount of this armament must give a satisfactory proof of the Company's resources in India, . . .
the perfect tranquillity which has been maintained in
the absence of so large a body of troops, principally
His Majesty's regiments, may afford views not less

---

[1] To the Right Hon. R. Dundas, Jan. 1, 1811.

favourable, first, of our political state without, and next of that more important point of our security, which depends upon the entire suppression of recent troubles within. The expedition against Bourbon, composed entirely of troops from the establishment of Fort St. George, sailed from Madras roads the day on which I myself took leave of the coast. I certainly could not have ventured such a measure, if notwithstanding some vexations and disgusts down to the latest period, which might be regarded as the dregs of former disorder, I had not confidently relied on the stability of those considerations, stated at the time to the Secret Committee, on which my conviction rested of the effectual suppression of insubordination and disloyalty in the Madras army. It cannot but be matter of public gratification that these sentiments have been confirmed by every subsequent event.

'Fort William: January 25, 1811.

'I have this morning received, by despatches from Mr. Farquhar, the happy accounts of the surrender of the Mauritius. I will not postpone my cordial congratulations on the fortunate accomplishment—with loss so much less considerable than might have been expected—of a service, the most important as it is universally considered here, and as in truth I believe it to be, that could be rendered to the East India Company and the nation in the East.'

CHAPTER XII.

IN a letter to Lady Minto, written before the armament destined to capture the French islands had sailed, Lord Minto wrote:—' I have still one object more, in the event of a prosperous issue to the present enterprise, which will fill up the whole scheme of my warlike purposes, and which will purge the Eastern side of the globe of every hostile or rival European establishment.'

The first letter of 1811 opens thus:—' We are now in the agony of preparation for Java; and I will whisper in your ear that I am going there myself, not to command the army, but to see all the political work done to my mind.

' "Modeste" is to be my state coach.'

'Calcutta: February 25, 1811.

' I am to embark in a few days for Madras. I shall then, I hope, proceed to Malacca on board the "Modeste."[1] . . . My going in person upon this service is not a very usual measure, and my motives not being generally understood, many ingenious conjectures are,

[1] The ' Modeste,' commanded by Captain the Hon. George Elliot, was expected at Madras from China on March 15.

must preclude all hopes of conciliating the confidence of Runjeet Singh.

'With regard to Cabul the objection is precisely similar. With the King of that country we have never had any intercourse whatever. I hope that a sense of common danger, and a real identity of interests, may in the very able hands to which that mission is committed, become a foundation of solid union and of zealous and efficient co-operation. But here the work of confidence is to begin. All is yet to do, and I rely for success—here as at Lahore—only on the candid explanation of our true and real purpose, countenanced and supported by a general sincerity of demeanour and by the absence of all those traces of indirect and collateral design which, while they frequently fail in their own object, are very apt to frustrate and disappoint every other with which they are in any way connected.'

The minute ends thus:—'Speaking purely of military advantages, my opinion, I confess, is that the movement and operation of troops, as well as the success of a campaign, would be more facilitated and favoured by the friendship and assistance of the country which is the theatre of their operations without a previous topographical knowledge of the ground, or military report of its condition and resources, than by the possession of that knowledge in a hostile country.'

Mr. Metcalfe [1] was the envoy selected for the mission

---

[1] Afterwards Lord Metcalfe. Late Governor General of India, Governor of Jamaica, and Governor General of Canada.

to the Punjaub, and a more difficult task than that entrusted to him can hardly be conceived—to woo the great Rajah to an alliance, while refusing him the increase of territory on which he had set his heart. Charles Metcalfe was at this time twenty-three years of age; he was a lad of nineteen when Lord Wellesley sent him as political officer to the head-quarters of Lord Lake, where a combination of tact and spirit had established his reputation as one of the most promising of the younger civilians. On Lord Minto's arrival in India no name was brought before him with higher encomiums; and when selected for the most delicate of political missions, it was entrusted to his sole charge. He 'was to move' we are told 'without secretaries, assistants, or attachés; a military escort was to be provided, and a proper establishment of moonshees, writers, and servants was to be furnished. But the work of diplomacy was left entirely to his unaided counsels.'[1] He was to be the pioneer of the mission to Cabul. Besides collecting and communicating every information, political, geographical, and topographical, concerning the country he was despatched to, together with the real disposition of its ruler, the state of his government, troops, resources, &c., he was to push his *reconnaissances*, by means of secret news-writers, to Cabul, Cashmere, Peshawur, Candahar, Herat, and as far as possible into the interior of Persia.

[1] Kaye's *Correspondence of Lord Metcalfe.*

in this manner, although I confess, since it is right, that I never engaged in any affair with greater interest or with more pleasure; and you will easily conceive what a gratifying break this kind of adventure must make in the monotony of my not less laborious life at Fort William.

'I expect to be absent from Bengal seven or eight months; and of that period I shall probably not pass above six weeks or two months on land, so that, as for sailing, I might as well go to England at once.'

The next passages from his journal are dated '"*Modeste*," *at sea :*'—'I have been reading "Ossian," and Crabbe's "Borough," &c. I have also with me "The Lady of the Lake," and the six volumes of Scott's works, besides Mr. Dugald Stewart's new volume. His matter is always attractive to me, and his style most captivating. Mr. Fox's History, the whole corpus of Latin poets, and Cicero's works, not to mention Dryden's, edited by Scott. These with many manuscript volumes to read, and some, alas! to write, will serve me for pastime for this trip.

'*March* 21.—We have thirty soldiers of the Company's Bengal European regiment sent on board as marines. They are all recruits just come out, and all boys of about sixteen or seventeen years of age,—fine-looking lads, but never having seen a firelock, without clothing, without an officer, commissioned or non-commissioned, or so much as a corporal—in short the *raw material* perfectly unsophisticated. John has undertaken to manufacture the article, and has accordingly been teaching them the manœuvres on deck in great style. . . . We caught a shark yesterday, and a most butchering business it was. The shark would not have treated one of us half so inhumanly, but would have put us out of our pain in half the time.

'*April* 2.—C—— told me at Madras that his plan is to consume what remains of life, whatever it may be, in the pursuit of fortune for his family, and to be overtaken by the gentleman who is coming up behind us all, before he has accomplished his object. My plan is somewhat like his—with this difference, that I have fixed a period, and that I propose to twaddle a space (I have not settled how long) amongst you all. I allow that the gentleman behind may put out a little, and win the race before I intend it; but this is no part of my plan, and I really hope he will not be so uncivil nor such a marplot. After all, if the fellow should be a brute, I hardly know how I should have the face to complain, seeing that on March 23 I turned the corner of three score, after a happy and prosperous journey so far, and seeing that much of my plan, by far the best and most interesting part of it, I mean what secures comfort to those who seem now to make me live beyond my life and survive myself, will have been accomplished, before the trouble-fête could come up to spoil sport.'

'" Modeste," at sea, May 1811.

'Dr. Leyden's learning is stupendous, and he is also a very universal scholar. His knowledge, extensive and minute as it is, is always in his pocket, at his fingers' ends, and on the tip of his tongue. He has made it completely his own, and it is all ready money. All his talent and labour indeed, which are both excessive, could not, however, have accumulated such stores without his extraordinary memory. I begin, I fear, to look at that faculty with increasing wonder; I hope without envy, but something like one's admiration of young eyes. It must be confessed that Leyden has occasion for all the stores which application and memory can furnish, to supply his tongue, which would dissipate a common stock in a week. I do not believe that so great a reader was ever so great a talker before. You may be conceited about yourselves, my beautiful wife and daughters, but with all my partiality I must give it against you. You would appear absolutely silent in his company, as a ship under weigh seems at anchor when it is passed by a swifter sailer. Another feature of his conversation is a shrill, piercing, and at the same time grating voice. A frigate is not near large enough to place the ear at the proper point of hearing. If he had been at Babel he would infallibly have learned all the languages there, but in the end they must all have merged in the *Tividale How*,[1] for not a creature would have *got spoken* but himself. I must say to his honour that he has as intimate and profound a knowledge of the geography, history, mutual relations, religion, character, and manners of every tribe in Asia as he has of their language. On the present occasion there is not an island or petty state in the multitude of islands and

[1] How, twang.

nations amongst which we are going, of which he has not a tolerably minute and correct knowledge.

'His conversation is rather excursive; because, on his way to the point of enquiry, he strikes aside to some collateral topic, and from thence diverges still wider from the original object. I have often tried without success to fix him to the point in hand, and the only way has been a more peremptory call than I like to use, especially to one whom I like and esteem so highly. But nothing can differ more widely from his conversation in this respect than his writing. His pen is sober, steady, concise, lucid, and well fed with useful as well as curious matter. His reasoning is just, his judgment extremely sound, and his principles always admirable. His mind is upright and independent, his character spirited and generous with a strong leaning to the chivalrous; and in my own experience I have never found any trace either of wrong head, or of an impracticable or unpleasant temper. The only little blemish I have sometimes regretted to see in him is a disposition to egotism; not selfishness—but a propensity to bring the conversation from whatever quarter it starts round to himself, and to exalt his own actions, sufferings, or adventures in a manner a little approaching the marvellous. I have indulged myself in this portrait because I feel an interest which I know you all share in so distinguished a worthy of Teviotside.'[1]

[1] Dr. Leyden was born of humble parentage in the village of Denholm, Roxburghshire. In his native district he is best remembered as the author of *Scenes of Infancy* and other poems. A graceful monument was erected to his memory at Denholm a few years ago.

'Penang, Prince of Wales' Island: May 12, 1811.

'Mr. Bruce, Lord Elgin's brother, was the last Governor of Prince of Wales' Island; and his death, which is much and justly lamented, placed the senior member of Council, Mr. Phillips, provisionally in the chair. We were received therefore by him, and carried immediately to his house about two miles from George Town, the only place to be called a town in the island. Mr. Phillips is magnificently lodged; and his house, which he built himself, is one of the handsomest I have seen in India. . . . This mansion is not quite proportioned to the island, and looks like the great lady in the little parlour. The situation is beautiful—on the bank of a running stream fresh from mountain springs. Beyond the stream the plain extends perhaps a quarter of a mile to the foot of a sublime mountain, and not more sublime than beautiful, steep, craggy, broken into smaller hills, and the whole covered with the most magnificent wood, interspersed with underwood, and here and there vacant spaces which are green and flourishing. On the other side of the stream stands *Kelso*—a bungalow or cottage built by Scott of Raeburn's eldest son, who gave his house and ground that name, because the little stream divides itself into two branches and forms a sort of microscopic Tweed and Teviot, principally I presume from love and affection for home, which is brought to mind by slight affinities. I experienced something of the pleasure which the giver of the name found in it, and felt comfort from the view the name found in it, and felt comfort from the view and neighbourhood of miniature Kelso. . . .

'The island is about ten miles long, and, like most high islands, has a space between the sea and the mountain flat enough for cultivation. The interior is all mountain. In Penang, however, the plain is narrow everywhere, and in a great part of the circumference the mountain comes down steep to the very water, so that of this small territory a very small proportion can be cultivated or even inhabited. The principal plain was made the seat of the settlement; and, considering that it was desert twenty-five years ago when it came into our possession, great progress has been made both in useful and ornamental improvements. The population is called in round numbers 30,000 souls—of which two-thirds are Chinese, the rest Malays, people from the coast of Coromandel and other parts of India, convicts from Bengal—a garrison of Bengal Sepoys of about 1,000 men, and about 100 English gentlemen and seafaring people. The whole of this community may be considered as industrious, for without industry they could not live; but the Chinese are superior to all other Easterns in industry and ingenuity. Agriculture and most of the handicraft and mechanic trades are in the hands of the Chinese. Georgetown is well and regularly built—the fort is little more than nominal. I presume you know that Pulo Penang is the native name of Prince of Wales' Island.

'Upon the cession of the island the English colours happened to be hoisted on August 12, the Prince's birthday, and hence this new part of Her Majesty's dominions received his name.

. . . .

'One of the favourite sights is a flour-mill and baking establishment invented and executed by a Chinese. There is nothing very curious or difficult in the machinery; but the establishment is on a great scale, and owes its success not only to the ingenuity, but to the capital and to the very liberal spirit of enterprise of the owner;—to crown all, the bread is preferred by the navy to anything they had even in England. There is a good, regularly built road from Georgetown to the furthest extremity of the island, and there are extremely pretty green lanes, smooth and safe for buggies or little phaetons. The horses are universally little Acheen ponies, an excellent and handsome breed of the smallest fairylike horses you ever saw, from the great island of Sumatra, and particularly from Acheen, one of its kingdoms. What struck my Scotch mind most forcibly at Penang is the timber which covers every inch of the surface not under cultivation. I am certain that your poor, diminutive European imagination never conceived such trees and such innumerable multitudes of them. They stand as close to each other over the whole mountain as a larch plantation that never was thinned. The height of the bole before it loses the character of timber may be called, one with another, 150 feet. They are thick enough at this height for the mainmast to a large ship. They are in general perfectly straight and without branch for seventy feet high. The thickness near the ground is magnificent. I am afraid though, this side the Cape and far ayont, to say what they measure, but thirty feet in the girth is common. When you see them down, they are stupendous sticks. Being straight, they do not furnish the most essential timbers for ship-building; but they are excellent masts, yards, spars of all sorts. The luxuriance and vigour of all the Eastern vegetation is scarcely to be conceived on your side of the Cape. The freshness and verdure are well maintained here by showers like the Flood every night in the year, or *thereby.* I have found the climate, so far, much more temperate and even pleasant than I expected; and I reckon that I shall skip a summer by this trip, for in Bengal it is at this time the height of the hot winds, which are no joke. Here we have grateful and refreshing winds during the greatest part of the twenty-four hours, and rain and *purgative* thunder, and the sting is taken out of the tropical sun.

'Mr. Seton was put in possession of his government the day we landed, and I took my seat at the same time as Governor General in Council, converting this small presidency into the supreme Government of India, and acting myself the part of the great lady in the little parlour. There were some few points of business to transact, and Penang will have upon its consultations some proceedings of the Governor General in Council, which is an odd accident in the history of both Governments. We landed here on the 9th, and are getting under weigh for Malacca on the 12th—a short space for so long a chronicle.'

'Malacca: May 31, 1811.

'We embarked at Penang on May 12, and arrived at Malacca on the 18th. Nothing remarkable happened on the passage. The weather was a succession of calms or light winds and squalls, with heavy rain and thunder. This is the case pretty generally through the year in the Straits of Malacca. . . . The passage through these straits is made pretty and interesting by the variety of islands, and by the high coast of the Malay peninsula, which is always in view, and often at a very discernible distance. Both the islands and the main are much in the same character as Penang—mountainous, and covered with timber, of which there must be inexhaustible treasures in these regions. We sometimes had the Malay coast and the mountains of Sumatra in sight at the same time, to our right and left. At Malacca we found all the Bengal troops arrived . . . the troops form two camps, in dry, healthy situations, on the sea-shore, close to the water. One is at two miles, the other and most considerable at six, from the town, which helps to defend them against the incursions of barrack-fever and dysentery. The camps very much adorn and enliven the scenery of this pretty bay. Malacca stands on the banks of a small stream, about the breadth of the Rule at Spittal, but resembling it in no other respect. The town is built along the right bank of the river, one side of the houses projecting a few feet over the stream, supported on piles, which elevate them seven or eight feet above the surface of the water. This gives the place in that quarter rather an amphibious appearance. The town runs down to the edge of the sea, and runs back in the direction of the beach, sometimes advancing into the tide upon piles, sometimes leaving a handsome terrace between the houses and the water.

'On the opposite bank of the river, close also to the sea, the Portuguese built a small fort, on their acquisition of the place in the sixteenth century. The Dutch dispossessed them in the following century, and maintained everything as it was. We came next, about sixteen years ago, and by orders from home have pulled down the fort. This work of destruction has been very recently accomplished, at considerable expense—a most useless piece of gratuitous mischief, as far as I can understand the subject. The ruins of the walls remain, and will long transmit a memorial of the narrow, and what is felt by the people here to be the malevolent, policy displayed by England to this new portion of her dominions. The Government House, however, built by the Portuguese, and a church erected by the Dutch within the limits of the fort, are still on foot, together with a few other buildings, public and private. I inhabit the Government House, which is not magnificent, but answers my purposes perfectly in most respects. But it stands at the foot of a steep hill, which covers the whole tenement from the sea. Now as the sea-breeze is in these climates the true *vital* air, and as delicious as the gas of Paradise, suffocation is our portion at the Government House. As I see you gasping at this account, and opening all the windows in spite of Elliot of Wells, it will give your ladyship great satisfaction to find that the hill makes amends for the harm it does below, by supporting up in the air very near the top a small bungalow, composed of one room and an open verandah, fronting the sea. George is the real owner; but the dutiful boy permits me to sit in the verandah from breakfast to dinner, and has thereby, beyond a doubt, prolonged my life almost a fortnight already. It is in this verandah that he and I are at present, writing love-letters to our absent wives. We swallow the breeze fresh from the sea, and the climate is entirely disarmed. The prospect, too, is a refreshing one to the eye, and possesses beauty on shore and on sea. We have the roads with all the shipping and a string of small islands in front; to the right we have a bird's-eye view of the little river and town beyond; the coast, wooded down to the water, runs curving and waving, and throwing out pretty projecting points, made interesting by the camps at different distances; the whole backed inward from the sea by an uneven plain, springing first into elevations, then hills, and at length high mountains in the distance; all clothed near the eye with the richest vegetation and verdure, and, far as well as near, with one universal wood. Of the distant mountains the most important is Mount Ophir, which has pretensions, of which I will not pretend to judge, to be the true Mount Ophir. Certain it is that gold is collected there at this day.

'Even close to Malacca the country seems a forest of

lofty timber. But the timber has been long since removed, and all that are now seen are fruit-trees, some of which are rather of the forest than of garden dimensions, and under their close, thick shade the Malay and Chinese peasants cultivate their grounds with industry and not without skill. There are many green drives from three to five and six miles round in these woods, and they pass through a great deal of beautiful forest scenery. The conveyance here, as at Penang, is in low buggies and phaetons drawn by Acheen ponies, which bustle on with great activity and at a good rate.

'Mr. George has made a number of sketches which will help to fill up my blanks.

'There are about 15,000 souls in the town and adjoining district. About two-thirds of these are Malays—that is to say, natives; the remainder are principally Chinese who have been long settled, and have colonised here contrary to their usual custom, which is to return to China when they have made a little independence to live on at home. The Chinese emigrants never bring women with them, but *foregather* with Malay females—mostly slaves—and leave them behind when they go home. At Malacca they have married the daughters of these Malay mothers, and these, intermarrying, have in a number of generations converted the Malay coarse clay into fine China; so that the colony is now *whole* blood on both sides of the house, and may be accounted curious in that respect as well as in that of the men not being emigrants from China, but descended from emigrant ancestors and born for several generations at Malacca. There are also some remains of the old Portuguese stock. These are very degenerate, and little trace of European origin is left, except their professing the Catholic religion. There are people, both Mussulman and Hindoo, from different parts of India; but the most thriving class, though not the most numerous, is Dutch, pure, and mixed with Malay blood. The better kind of Dutch are the only substantial part of the community. They continue, under our Government, to fill the principal offices, particularly the judicial, Dutch law being established by the capitulation. Some are merchants, several of them are well-informed, respectable people, and one or two are polite, accomplished men. Of the ladies, the elder matrons preserve a smack of the primitive Dutch colonial fashion in dress and manners. The daughters dress, dance, and flirt very much as well-educated young women do in Europe, with the advantage of being intensely and beautifully brown. You are *lily-fair* compared with the fairest of the Batavo-Malaya fair sex. My fidelity, you see, is put to the test. Of English there is but a commandant with one or two officers and medical men attached to the small garrison, which consists of two companies of Sepoys from Bengal. Malacca is a dependency of the Penang Government.

'This account of Malacca is for ordinary times. At present we have a great fleet and army officered by English gentlemen; we have also my establishment, including Mr. Raffles, who has a pretty numerous family. Mrs. Raffles is the great lady, with dark eyes, lively manner, accomplished and clever. She had a former husband in India; and I have heard, but am not sure of the fact, that she was one of the beauties to whom Anacreontic Moore addressed many of his amatory elegies. . . .

'I have mustered the whole female community of Malacca at a ball, for I am now writing on *June* 7. I celebrated the King's birthday by a levée in the forenoon, a great dinner to all mankind, and a ball in the evening to all womankind. I escaped during the first dance, having had enough of the day by the earlier festivities; and I slept that night up in George's bungalow to be out of earshot of the fiddlers. One of the pleasantest parts of the celebration took place privately after the levée. I released all the Government slaves at Malacca, presenting to each with my own hand a certificate of their freedom, and four dollars to provide for their immediate subsistence till they can get into some way of life. They have also the option of resuming their former state if they find a difficulty in maintaining themselves. They are only nineteen in number, male and female, of all ages, from infants in arms to old, helpless people. Most of them were *born* slaves to the Dutch Company, some to the English, and all their children would have continued slaves. Slavery is established in all these countries to a shocking extent. An insolvent debtor, however small his debt, is condemned to be the slave of the creditor. Some have been slaves for life for 100 or 200 dollars, and if the sum is considerable the whole family shares the same fate. Men may gamble their children, their wives, and lastly themselves into slavery, in satisfaction of bets upon fighting cocks, or any other gambling debt; and nothing is more common. If a criminal is condemned to slavery, his whole family goes with him; or, if he is put to death, the wife and children, young and old, after witnessing the execution, are sold into slavery—the mother to one master, the children to others. I speak now, not of Malacca, but of other Malay countries, including Java. I hope something may be done—partly by authority, partly by influence—to mitigate these horrors; in the meanwhile the people of Malacca have been told and have seen that the English think no man should be deprived of his liberty except criminals. Another proof has been given to them that we dislike cruelty. Finding some instruments of torture still preserved, although they have been long disused, I had the cross upon which criminals were *broken*, and another wooden instrument that had served as a sort of rack, burnt under the windows of a room from which executions are seen by the magistrates, where I and the magistrates were assembled for the purpose; and at the same time various iron articles for screwing thumbs, wrists, and ankles, and other contrivances of that diabolical sort, were carried out in a boat by the executioner into the roads, and sunk in deep water, never to rise or screw poor people's bones and joints again.

'Talking of slaves, I must tell you that I am myself the master of several. A Rajah of Balli, an island adjoining the east end of Java, has sent me, amongst other presents, five boys and two girls, all slaves, at my service. They have been some time kept at Mr. Raffles's house, who has agreed to take one or two. They are all emancipated, of course, but remain an orphan charge upon us. The boys are from about eight to thirteen years old, and are all fine, spunky-looking boys. The girls are four or five years old. Now to give you a notion of the manners and scenes they are accustomed to : they were all dressed in their bettermost upon the occasion of their being first shown to me. They perceived that there was a sort of solemnity, which seemed to give them some uneasiness. While they were paraded in this manner, and they were all gazing round them, two Malay spears unfortunately caught Taylor's eye, in the corner of the room, and *of necessity* he began tossing and brandishing them about, and at length the scabbards were pulled off the bright blades at the ends of the weapons. The moment this happened the poor boys all huddled together, and the youngest left the rest and came with his little hands joined together, in the most supplicating manner, and with the most imploring face, walking from one of us to the other, and evidently begging for his life, though he did not utter a word, nor even cried ; but he appeared terrified. It was like one who had little hope of obtaining his request, and who had been accustomed to consider the thing he feared as a sort of natural doom that was to be expected. It was with some difficulty, even after the spears were removed, that the children were reassured. They certainly thought that they had been dressed out to be sacrificed or put to death for some cause or other, and when they saw the naked points of the spears they thought their time was come. This is the less surprising, as there is every reason to believe that each of them had seen his father put to death by a number of spears, which is a common mode of execution. Next day they were all very merry and happy. George has taken one of the boys to serve him on board of ship, and that boy has fallen on his legs. Mr. Raffles will take care of one or two, and the rest have fallen to my lot. They will probably grow into very good servants. The girls will puzzle me most. I have some thought of baking them in a pie against the Queen's birthday, unless I should strike out some other idea in the meanwhile. Upon the whole, this present from the Rajah of Balli is providential for the poor children. The Rajah has sent two Vakeels, or Ambassadors, to meet me here, and I gave their Excellencies audience on June 4. They are young, well-looking men. I do not remember having seen the same costume at St. James's. They were naked down to the middle; but the garments, when they once began, were rich enough. I have one slave more who was given me *in* a present from the Sultan of Pontiana, a great chief in the island of Borneo, whom I am likely enough to thank in person on my way to Java. This gentleman is Lord Monboddo's genuine oran-outang, which in the Malay language signifies literally wild man. He is really too like a man—that is to say, a Malay man. His features and the whole cast of his face are identically the same, for Malays are all exactly like each other. Some people think very seriously that the oran-outang was the original patriarch and progenitor of the whole Malay race, and there is certainly a good deal to be said on both sides. It is true the oran-outang has one manifest advantage over his degenerate posterity, having four hands instead of two, and this is the principal difference. My wild man is but a boy—indeed, a baby; but he is much larger than any monkey I ever saw. He is also too much civilised to deserve the name of wild. I saw him yesterday sitting on a stool, and eating his rice on a table like a Christian gentleman.'

While Lord Minto was watching the gay and moving scene from the bungalow on the hill, it was attracting the curious gaze of the natives of Malacca, who had never before assisted at *pareille fête*, and he himself was more closely scanned by an observant eye than he was at all aware of.

A most entertaining narrative of the arrival at Malacca of the expedition, consisting of ninety sail, carrying 6,000 European and 6,000 native troops, forms a chapter in the autobiography of a Malay, Abdulla by name, which was translated by the well-known writer Mr. J. T. Thomson, F.R.G.S., and published about six years ago.[1] From it we shall venture to quote a few passages to complete the narrative contained in the letters.

[1] Under the title of 'Hakayit Abdulla.'

Abdulla was only fourteen years of age at the time; yet, in his description of their camps, he is said to have painted the Sepoys to the life; and in the few lively touches with which he puts before us the English officers, and the Governor General himself, we are able to recognise the photographic fidelity of his sketches.

'They erected their tents from Lambongan as far as Tanjong Kling, this without break, each with their entrances. And amongst these were various races of Hindoos and Mussulmans; and I saw some who ate like dogs, to wit, they licked their food with their tongues; while there were others who, on being seen eating, would throw the food away, and chase you as if they would kill you, they were so angry. There were some who only half-heated the food, and ate it then, covered with perspiration as if bathing in it. And when they had eaten, they buried the rice and curry that was over in the sand. And there were others who tied three strands of thread round their body before they ate, nor did they stop eating till the thread had broken. There were others who took white and red earth and smeared it on their breasts, with three stripes on their arms and brow; then they bowed themselves in front, then to the right and to the left, then to the back, then off they ran into the sea, and worshipped the sun for some time, turning their faces to the right and left. Then they came ashore, and went to eat within white cloth screens, so that no one could see them at their meals. But if persons should happen to see them, they would cast out their food, and break the earthen vessels in pieces, buying others for the next time. Others there were who could eat before people, but they could not speak. . . . I saw many foolish customs. . . . How many forms of people did I then not see, and kinds of dresses that I had never in my life seen before! And it was to be perceived that the English had provided their leaders with different dresses: some had tigers' skins for coats, others had hats covered with fowls' feathers, dyed red, white, or black, while others had beasts' skins for trousers; there were others who had clothes spotted like leopards.'

To their young co-religionist—for Abdulla was a Mussulman—the Mahometan Sepoys from Delhi and Oude wore a far more dignified aspect than the Hindoos with their strange and 'foolish' customs. 'These Sepoys were well acquainted with the Koran; amongst them were many descendants of the Arabs of the race of Syeds. They were gracious, manly, and courteous.' 'They were under the command of English officers, who drilled them every day.' Here follows a trait as characteristic of the Englishmen as any of those attributed to the men under their command. 'And when they had done drilling and were returning, the officers did not take their horses through the gates, but leaped over the fence, which was seven cubits high.[1] The Malacca people came in hundreds every day to see this feat, and the officers leaping the fence; loud were

---

[1] The Editor informs us that this must be taken as Oriental hyperbole, since seven cubits would be ten and a half feet.

they in their cries of astonishment at seeing the skill of the horses—equal as it was to that of mankind—in understanding the sound of the trumpet. Says one, "This is not men's but *jin's* work."'

When at last came the ship with Lord Minto on board, 'there went out an order for everyone to clean their frontages in all the streets. Then thousands of all races collected at the sea-shore to have a sight of him and his dress, his name being so great. After this a great noise was heard of the regiments coming in full force, with the music of drums, fifes, and other instruments. . . . And the multitude in Malacca increased so greatly that there was no knowing who they were, but that they were of the human race. . . . At the time of his leaving his ship the cannon roared like thunder—the sea became dark with smoke. And when I had seen the appearance and circumstance of Lord Minto, I was much moved; for I guessed in my mind as to his appearance, position, and height, that these would be great, and his dress gorgeous. . . . But his appearance was of one which was middle-aged, thin in body, of soft manners and sweet countenance, and I felt that he could not carry twenty cutties (about thirty pounds), so slow were his motions. His coat was black cloth, trousers the same, nor was there anything peculiar. And when the leading men desired to pay their respects they remained at a distance, none daring to grasp his hand; but they took off their hats and bent their bodies. . . . When he landed he bowed to the right and to the left. Now he had not the remotest appearance of pomposity or lofty-headedness; but there was real modesty and kindly expression. . . . Now as long as Lord Minto remained in Malacca he took a round in his carriage every evening, one day visiting the mosque, another the Chinese Joss-house, another the Dutch and Portuguese Churches; and wherever he was met by rich, poor, or low, they stopped to make their bow, which he returned with good-humour and courtesy, without the slightest shadow of pomposity.'

Lord Minto's visit to the debtors' prison is related with much sympathy and great amplifications. One fact told by Abdulla, which we do not find in the correspondence, is worthy of mention; namely, that when the cells of the filthy dungeon were destroyed, a new gaol was built in its place which was 'a residence free of all annoyances but one, that you could not get out of it.'

We learn from the editor of Abdulla's autobiography that, 'as a memento of the deliverance of the prisoners, and of other high-minded acts at Malacca, Lord Minto's portrait was procured and hung up in the resident magistrate's office, where he is represented as breaking the shackles of cruelty. When I saw it in 1848 I viewed it with great curiosity. The climate had so destroyed the colours that it might have served for a black Madonna.'

'H.M.S. "Modeste," off Java: ended August 3, 1811.

'The fleet having at length assembled at Malacca it was despatched towards its destination in a number of small divisions, which sailed successively, each under charge of a frigate, and attended also by sloops of war or Company's cruizers. The "Modeste" was not attached to any division, and, being sure of overtaking the earliest and swiftest, we remained at anchor till the whole had departed. The fleet consisted of 81 sail of all descriptions, and it was despatched in many divisions because we had several narrow straits and difficult passes before us, which must have occasioned confusion, and probably accident and loss, if so large a body of shipping had kept together. This voyage is made interesting by the very positive opinions which Admiral Drury had given himself, and had managed to obtain a countenance to from several quarters of authority on such questions, that it was absolutely impracticable to make a passage to Java with a fleet of transports, if it should sail from Madras later than March 1. It was with this opinion that I had to contend, pushing forward the expedition in the present season, although it could not take its departure so soon as the day fixed by the Admiral, by six weeks according to my expectations, and, as it has proved on trial, by two months. The result has furnished another testimony in favour of the virtue called obstinacy, which is entitled by success to the more polite name of firmness. The difficulty was this. As soon as what is called the south-east monsoon in the eastern seas sets in, the wind blows hard and pretty steadily from the east along the channel between the north of Java and the south of Borneo; it blows to the north-west

along the east coast of Sumatra, and between that
coast and the Malay Peninsula; it blows to the north
between the west coast of Borneo and the straits of
Malacca. So that, starting from Malacca, the wind was
directly contrary in every part of the course to the
northern coast of Java. Besides this difficulty there is
a current in the same direction as the wind throughout. To carry a great fleet of transports, not famous
in general for working to windward, a long voyage
directly against wind and current, did not appear promising. It was known, however, that with a little
patience a fleet can at that season make a passage
down the Straits of Malacca by any one of the several
passages which lead to the eastward. This is done by
the help of squalls which generally blow from the
northward; by occasional shifts of wind; and by alterations of tide or current which afford a favourable start
to the eastward. It was ascertained by investigation,
enquiry, and actual survey and trial recently made for
the present occasion, that after making the west coast
of Borneo, land winds at night, and the sea breeze
during part of the day, together with a slackening of
the current, and even a favourable current during
particular periods of the tide, will enable ships to make
a passage along the coast to the southward without
much delay; and from the south-west point of Borneo,
having the wind at east, you may stand at least as high
as south to Java, and make that island as far to the
east as Samarang—which is more than we desire. The
plan was therefore settled upon this foundation. The

It may nevertheless remain an open question whether the friendly relations established between the Company's Government and Afghanistan might not have been cultivated with better success if the far-sighted policy inaugurated by Lord Minto had been pursued and developed, and due importance attached to the movements of European States in that quarter: in such a course there might have been more of statesmanship and less of saltpetre.

One undeniable and important result of the scheme for the defence of India was the greater knowledge obtained by the missions of the countries and populations to which they were sent, and Mr. Elphinstone's 'History of Cabul,' Colonel Malcolm's 'Persian History' and 'Sketches of Persia,' and Sir Henry Pottinger's work on Beloochistan were conceived during the embassies sent out by Lord Minto. The first two works were compiled and published at the expense of, or with the assistance of ample and liberal aid from, the Indian Government, at the instigation of the Governor General.

is in the possession of Mir Hasham Khan, native officer in the 12th Bengal Cavalry, and grandson of the Vizier of Shah Soojah. The fact became accidentally known to Lord Melgund, the great-grandson of Lord Minto, while with the column of General Roberts in the Kurrum valley in the spring of 1879. He did not see the treaty, but he was informed that the original signature of Lord Minto was attached to it. Mir Hasham Khan is described as a very smart officer in one of our best cavalry regiments. This *rapprochement* between the descendant of the Governor General and of the Afghan statesman, was related in a letter from India while the foregoing pages were being written.

NOTE.

The State of Scinde had come within the scope of the defensive arrangements proposed by the British Government, but the indiscretion of their agent, Captain Seton, led to the annulling of the treaty concluded by him with the Ameer of Scinde.

It was found that Persian agents were negotiating with the Government of Scinde at the same time as the Envoy of the Indian Government; that they had authority to act for both France and Persia, and that the bait held out to the Government of Scinde was military aid to throw off the yoke of the King of Cabul, to whom they owed a nominal allegiance, and the possession of the Afghan fortress of Candahar. 'The chief ruler of Scinde informed Captain Seton distinctly that, despairing of the good-will of the British Government, he had intended to close with the offers of the French and Persians, but preferred the British alliance on the same terms.' These terms, agreed to by Captain Seton, were not consistent with the endeavours making to secure the friendship of the King of Cabul; hence the Indian Government repudiated the engagements made by Captain Seton, and sent another Envoy (Mr. H. Smith) to Scinde, to renew the negotiations with that Government, on the footing on which alone Captain Seton had been empowered to treat—namely, the admission, as a preliminary step to all further transactions, of a resident agent of the British Government (the commercial resident having been expelled in 1802).

'This measure is necessarily preliminary to the accom-

Edgell's *works*. They constructed dams across the stream of fresh water, to raise the surface higher than the tide at high water. The *pond head* was carried down every shower that fell, which were not a few, but they renewed the work next morning indefatigably, having plenty of hands; and in fact their labours answered the purpose, and a full stock of excellent water was obtained. The Sepoys are particularly happy on these short visits to the land. Their religion makes it difficult to supply them with food at all on board, and it is always attended with inconvenience and privations of various sorts, the whole heightened by uneasy scruples by way of spice. When they get on shore, each man cooks his own meal according to his taste and prejudices, and they bathe comfortably both to their skins and consciences. The whole scene of black and white men, of trades and occupations, with the sort of spirit, energy, and cheerfulness which belongs to British seamen, made this Panambangan beach a most lively and agreeable spot.

'From Malacca the "Modeste" was accompanied by the schooner "Minto," a vessel attached to me, and containing Dr. Leyden with a number of Malay moonshees or interpreters and writers of that learned language. She is commanded by Captain Greig, a remarkably intelligent country ship-master, who is perfectly at home in the eastern seas. He has already been of the greatest use, both by missions to some islands adjacent to Java; and more particularly by having pointed out the passage which we are now making to Java, and ascertained its practicability by actual survey himself. While thus engaged he was attacked by a very strong Pirate Prow, whom he beat off with difficulty and with the loss of several killed and a greater number wounded. . . . Greig is a plain, modest, unassuming Fife-man, with excellent natural parts and character, such as " Calydonia, altrix terra exuberantium virum,' so often sends from her lower ranks to all the quarters of the globe. Greig is ennobled, however, by another exuberant member of his family, who sent home honour and reputation to his stock from Russia and the Archipelago,—Admiral Greig himself, who was a near relation of our Greig of the " Minto " schooner. . . .

'. . . I return to Panambangan, where our gay fleet encampments on shore, and all the occupations which this halt afforded, would make a mighty good engraving to illustrate this chapter of my journal when it is published, as it will be by my executors, in quarto, price ten guineas.

' You must know, fresh fish is a great treat at sea, and with this luxury we solaced ourselves and the crew. There were oysters also, but none fell to my share ; but do not imagine our pleasures were confined to the table ; for we gratified our higher tastes and improved our minds and morals at the Theatre. A play has been performed every Saturday evening by His Majesty's servants on board His Majesty's Ship " Modeste," and when the fleet was collected at Panambangan the house was crowded with rank and fashion. I omit beauty, because the manager admits no female either before or behind the curtain; so that we enjoy the moral entertainment of stage plays in all its purity. I was never near so well amused at any other performance of amateurs. It is really surprising to observe the *propriety* with which these rough, uninstructed, unassisted sailors represent all the varieties of character which are found in comedy, and, amongst the rest, young, accomplished, and generally sentimental ladies of quality; rendering with perfect justness all that concerns nature, failing only in what is artificial and arbitrary, as in the extraordinary work they make of what appears to us very ordinary words of the English language. We now hear *exquisitive* for exquisite, *etiquity* for etiquette, and *axe* for ask, with as little prejudice to the play or the performer as a Scotch vowel or phrase is heard in the House of Commons from an eloquent member for Scotland. . . .

'From Panambangan anchorage we were to pass between that island and an adjacent one to the eastward in order to make the west coast of Borneo. But no part of this track had been examined. George accordingly sent Captain Greig with the "Minto" schooner to perform that service, and he made a perfectly satisfactory report before Commodore Broughton had arrived at Panambangan with the bulk of the fleet.

'Commodore Broughton,[1] who is the most cautious navigator that ever wore a blue coat, was not satisfied

---

[1] Commodore Broughton had taken the command of the naval force on the death of Admiral Drury, which occurred before the expedition left Madras.

to abide by Greig's report, but ordered the "Modeste"
to go ahead and reconnoitre the whole passage to the
Rendezvous, thinking very properly that I had better
be drowned than he. As I was entirely of the same
opinion I accepted the service very thankfully. In
reality I knew that George was much fitter to perform
this duty than any other officer in the fleet, and I
thought it would be amusing to myself.

'. . . We made the coast of Borneo as far to the
north as we could, and then zigzagged our way along
the shore in five or six fathoms of water to the point
proposed.

'. . . The Commodore had also ordered George to
survey the neighbourhood of Pulo Mancap, which is
situated beyond the rendezvous, and is surrounded with
shoals. This duty we also performed, returning to the
Rendezvous before the Commodore and fleet reached
it.

'We had fallen in with a fleet of nine Buggese Prows[1]
when we went out towards Pulo Mancap, and from
them George was informed of a shoal which lay somewhat in the course to Java. George, in communicating
the rest of his information to the Commodore, mentioned this shoal. Upon this he ordered the "Modeste"
to explore it, whereupon we sailed again, but returned
the second day without having found it. Immediately
after, accounts were received that three French frigates,
with 1,000 troops, had got into Java, and again the

[1] Another letter says, 'Buggese, properly Bouginese, Prows,
belonging to the Rajah of Pontiana.'

Commodore stood my friend and gave me the post of honour, which I accepted with real pleasure. He ordered the "Modeste" immediately to Java. We sailed that night and fell in with the very shoal, which we had missed by one mile of longitude a couple of days before. But as the Commodore would not allow us any small vessel to send back with intelligence, if we should meet with any, we could not convey notice to the fleet of this danger. However, there is little risk, for it lies further to windward than they can well keep up to. In less than forty-eight hours from Rendezvous Island we were near enough Java to have seen the land if it had been daylight. On the next morning, July 25, we got a sight of the Land of Promise.'

That afternoon Lord Minto received from Captain Sayer of the ' Leda,' the intelligence that Rear-Admiral Stopford, on learning the death of Admiral Drury, had determined to proceed at once to Java, and was actually within a few days' sail of Java.¹ 'The little Commodore's brief hour of authority came to an end to the great relief of all in the fleet and army. There could

---

¹ Another piece of intelligence derived from Captain Sayer is recorded thus : 'He brought the news of *the Empress having an heir.* The Empress Maria Louisa, daughter of the Emperor of Austria, granddaughter of Maria Theresa, niece of the Queen of Naples, wife of Bonaparte ! ! !' It was no doubt strange news to the late Envoy Extraordinary to the Court of Vienna, and it was scarcely less strange that it should have reached him in a remote island in the Java Sea, on his way to wrest an important conquest from the grasp of Bonaparte. 'It seems to me,' wrote Lady Malmesbury, 'that while you have taken to make conquests, Bonaparte is becoming quite a family man.'

not be a man less fit for the important situation into which chance had brought him.

'What information we have is all favourable to our views, and I do flatter myself that my last military labour will terminate as successfully as the former have done.

'Having met a prize vessel, very lately from Grissy in the east of Java, we have learnt that the new Governor General Janssens, (formerly Governor of the Cape) arrived in one of the French frigates, and that Marshal D'Aendels, whom he has superseded, has since departed in the same frigate. The other two frigates are blocked up in Sourabaya. We have been long expected in Java, and the disposition of all tribes and nations, including the Dutch, is entirely favourable to the establishment of our Government.

'Having now brought these annals down to the present hour, *dinner-time*, July 27, cruising till our expedition comes on, I shall conclude with the event whenever it happens, and open a new number for our exploits on shore.

'*August 3.*—We cruised to the eastward, and George sent his boats in the night to a small place, called Taggul, to cut out some Prows of which he had intelligence, lading rice for Batavia by the order of the Dutch Government. Instead of that sort of quiet craft, the boats fell in with four strong gun-boats, each carrying thirty-two pounders and full of men. Not being equipped for that sort of contest our boats returned without attacking. We returned to the Rendezvous, and the fleet not having yet arrived, we stretched out again to the eastward, and the boats of the "Modeste" and "Leda" went in again to Taggul prepared to carry the gun-boats. But this time these warriors had retired and sailed towards Batavia; so that our boats only brought off a small brig and two Prows laden with rice for Batavia.

'On returning to the Rendezvous, we found yesterday morning, at daybreak, a ship looking out for us to say the expedition had arrived on July 30, and had sailed towards Batavia early that morning. We soon came up with them, and are now approaching the place of disembarkation which will take place this morning or at daybreak to-morrow.—God bless you.'

The expedition arrived on July 30, and on August 4 the disembarkation was effected at a small town called Chillinching in Batavia Bay.

'Chillinching, Java: August 6, 1811.

'The disembarkation took place without any kind of opposition. All the troops, a few field-pieces, and part of the stores were landed that evening and in the course of the night. The horses, ordnance, and additional stores were put on shore next day. . . . This village is principally Chinese. They made us welcome, and brought their articles out for sale with very flattering confidence. This was justified by the exemplary behaviour of the troops, who paid their way and did not even kiss an old woman without her consent. There has been but one drunken man in two days.

'*August* 7. As everything has been quiet, and the army remains at Chillinching, where the General[1] occupies the only gentleman's house, I have continued on the "Modeste," and go on shore when I like. Yesterday I took a ride with the General to the advanced post, about four miles, and then returned to the "Modeste." The country is like Chinese paper on a wall. Canals, tanks, and narrow ways between; here and there a little dry ground, and these spaces are in a state of high cultivation. Every now and then we found a gentleman's house with no appearance of splendour, but always marked by the characteristic neatness of the Dutch. Our road ran westward parallel to the sea; the right of the line of the troops on the sea, the left inland. I had an opportunity of observing what may be deemed, I believe, a pretty nearly unexampled degree of discipline in the troops. They do not use tents, and have as yet had only their salt provisions. They are posted in gardens and orchards with cottages and houses of a better description, surrounded with poultry, fruit, and vegetables. No fresh beef or pork was to be procured. the cattle and pigs having been very generally removed by order of Government. In these circumstances we saw the peasants living as quietly in their own houses, and carrying on their usual occupations with as little annoyance, apprehension, or even notice of an invading army in the midst of them, as if we were all their near relations on a visit. You see the trees laden with cocoa-nuts and plantains, acres of onions, cabbage, and

[1] Sir Samuel Auchmuty.

many tempting things, not one taken, nor the slightest offence given to a single inhabitant. Not a duck or a hen made free with, money offered and given in every instance for what the people are willing to spare. . . . The gentlemen's houses and other habitations of a middling kind being deserted, with some old slave or servant left behind to look after them, the officers have astonished these guardians by refusing to occupy the houses with clean beds and neat furniture, and sleeping sometimes in the verandah, sometimes in a separate pavilion, and never in the house; and the cocks are seen fighting, the hens and chickens pecking about, and the ducks gobbling and dabbling, just as if they were our own fellow-subjects. I observed yesterday to the General, as we were passing the house of the Dutch Paymaster General, that a battle which we saw between two of his cocks was the only thing like war that I could perceive in our invasion.

. . . .

'*August* 9. The advance of the army having moved forward to a place about three miles from Batavia, the General sent a summons to the city which was immediately answered by a surrender at discretion. The enemy, in order to concentrate their force at a place called Cornelis, had withdrawn their troops on the 6th, and set fire to some public stores and to the citadel; the town was therefore glad of our protection against a disposition to plunder and disorder manifested by the slaves and lower class of Malays. We were thus in possession of the metropolis of the Dutch East Indian

Empire the fourth day after our landing. Not a gentleman, not a person of any note was left in the city. The Dutch, that is, the French Governor, had required them under pain of death to quit their houses and repair to the head-quarters of the army, where they are narrowly watched. They have left their houses, however, richly furnished, their wives, children, and slaves to the safeguard of the invaders' generosity; and we are all Scipios. The deserted women were in terror, not of us but of their own slaves, who have a slavish trick of using the opportunity of public disorder to gratify their private passions by rising on the defenceless whites and murdering those they rob. . . . Everything portable of public property had been removed from the town, but much valuable public property was consumed, and much plundered. In some streets people walked during the first days of our occupation over the shoes in sugar, coffee, spices, and rice. But much has been preserved. In that great city were found only six horses (ponies) and not one head of cattle.

'I sent a letter yesterday morning to General Janssens, the Governor General, containing a summons, and distributed at the same time a sort of manifesto to the Dutch inhabitants to remove their apprehensions and invite their co-operation. The summons was refused, and I received the answer that night.

'*August* 12. I went on shore on the 9th about noon to speak to the General. Admiral Stopford had joined the fleet that morning, and landed for the purpose of visiting the General and myself.

'Captain Robison, my aide-de-camp, who carried my summons to General Janssens found him at Cornelis, a strong post about six miles from Batavia. He went to Weltevreeden, halfway, without molestation; but was blinded the rest of the road. As far as Weltevreeden he *saw* that there was no obstacle to the advance of troops; from thence to Cornelis he perceived by the motion of the carriage that the road was smooth and the bridges, if any, were standing. Upon this report, confirmed by their information, the General determined to push on and take post at Weltevreeden. Weltevreeden is an immense and magnificent military cantonment, but not fortified. Cornelis is a military post of great strength, on which all the art of French engineering has been long bestowed. It is considered as the citadel of Java, in which the colony itself is to be defended. The advance of the army moved forward accordingly on August 10, and were followed by other troops.

'They met no opposition till they had passed through the cantonments of Weltevreeden, but immediately afterwards a very sharp action commenced. It lay principally between the riflemen and the light troops in the jungle on each side of the road, and in this contest the superiority of our men was immediately decisive, driving the enemy from the woods with great loss. Another principal feature of the day was the capture, sword in hand, of four of the enemy's field-pieces, which had been planted in the road behind an abbatis. They were deserted by the men, but well defended by an officer or two and a non-commissioned officer who were cut down at their guns. Our troops suffered principally on this road from grape and musketry under cover of the abbatis; but they drove the enemy in such confusion before them that Colonel Gillespie was prevented only by repeated orders from the General, from dashing at once into the place along with them. Our troops halted, and took post under the guns of Cornelis. This was a most important and most honourable success. It gave us every imaginable accommodation for the army in the barracks and cantonments of Weltevreeden, great stores and magazines, some hundred pieces of artillery, mostly brass, of all calibres, horses, labourers, and an easy conveyance of every article by water.

'.... The loss of the enemy was great, ours inconsiderable. Taylor, who is attached to Gillespie, distinguished himself on this maiden occasion by the greatest activity, courage, coolness, and judgment.

'*August* 15. I continued on board the "Modeste" till the 14th, when I landed privately, and settled, with all my friends, in a good spacious house near the cantonments of Weltevreeden. Cornelis is found too strong to be carried without heavy artillery. The battering train is therefore landing from the transports, and nothing material has happened since the 10th. The humanity of the men to their wounded prisoners on that day was admirable. No distinction of colour on that occasion. Our soldiers picked up English, Dutch, and Malay, without distinction, in the jungle and carried them with great labour to the hospital. The Malays and other native troops are all in amazement, having been made to believe that we are savages, and should treat them with all sorts of barbarities if they fell into our hands.

Batavia shines in the national neatness of the Dutch. The streets wide, not paved, but the roads formed of very fine gravel, and excellent. From the town the roads run along canals, or streams of water, in some places quick and almost lively, mostly, however, slow, dull, and *always* yellow. On the other side of the road there is a succession of garden houses; the garden gate and rail close to the road; the houses more or less retired, and standing each in an open space of its own. They are not remarkable for show and cheerfulness, and the architecture is not Vitruvian; but they indicate the neighbourhood of a great capital, and they convey a strong idea of opulence and luxury. The houses, indeed, are to be admired for space, loftiness of rooms, and fitness for a warm climate. In the house that I inhabit there is a high open gallery of 100 feet by 32. My bedroom is immediately over it, and of the same dimensions. A great hall crosses from the gallery to the front, so that the winds blow in and through from four quarters.

'*August* 23. The batteries have been very tedious, and there does appear to have been a good portion of fiddle-de-dee twaddlification in the departments connected with our works.

. . . .

'*August* 28. Nevertheless, the enemy's impregnable

works were stormed at daybreak on August 26—a new day in our military calendar. The place was most formidable in strength, and it really seems miraculous that mortal men could live in such a fire of round, grape, shells, and musketry long enough to pass deep trenches defended by pointed palisades inclining from the inner edge of the ditch outwards, force their way into redoubt after redoubt, till they were in possession of all the numerous works, which extend at least a mile. . . . The slaughter was dreadful, both during the attack and in the pursuit, when the total destruction of the enemy's army was prevented only by their surrendering prisoners, or dispersing and finally deserting the French. We have upwards of 5,000 prisoners, including all the Europeans left alive. General Janssens escaped capture most narrowly, by the most precipitate flight, leaving all his official papers behind him. General Jumelle, a Frenchman sent out to watch and succeed Janssens, was glad to get into a bog up to his chin till the heat of the pursuit was over, and then crept out in a dirty plight to a hospital, where he remained till dark, and then made off as hard as he could gallop to Buitenzorg, to join poor Janssens. There never was such a rout.

'The General immediately despatched Captain Robison with a second summons to be delivered verbally. It was again refused. But the affair is not the less decided. Janssens has not 600 men, out of 7,000 or 8,000 whom he commanded in the morning, and his government is at an end. Troops will advance to-morrow morning to Buitenzorg, and on their arrival, two days hence, he must either capitulate, or fly *alone* to the eastern part of the island, where he may affect to hold out till he is pursued. . . . I do really believe that August 26 is a glorious day to Sir Samuel Auchmuty and the army. . . . . The seamen have afforded entertainment as well as acquired honour by their eccentricities and courage. They fell in with a galloper of the enemy's, of which they took possession, when they mounted the four horses, and drove the gun on in the character of horse artillery. They were very soon all mounted at the expense of the French officers and troopers, and have obtained the title of His Majesty's Marine Light Dragoons. In short, Johnny has maintained a consistency of character with no feature of which I hope he will ever part.

'I knew the night before that the storm was to take place, and you may imagine the anxiety with which I heard the cannon and the musketry rather before daylight. By its long continuance and violence I perceived that the enemy had not instantly fled in a panic; and if they stood, with such an advantage as their works gave them, I dreaded the loss which must be sustained even with success. Taylor and Robert were constantly in my mind. On the event of this enterprise depended also the issue of this grand undertaking. George slept in my room. He soon got on horseback, and I into my buggy with Mr. Hope as expeditiously as I could. We drove on briskly to the field; the action still lasting; but at a mile distance I met a wounded officer and soldier walking to the hospital, a mile back. I therefore sent Mr. Hope to drive them to the hospital, and walking on myself soon came to the field, where the victory was by this time decisive, and the enemy in full flight. The General hearing I was there rode to meet me, and reported his triumph with a most radiant countenance. I then inquired after Taylor and my particular friends, and most happily found all unhurt.

.   .   .   .

'Next morning I went, before daylight, to visit all the works—our own as well as the enemy's. A field of battle seen in cold blood the day after is a horrid spectacle, but is too horrid for description. The number of the dead and the shocking variety of deaths had better not be imagined. In this instance, besides the objects scattered along the road and over a wide plain, there was a crowded, accumulated scene of slaughter and destruction, in all their worst shapes, collected together in a small space within each of the many redoubts that had been taken from the enemy. In one of them the dead, more mangled than can be described, were the conquerors themselves. They were the Grenadiers of two English regiments, and of course the finest men in the army. After forcing their way into the works, and having given three cheers for their success, the explosion of a magazine in the centre blew them into the air.

.   .   .   .

'When Hope and I visited this place, there was a

corner or bastion still burning violently. We looked into the fire, standing close to its edge, and going afterwards a few paces towards another corner, we were surprised by a loud explosion from the place we had just left. This proved to be a blind shell which had become red hot, and went off close to us, so that we might have paid for our peeping. Many officers were killed and wounded by the explosion of this magazine, which, I am disposed to think, happened by accident.'

In a despatch addressed by Sir Samuel Auchmuty to the Governor General, after the capture of Cornelis and the subsequent dispersion of the enemy's forces, he stated that, in the action of the 26th, near 5,000 prisoners had been taken. Among them three General officers, thirty-four field officers, seventy captains, and one hundred and fifty subaltern officers. General Janssens made his escape with difficulty during the action, and reached Buitenzorg, a distance of thirty miles, with a few cavalry, the sole remains of an army of ten thousand men. This place he subsequently evacuated, and fled to the eastward.

'*August* 29.—Janssens is gone with a fragment of his force, under two thousand of all sorts, towards Samarang. Two frigates have already sailed with a small force, and will be followed by more, to intercept him. The game is ours. . . . The General considers the affair as so entirely decided that he proposes returning to Madras after visiting Samarang. I have, on my part, published a proclamation declaring the French Government to be dissolved and the English established. Such is the state of our affairs at this date.

'I have now a melancholy account to send you of the heavy loss we have sustained in my poor friend Dr. Leyden. He was seized with fever a few days after I landed at Batavia, and struggled hard with it till yesterday morning, when he expired, and I assisted at paying him the last honours in the evening of the same day. He had been subject to bilious attacks from the time of leaving Calcutta, and indeed long before; but he was frequently ailing on the voyage, and always making great efforts of mental and sometimes of bodily labour. In Java he pushed his exertions of every kind far beyond his strength, and was totally regardless of the precautions against the sun, which are indispensable in these climates. He was seized, after great fatigue in the examination of a public library which I had committed to his charge; and having gone heated from the library into another room, which had not been opened for a long while, he was suddenly struck with a chill. He ran out of the place saying it was enough to give any man a fever; but, in truth, his habit was predisposed, and he never surmounted the first attack, though he struggled against it longer than is usual, for fevers are rapid here. This must be accounted the illness of a hot climate, but not of Batavia in particular. The climate, indeed, in this place, a little above Batavia, seems to us milder and more favourable to health than Bengal, and this is not reckoned a healthy month by the inhabitants. September and October are among the best in the year. I am myself perfectly well.

'*September* 4.—The despatches for England are to be sent on board this day, and I must close here. Sir Samuel has embarked for the eastern expedition, with 3,000 men, which far exceeds the force required, but they will garrison that end of the island. The "Modeste" carries the General to the eastward, and, when she has landed him, will return to be ready for me. I still think October 15 the likely time for my departure. This country is annexed, like the East India Company's territories. I leave Mr. Raffles with the title of Lieutenant Governor, and this Government is subordinate to the Governor General in Council in Bengal. All these arrangements, however, are hitherto made provisional by me, subject therefore to confirmation or alteration at home, for I have been obliged to deviate materially from my instructions. The country is great, fertile, and flourishing beyond my expectations, and, with all that depends upon and is connected with it, will, I hope, prove an acquisition of great value and importance.

'Colonel Gillespie will be left in command of the troops on the island. He has been the great hero, and the chief means of our success. He was very ill of a fever the day he led the storm of Cornelis, but is better; and I think this appointment, which I sent Taylor to communicate to him yesterday, will prove a good medicine.'

'Java, October 3, 1811.

'This letter accompanies the final surrender of Java by capitulation, and the successful termination of my last martial labour. I am certainly relieved from many cares which have been my companions from the moment of losing the grand care of the Madras mutiny; and these comrades have made room for a most comfortable quiet consciousness of having done well, and employed the powers that have been placed in my hands profitably to England, from which I held them. Gilbert tells me I must not expect any great rewards. This was last February, on the occasion of the conquest of the Mauritius. I do not expect them now, and I feel little concern in that affair. I have certainly deserved some public acknowledgment or other by a very unusual train of successful and of unusually important services.

'The withholding the usual recompense of service is one thing, but to conceal or equivocate about the nature of a service is another. I should certainly not become a suitor for reward, which loses its very substance if given to importunity or favour; but I would, on the other hand, assert my right simply to the *public knowledge* of what I have done. I cannot help suspecting that an attempt has been made by Ministers to cloke themselves in my feathers, and if they have done so, it must have been by nothing more noble than a juggle.

'I have seen English papers down to the middle of

March, and I certainly cannot perceive that any mortal has suspected my having any concern with the French islands, beyond the execution of an order sent out by Government. That order was not received by me till the army sent by me was landing in the Isle of France. That order was for an expedition in April 1811: The Isle of France surrendered on December 3, 1810, to the army I had sent. If I had not pushed the thing forward, through a thousand difficulties, and at an immense personal hazard, just at the moment when I did, the expedition ordered by the Government could not have been sent, or if sent could not have been successful; for the island would have been reinforced —the certainty of which has been demonstrated by the arrival of French squadron after squadron since the capture—and would have been impregnable in April to any force it was possible for India to furnish. If I had failed in my own expedition, from whatever chance, and without any fault of mine, I should have been torn to pieces by the very same Ministers, who would have told the world very distinctly, and without any equivocation, whether the calamitous expedition had been sent by me or by themselves. . . .

'With regard to Java, I acquainted Government with my intention to follow up the reduction of the French islands with an expedition against Java. This was done in my first communications concerning the French islands; and I pressed hard for *instructions* on the latter undertaking, saying that I should wait as long as I could for their answer without hazarding the success of the plan, and if I should receive no orders, when there had been time sufficient to send them, I should conclude my design was not disapproved, and should proceed to the execution of it. In the meanwhile, everything was concerted for the return of troops and transports from the Isle of France to India, for the purpose of serving against Java. This was executed accordingly, and these resources arrived in time. Arrangements were made at all the Presidencies of India, and every preparation was put in motion the moment the news arrived of our success in the Isle of France. Everything was in forwardness when I received the orders of the Secret Committee to attack Java; and I should have gone on that expedition when I did if no orders had come. Java, therefore, so far as credit is concerned, is as much my own as the French islands; for the plan was formed, and the resolution taken, and the preparations made, and the service would have been performed precisely as it has, on my own judgment and at my own risk. I do not think Government has neglected anything either. They could not have sent their orders sooner. But circumstances were such that if I had not taken the whole thing upon myself, and despatched it in the shortest imaginable time, the orders from England would have been too late in both cases. This is, I think, enough on the first pronoun personal.

'This country far surpasses all the expectations any stranger had ever formed of its fertility and the richness of its produce, its population and *civilisation*, a praise which you probably did not look for. I have pleasure in seeing also that the worst system of government and of laws imaginable present a wide field for active improvements, which better principles of policy and a purer administration cannot fail of producing. If I am happy enough to see some progress made in these views, and to witness a substantial amelioration in the condition of the five millions who inhabit this beautiful country, or even a tendency to that result, from the foundations I shall have laid, I shall bear the want of rewards with the greatest equanimity and indifference.

'I am a great philosopher of late, having studied hard in all the leisure moments of this expedition, by sea and land, under the best precepts and the worst practice that were ever united in the same master, Cicero himself. I am near the end of his twenty volumes, and have had great delight in *almost* every page. Let Gilbert read you the " Somnium Scipionis," one of the finest works of antiquity; or at least this passage, which is near the end, and the parting advice of the elder Scipio to his son, before the close of the vision, when he returns to the regions of light and immortality.

'Igitur alte si spectare voles, atque hanc sedem, et æternam domum contueri : neque te sermonibus vulgi dederis, nec in premiis humanis spem posueris rerum tuarum : suis te opportet illecebris ipsa virtus trahat ad verum decus.' 'Verum decus' is Latin for nobility without a patent; and the last passage, beginning ' suis te opportet ' and ending ' verum decus,' is most beautiful. I have chosen it for the family motto, if not on our seals and panels, on our lives. In the meantime I have put this discourse of Scipio's apparition to his son, in the mouth of our family genius in " the Minto vision." [1]

> Let Reason's torch on zeal attend !
> Her calm undazzling light to lend :
> With patriot ardour wisdom blend.
> > Be these your guides !
> Your country's good the noble end,
> > And nought besides.
>
> Heed not the bellowing crowd's acclaim,
> And fleeting roar of vulgar fame,
> Powerless to grace an honest name,
> > Or to defile ;
> The drunken praise or ruffian blame
> > Of clamour vile.
>
> Guerdons that prompt the worldly race
> Thy generous toil shall ne'er debase ;
> Won by fair Virtue's inborn grace,
> > Her smiles alone
> Shall woo thee to the lofty place
> > Of true renown.
>
> Oh, treasure in thy filial breast,
> My parting counsel, last and best.
> Be Virtue for herself caress'd ; [2]
> > Her heavenly love
> Such transport yields as Spirits blest
> > Enjoy above.

'I shall *positively* sail by the 20th inst. (October) ; I hope sooner; and shall be most happy to turn my

---

[1] A poem written by himself in India and dedicated to his family.

[2] Concluditur profecto, et virtutes omnes, et honestum illud, quod ex his virtutibus exoritur, et in his hæret, esse *per se* expetendum.—Cic. *De Finibus*, v. 23, et passim.

head towards one of my homes, till the grand departure of all arrives. That will happen at latest in twenty-seven months from October 1. I reckon to January 1, 1814.'

'Java, October 13, 1811.

'Nothing has happened since my last at all memorable . . . This letter goes by a transport, the "Countess d'Harcourt," which carries General Janssens and his suite to England as prisoners of war. If you should by any chance come in his way, *Palm, be civil*[1]—for he is one of the very best and most estimable men I ever knew. He has suffered a great and severe reverse, which he has felt so deeply as to affect his health. His predecessor was a wretch in every imaginable way, one of the monsters which the worst times of the French Revolution engendered, or rather lifted from the mud at the bottom, to flounce and figure away their hour upon the surface. He was greedy, corrupt, and rascally in amassing money for himself, and equally unjust and oppressive in procuring public supplies. He was cruel, and regardless of men's lives beyond most of the revolutionary tyrants in the Reign of Terror. He forced the Javanese to cut a road through a morass at the expense of 6,000 lives for that short space. He ordered two Javanese Princes, confined by him as state prisoners, to be privately murdered, and became savage from the delay which arose from the scruples of the officer in whose custody they were; a providential delay; for Janssens arrived in the interval, and passing

---

[1] A phrase frequently addressed by Lady Palmerston to her lord.

through the place, on his way to Batavia, saved the
victims. D'Aendels was as great a brute as tyrant in
his pleasures—no man's family was safe. . . . In short,
none of the worst of the Roman pro-consuls ever vexed
and scourged their provinces, too distant for control,
with more extortion and cruelty than this villain. His
successor is his opposite in every point—a virtuous, just,
and humane man ; a brave and good officer ; and, I think
from his conversation, a wise and even enlightened
statesman.

'Bonaparte certainly did one good action in sending
a character so respectable to supersede D'Aendels at
twenty-four hours' notice ; for he was peremptorily
ordered to resign the government in that time, and to
embark inmediately for Europe. As soon as the ship
was under weigh, it is understood here that the captain produced an order to carry him to France as a
prisoner. The attachment of all ranks of men to
Janssens is remarkable ; and he certainly deprived us of
the support which, if we had found D'Aendels in the
government, the Dutch part of the colony would have
given us. So pray be civil to my virtuous predecessor
in Java, if you have an opportunity.

'George sent you the history of my orgies at a
dinner given by me to Sir Samuel Auchmuty and the
army. The army has since given a ball and supper to
Sir Samuel and me jointly ; and we entered hand in
hand, like the two kings of Brentford smelling at one
nosegay. This festival was at the residence of the
former Governors General, and the decorations had been

all or nearly so in a state of preparation for the celebration of Napoleon's birthday, which we disturbed like *trouble-fêtes* as we were, by landing and getting possession of Batavia, Government House, decorations and all, a few days before the grand occasion. . . . It is impossible to give you anything like an adequate notion of the total absence of beauty in so crowded a hall. There never is a dozen of women assembled in Europe without a few attractions amongst them. Here there was no difference, except in some few varieties of ugliness and ordinariness of dress and manners. The Dutch did not encourage, nor indeed allow freely, European women to go out to their colonies in India. The consequence has been, that the men lived with native women, whose daughters, gradually borrowing something from the father's side, and becoming a mixed breed, are now the wives and ladies of rank and fashion in Java. The young ladies have learnt the European fashions of dress, and their carriage and manners are something like our own of an ordinary class. Their education is almost wholly neglected; or rather no means exist here to provide for it. They are attended from their cradles by numerous slaves, by whom they are trained in helplessness and laziness; and from such companions and governesses, you may conceive how much accomplishment or refinement in manners or opinions they are likely to acquire.

In dancing, the young beauties seemed lame in English country dances, of which they knew neither the steps nor the figures; but in their own dance, which was to a very slow valse tune, the figure much the same as ours, with a valse embrace however, instead of an allemande, they were at home, and not without grace; while our English damsels and cavaliers were all abroad, and about as awkward and crippled as their Dutch fellow-subjects had been before. Mrs. Bunbury, the wife of an officer, a young pretty Englishwoman, stood up in the dance; but seeing, when the first couple reached her, the Dutch gentleman take his partner fairly in his arms and hug her, as it appeared to her as a bear does his prey, she fairly took to her heels, and could not be brought back again by any means, to see or share such horror. The Dutch valsers certainly deal in very strict embraces, but our English gentlemen, to their shame be it said, appeared so entirely unpractised in that art, that their Dutch partners gave the point up as a bad job, and were forced to content themselves with merely taking hands and swinging the loobies about. The chaperons and older Dutch ladies are a class not yet described in Europe. The principal mark to know them by is their immense size. The whole colonial sex runs naturally to fat, partly from over-feeding—partly from total want of exercise. The morning air is the grand pursuit of the English Orientalists; the Dutch of both sexes have a horror for it, and prefer their beds. In the rest of the day nobody can go out; and in the evening they think a drive in a carriage too great an effort. They pass their time as follows. There is a canal opposite to every door on the other side of the road. Each house has a little projecting gallery supported by posts in the canal. The lower part of this, that is to say, from the level of the road down into the water, is made in some small degree private, by upright bars at a little distance from each other, and with this bath the road communicates by wooden steps. Here the lady of the house, her relatives, and female slaves, lave their charms, and here you may behold the handmaids of Diana sporting on and under the wave in sight of all passing Actæons. This is the morning scene. In the evening, as I was saying, they have chairs brought out in the gallery above, and sit with their *beaux* in conversation and repose. Suppose an immense woman sitting behind a stall with roasted apples, and we have an old Dutch lady of the highest rank and fashion. Her upper garment is a loose coarse white cotton jacket fastened nowhere, but worn with the graceful negligence of pins and all other fastenings or constraints of a Scotch *lass*, an equally coarse petticoat, and the coarsest stockings, terminating in wide thick-soled shoes; but by standing behind her you find out her nobility, for at the back of the head a little circle of hair is gathered into a small crown, and on this are deposited diamonds, rubies, and precious stones often of very great value. It is well with this if they can speak even Dutch, many knowing no language but Malay.'

In the instructions sent from the Court of Directors to Lord Minto respecting an expedition to Java, no provision was made for any permanent occupation of the island: no such measure had been in contemplation previous to Lord Minto's arrival in Java, and to the personal acquaintance he thereupon attained with the condition of the population. The Court of Directors had simply intended an expedition to expel the Dutch Power, to destroy the fortifications, and to distribute the arms and stores among the natives. These instructions Lord Minto took it on his own responsibility to disobey, preferring to give time for reconsideration of orders issued in ignorance of the facts, to their execution at the cost of bloodshed and anarchy, if not of certain destruction to the colonists.

It would be mere waste of time at the present day to enter into any detailed account of the measures inaugurated by Lord Minto for the administration of Java, thus incorporated into the British Empire.

A few extracts from his despatches will suffice to show the condition in which he found the island and the nature of the amelioration he proposed to effect. The 'History of Java,' by Sir S. Raffles, and other works demonstrate that the brief period during which the connection of Great Britain and Java existed, was one to the island of prosperity and tranquillity.

In a despatch to the Secret Committee dated September 3, 1811, Lord Minto stated that he had taken possession of the Island of Java in the Company's name.

'I am aware,' he said, 'that all conquests of territory from European Powers accrue by the constitution of the Empire to the Crown ; and, if I had been under the necessity of prosecuting this enterprise on my own responsibility and without orders, Java must have been simply annexed to His Majesty's dominions subject to any arrangement which might afterwards be adopted by His Majesty with the Company. But since the establishment of the Board of Control, every order that issues from the Honourable Court, or your Honourable Committee, bears with it the sanction of His Majesty's Government, and I am therefore to consider the commands with which I was honoured respecting Java, as importing a transfer of His Majesty's rights of conquest in this instance to the Honourable Company.

'I shall appear on first sight to have departed from the tenor of your Honourable Committee's instructions, by keeping possession instead of dismantling and evacuating the island.

'This is a much greater country than I believe is generally conceived, and the destructive field of massacre and ruin, to which the disarming of the colony and arming the natives must have led, is too extensive, and the scene would have been too shocking to every virtuous and natural feeling, to remain for a moment in the contemplation of minds to which the object should have been presented in its true colours. In deviating from this part of the plan I have, therefore, most assuredly been long since approved.

'I have presented no exaggerated view of this subject, but am more than ever confirmed in the truth and justice of the picture that has been set before you.[1] by

---

[1] In an earlier and fuller despatch.

what I have witnessed of terror created in this populous and flourishing quarter of Java by the absence of military protection for the short interval of two days only, which passed between the departure of the French and the arrival of our troops; as well as by the actual massacre and pillage which in the circuit of a few miles have followed the dispersion of Janssen's army, before a detachment of our own could be advanced to Buitenzorg.

'It would have been an abuse therefore of the word obedience, and offensive above all to the authority from which the order had been issued under a defect of local information, to have carried into effect a command of which the consequences described were manifest on the spot to those who were charged with the execution.

'The only modification of which the measure was susceptible, would have been to provide the means of retreat and of future security and maintenance to the multitudes whose lives and property were concerned. This would have entailed an immense burden on the British Government, and would have required pecuniary sacrifices and arrangements which could have been hazarded by no subordinate authority abroad.

. . . .

'The three courses which are open to your choice are—to withdraw the whole European population and to make a provision for their support; to restore the colony unweakened to the Dutch; or to retain it under the British protection and Government.

'I have found here the favourable disposition which I expected from the Dutch inhabitants. They are generally repugnant to the French usurpation both of the mother country and of the colonies. . . . But the French Government had established so strong a power by a system of severity and terror, and there still exist so many collateral means of influence by connections both of family and fortune in Europe, that we have experienced only silent and inefficient favour, and derived no active aid whatever from the friendly disposition of the people. Our difficulties have been considerably increased by this neutral spirit; but, had the Dutch been apprised that, in the event of success, it was our design to deliver them up disarmed to the Javanese, we should have had to contend with all the energies of despair, and I am quite persuaded that we should have found our force inadequate to the enterprise.

. . . .

'The multitude of arrangements, especially for the public security and tranquillity which the sudden assumption of the government demand, do not in the present moment leave me at liberty to prosecute inquiries and pursue deliberations concerning your more general interests in this quarter.

. . . .

'I propose to vest the chief authority in Mr. Raffles, under the title of Lieutenant Governor; . . . . that the Government of Java should be subordinate to the supreme Government of Bengal; that a regular report of all proceedings should be made there; and that the orders of the Governor General in Council should be binding in Java, subject to the higher authority of the Honourable Court of Directors.'

'I can say[1] with certainty that the value of the island and the face of prosperity which every part of the island wears, even weighed down as it has been by a most oppressive system, and after a most iniquitous and grinding administration of government, very far exceeds any other which had ever been conceived by strangers, and is a constant and general subject of observation amongst ourselves. Yet every acknowledged principle of good government is unknown in Java, and all the mischievous, deteriorating, and grievous maxims of a narrow, monopolising, and harsh policy are in full force and vigour in every department of affairs. No man's interest in land exceeds the term of one year. This admits of a small number of partial exceptions, but is generally true. The whole surface is the property of Government, and very extensive territories are cultivated and managed on the account of Government under the direction of public affairs. Government exacts a pre-emption at an arbitrary price in the produce of many other lands.

'In a word the whole system of property is vicious and adverse to the interests of Government and people.

'The revenues, &c., have long been all *in farm*: the farmers are universally Chinese, who have no competitors. Hence arises necessary loss to Government and

[1] To the Secret Committee of the Court of Directors, October 5, 1811.

oppressive extortion on the subject. I have nevertheless been obliged to renew the farms for the remaining months of the present year. A change in the system of collecting will require considerable preparation both in regulation and in providing instruments, who are now entirely wanting. The duties of export and import in the harbour of Batavia have, however, been placed under a custom-house, collection being immediately under the vigilance of Government.

'On this subject it may be satisfactory to your Committee to observe that I have abolished the duties and suppressed the farms on gaming and cock-fighting, leaving Government free by that sacrifice to employ such prohibitory means as can be devised to check this prevailing and destructive vice of the native population.

'The state of slavery has attracted my serious and anxious attention. That monstrous system prevails to a calamitous extent throughout these Eastern regions of India, and produces, as it cannot fail of doing, most of the miseries incident to that mode of procuring the service of men. But it is too general to be suddenly suppressed by any one Power in so many separate and independent countries. In Java it is fortunately not grievous to the slave; servitude being almost wholly domestic or menial. I hope something may be done immediately for modifying this evil, and I propose that Government should set the example in this reform by abstaining entirely from the future purchase of slaves. A return is preparing of the public slaves of Government now existing, and if the number should prove inconsiderable, as I hope it will, I have it in contemplation to hazard an anticipation of your approbation, which I shall surely receive, by emancipating all those to whom that change would be advisable. The importation of slaves may also be checked, although it cannot yet be abolished.'

'Weltevreeden, Java: October 6, 1811.[1]

'I consider the main point as ascertained, and that Java will supply resources at the least for its own expenses. I need not say to you how great a benefit, not reducible to the columns of an estimate in dollars, will in that case accrue to the Company and the nation. We now know from proof that it was the policy of the Dutch to conceal the value and to exaggerate the defects of their possessions, especially of Java. This will account for the inadequate opinion entertained, at least I imagine so, at home of this island. It is now most flourishing; but the field for improvement is inexhaustible. All that I fear is the general peace. This ought not surely to prevent us from beginning to perform the first duty of Governments in improving the condition of a people that has become tributary to our authority and tributary to our prosperity. All we are justified in avoiding is the prosecution in this interval of expensive works. The exclusion of European masters from Java is impossible in the present state of things. To make them richer, happier, and to give the people itself a feeling of independence, which they are now

[1] To the Right Hon. R. Dundas.

totally without, would be the best receipt for making their country less accessible to European invaders. But in our own times this cannot be looked to, and the Government we have established must instantly be replaced by the French whenever it is withdrawn. The more flourishing the country may be at the time of such a revolution, the better, I think, for the nations without, although it may also be advantageous to the ruling European power within. But I feel assured that you agree with me in thinking our policy should lead to the improvement of the country, and, if not our policy, the eternal and fundamental law by which Governments and subjects are united. I think we ought to make it an English colony as soon as we can, by the introduction of English colonists, English capital, and, therefore, an English interest. This does not require the exclusion of the old Dutch, who will not bear a great proportion to the whole, and who will become English the more readily as they are now without a country.'

'I shall embark to-morrow evening, and hope to make the passage in about thirty days.[1] Local business, and the extreme pressure of such affairs as concern either bodies of men or individuals, have, as is usual, accumulated upon me to such a degree for some time past in the expectation of my approaching departure, that it would have been entirely impossible for me to throw the information I possess, or the resolutions and

[1] Extract from a despatch of Lord Minto to the Secret Committee October 18, 1811.

opinions I have been able to form, on the affairs of this new Government, into a shape fit for inspection. . . . The leisure of my voyage to Bengal will enable me to digest the material I take with me, and to present to your Honourable Committee by the first ship from Bengal after my arrival there, a full, and I would anxiously—fondly hope, a satisfactory report of my proceedings in this country.

'In the meanwhile, conscious that in the share which has fallen to my lot in the arduous but successful measures which have placed this important territory at your disposal, I have looked only to the general interests of the nation and the East India Company, and that in every point of the arrangements which I have provisionally adopted since the acquisition was made, the advantage of the Company and the improvement of the country have been the united but exclusive objects of contemplation, I cannot help entertaining an earnest wish, which I should be happy indeed if all circumstances authorised me to call a hope, that sufficient confidence might be felt in the judgments which I have formed, with much inquiry and reflection on the spot, to make at least a trial of the system and arrangements I now presume to recommend. . . . I will therefore specify two points at least of the present system in Java, which in my faithful and deliberate judgment it would be prejudicial to every interest of the Company or the public in this country to alter or reverse in the present period of our connection.

'First, I strongly recommend that the arrangements

now established may not be superseded for the purpose of uniting the Government in the same person with the command of the army.

'Secondly, that this island and all its affairs, civil and military, may be left under the superintendence of the Governor of Bengal, and not transferred to any other authority in India.

'I am happy to confirm the opinion I have already submitted to your honourable Committee that the resources of the island will assuredly cover all charges, civil and military.'

Before quitting Batavia Lord Minto remarked to one of its chief residents, that it was not certain whether England would retain permanent possession of Java,— 'but,' he added, in words which were long remembered, 'while we are here let us do as much good as we can.' To the close of his administration of the government of India he watched over the welfare of Java with unfailing solicitude—a fact recognised in feeling language by Sir Stamford Raffles when, addressing the Batavian Society subsequently to Lord Minto's death, he said:

'A tender and parental care for the island of Java was publicly avowed on different occasions; the proofs of it were received; the European community was saved and preserved by his humanity, and on his responsibility; for the native administration principles were laid down on which the whole of the present structure has been raised; and in every instance a wish was evinced of improving the successes of war, as much in favour of the conquered as of the conqueror.

'It would not be proper on this occasion to enter into particulars, but who does not gratefully recollect the general tenor of his conduct and demeanour while in Java? administering aid and assistance with his own hands to the maimed and wounded of his enemies; setting, in the midst of his successes, an example of moderation and simplicity of manner even to the vanquished; proceeding often in public without any other signs of greatness and distinction than what the whole community singly and jointly were eager to show him; never missing an opportunity of doing even a temporary good; and conciliating by these means the minds of the public to such a degree, that enemies were rendered friends, and that the names of conqueror and subduer were lost in those of protector and liberator.'

The energy and devotion which Lord Minto brought to bear on the affairs of Java were all the more praiseworthy, because of the acute grief he endured during the months passed by him in the island. There he learnt the death of his youngest son, William, who had been left at Madras, having already shown symptoms of the illness which was the cause of his death—an attack of congestion of the lungs.

Of this sad event Lord Minto said to those who were near him when he learnt it, that 'it was the first and only grievance which either this son or any of his children had ever inflicted on their parents.'

CHAPTER XIII.

Heavy and numerous were the letter-bags which awaited at Calcutta Lord Minto's return from Java. It was therefore with no small share of surprise that he found the official letters addressed to him absolutely silent on the most important transactions of the preceding years, namely, the Madras mutiny, and the conquest of the French islands.

'It does not appear,' he wrote to Lord Melville, in a private and confidential letter dated December 10, 1811, 'it does not appear from anything official that the Court of Directors ever heard that the French cruisers had been for ever excluded from the port of Mauritius, and that the French islands themselves had been captured by an army of their own under their own Government. This seems strange to us, to whom no doubt those events have appeared of greater moment than they are, owing, perhaps, to their having so long occupied our whole hearts and souls. I have not been able sometimes to help asking myself whether the same silence would have prevailed if I had failed, and whether the public would not in that case have been very distinctly informed whose expedition it was.'

In another letter to the same correspondent, he wrote: 'I do not foresee that in what may remain of my public life any occasion can ever occur again in which the interests confided to me shall require the assumption at my own hazard of unauthorised powers. I am far from thinking that measures undertaken on responsibility are by any means meritorious on that account. On the contrary, success itself should in my judgment be put on its defence, and it is not till after acquittal that the irregular service, however important, can obtain acknowledgment. . . My defence is, first, I knew in an authoritative way (I include the French islands in this argument) that the objects proposed by the measures I hazarded were deemed desirable by Government. I knew, secondly, that they could not be obtained in any other way. Thirdly, I had good grounds, since established by success in each instance, to believe that they might *then* be accomplished. Fourthly (and this is the strong point of my defence, without which all the rest would be invalid), I was intimately convinced, and I am now sanctioned by the events, that the service would have become impracticable by delay.

'It has been made manifest that if the French islands had not been reduced before the last hurricane month, that conquest would never have been accomplished by any scale of force or measures which have hitherto been in contemplation. . . . Three thousand, or four thousand, indeed a smaller number of French troops of the line – and that succour, we have now reason to know, would have been actually thrown in—

would, in all the opinions I have heard, have rendered the Mauritius impregnable to any expedition from India.

'Again, if the Mauritius had not fallen in December, it would have been totally impossible to prosecute the views against Java, always combined with the former, before the rainy monsoons in the Eastern seas. And if we had waited for the succeeding favourable season, we have now seen that Java would also have been reinforced beyond any means we could have employed for the conquest. In a course of measures, therefore, necessarily to follow each other, depending all through upon a chain of success without a broken link, and each limited to the narrowest period of time, and treading upon the heels of the other, I had,—first, to be reasonably satisfied that by great exertion success was possible and probable,—and next, to push on without delay. "Nos quidem hoc sentimus"—this is the sentiment of Cicero to Lentulus when he advises him to undertake the conquest of Egypt—"si exploratum tibi sit, posse te illius regni potiri, non esse cunctandum; si dubium non esse conandum."

'... and in the progress of these successive anxious events I have been more than once reminded of what Lentulus is told in the same epistle from his friend: 'Totius facti tui judicium, non tam ex consilio tuo, quam ex eventu, homines esse facturos.

. . . . . .

'I have been most fortunate in Sir S. Auchmuty, not only as a General but as a gentleman. Collision has

been entirely excluded from this joint service, and the
most cordial harmony has prevailed between us.
Indeed, I have taken care there should be no collision
by effacing myself entirely till the conquest was made,
and the moment came for assuming the government;
taking care that one sun should be in eclipse
while the other was shining in the same hemisphere.
. . . You cannot well imagine the discomfort I feel in
writing a line that expresses even a shade of discontent,
and especially in addressing it to yourself, whose whole
conduct towards me has been calculated to inspire sentiments
of the very opposite kind; but in truth I have
had occasion to perceive for a certain time back a
change in the comfortable footing on which I stood at
home when I left England.' After alluding to certain
measures which in his judgment appeared to claim an
acknowledgment that they had not received, Lord Minto
continued: 'At the head of these I place all that relates
to the Madras troubles, on which I am anxious to say
beforehand that I join issue with any adversaries I may
appear to have, and to assert for myself that from the
first origin to the last date of these events I acted the
part that became me, consulting alike the duty I owed
to the public, and the justice or indulgence which it was
fitting to administer to individuals. A mutiny of officers
and gentlemen was subdued; the distracted army was
tranquillised and reconciled; the same army has since,
and did indeed instantly evince, not merely its fidelity,
but its courage and discipline in action and distinguished
service.'

And to the Chairman of the Court of Directors[1] he wrote in the same strain:—

'If I had acted on any feeble and false principle—if I had weakened my support to the Company's government by any refined or capricious modification—if I had but wavered and suffered a shade of doubt to exist concerning me, Sir George himself has often acknowledged, since the event has been closed, that all was lost. After the submission of the guilty I claim to have done all that was necessary for discipline and future security; and it is my boast, and always will be, that *I did no more*; that I stopped the torrent of individual calamity at the point where it ceased to be indispensable for the public interest and safety. I claim to have tranquillised the army as quickly after the tempest as the swell that survives tempests allowed; and from a condition dangerous to the existence of our nation, I sent out that army instantly, entitled to our confidence when it went, and to our thanks and applause when the service was performed.

'In the last days of 1811 I have still to say that I do not know by a single official word that my residence at Madras during eight months of the years 1809 and 1810 has ever reached the ears of the Court of Directors. I hazarded from thence several important suggestions for the public good, but they have lain without notice until the present time.'

Again, as in his differences with the missionaries,

---

[1] Dec. 12, 1811.

the Court of Directors was a house divided against itself. Sir George Barlow's friends were offended by the leniency shown to the officers; his opponents resented the approbation bestowed by Lord Minto on Sir George Barlow for the energetic measures by which he had stemmed the tide of mutiny.

The Governor General had strongly recommended Sir George, 'and other faithful servants of the Madras mutiny,' for some mark of public approbation. 'If this is not done, I must say that Government will be deficient in a just estimate of the evil that has been averted, and of the service that has been rendered to the empire.' But though the despatches, when at last they arrived in India, contained a cordial approbation of the part taken by the Governor General, the conduct of Sir George Barlow was commented upon in terms which foreshadowed his recall in the following year.

Some passages from a letter written by Lord Minto's eldest daughter, give an amusing and probably an accurate view of certain circumstances which deprived her father's services at this period of their just meed of approbation.

'Minto, May 1, 1811.

' I think it has been the way all along for the Foxite Whigs to take part with the officers at Madras; and I was convinced, from the time Cecil Smith came home, that not only the 'Edinburgh Review' would take that side, but that Sidney Smith would be the oracle upon the subject at Holland House, &c.; and so I verily believe it is.

'There is such a complication of plots and wheels in the political world that it is not very easy to say at any time what will be thought or done by those who call themselves your friends. I believe that if the present Government brought forward any proposal of rewarding you, or Sir George either, for the Madras business, or had even voted thanks for the Isle of France, Opposition would, as in duty bound, have opposed the measure; and the Directors, amidst the variances in their Court on all the late Indian business, may think like Mrs. Beaumont, in "Manœuvring,"[1] that *in general it is safest not to mention things.* As for the Isle of France, they wish it had been taken for them, instead of the Crown. The Crown, or at least the Ministers, seem determined not to approve too hastily of anything you do; and therefore General Abercrombie goes without his thanks, all Melvillite though he be. Lord Grenville, &c., think, I suppose, that it might have been done during their Administration (as Lord Wellesley knows he might have done it). Lord Grey is, they say, displeased that his brother did not command the Expedition; and while in their eyes your measures are those of the present Ministry, and your honour and glory theirs, consequently not to be promoted—in the eyes of said Ministers you are an Oppositionist, and equally an unfit person to be exalted

---

[1] One of Miss Edgeworth's Tales of Fashionable Life.

by their approbation. The great men of the age are certainly not governed by great motives. So much the worse for them. . . . Certainly if it were possible to unravel such mysteries, one would think that one had the key to the hearts of the Directors, when one praised Sir G. Barlow; yet G—— always seems to think his friends in the Direction are least friendly to you. The thing I dislike is the apparent indifference of the Whigs; but mamma says she is used to that, and that it is the way of the world and of politicians; and we certainly don't worry ourselves about any part of it. We never can be sufficiently thankful that the Isle of France business succeeded. If we had received your letter and the account of a failure at the same time, and in these times, we should really have been in despair. I am not much apt to think about politics; but lately they have come in everybody's way to observe, and I am like the rest of the world, and look and wonder how it will all end.

'The King seems regaining his bodily health; but, as no one seems to expect his mind really to recover, I cannot see any reason, public or private, for wishing his recovery; excepting that in that case Lord Eldon has almost promised *to depart in peace,* which certainly would be a pleasing circumstance. I think there would be some pleasure (enough to make up for many disadvantages) in laying one's hand upon his lordship's head, and, like the old Abbot in " Marmion " dismissing him with—" Sinful Brother, part in peace."'

As in 1811, so in 1812, the state of affairs at home absorbed all the interest which in more fortunate times might have been extended to the empire at large. After the death of Perceval and the various abortive attempts at the formation of a new ministry which followed on that tragical event, Lord Holland wrote to Lord Minto that 'whatever indifference may have been shown to events in India, has been extended also to the war in Spain, the concerns of the North of Europe, the Catholics in Ireland, the Orders in Council at home, and the events in America; for while the various negotiations for forming a ministry were pending, it is true that they so entirely engrossed all the attention of the public, that victories and defeats, peaces and wars, insurrections and scarcities were overlooked as matters of inferior importance; and a newspaper which contained nothing but extraordinary gazettes, and no minute of a conversation between private gentlemen on their views of policy or party connections, was a dull, insipid, and uninteresting production. I do not know whether we are quite come to our senses yet—there are strong suspicions that Lord Liverpool has said something to Mr. Canning, and Mr. Canning answered something to Lord Liverpool, with which the public is unacquainted; and, in the language of the newspapers, the world has much reason to complain of this suppression of intelligence.'[1]

At the present time news from our distant dependency comes to us with the rapidity of the lightning's

[1] Lord Holland to Lord Minto, September 1812.

flash, and not seldom with something of its dread effects. In the time of Lord Minto it travelled like light from a distant star—paled by distance ere it reached our shores. Besides this unavoidable disadvantage attending on the imperfection of communication between England and India, the brilliant results of the expedition to Java were made known in England at a moment, not only of political anxiety, but of great national depression. The prolongation of the war, the consequent rise of prices, the prevailing disaffection in the country towards the person of the Regent, had created a general sentiment of uneasiness among the best-informed portion of the public. Lady Minto's letters from London in 1812 give a vivid impression of the troubled condition of the times.

'April 22, 1812.

'You will see by the papers that the whole country is up in arms at the immoderate price of everything. Bread is double what it was last year, and four times its original price, and all other necessaries equally high. As to luxuries, they are beyond imagination; but you may guess that of necessaries when I tell you I am obliged to give the maid-servants *five shillings* a day,[1] which with difficulty will suffice. Riots have taken place in most of the great manufacturing towns, of a most formidable character; they are increasing rather than diminishing, and there is a most general dread of what will be the result of the present state of things.

[1] For their Board.

Royalty seems to court its downfall, and has already forfeited even artificial respect. *He* seems determined to leave the nation to its fate, and will not even go through the labour of signing his name to one paper in twenty that awaits his signature. He gets up at three; has jewellers, tailors, and all sorts of tradesmen as soon as he is up, whom he receives before he dresses; and metamorphoses the dress of the army and navy, and fiddle-faddles away an hour or two, dresses and goes to Hertford House, drinks the hottest and strongest mixtures of spirits and strong wines, and forgets the pleasures and the cares of life.'

'May 21, 1812.

'I have long been holding forth on the badness of the times, but the horrible and atrocious murder of the Prime Minister [1] last week has really made everybody's hair stand on end. I need not describe it, as every circumstance is most truly detailed in all the newspapers. It does not appear that the assassin was connected with any of the great variety of discontented or riotous mobs which exist in different parts of the kingdom; at the same time his conduct has been applauded and commended, as you will see at Nottingham, by huzzas and ringing of bells.

'In London, I am very sorry to say, the lower and even the middle classes rejoice in the event, and make no scruple of saying openly, "It is all the better; more should go the same way." There have been, and still

[1] Mr. Perceval was shot by Bellingham on May 11, 1812.

are, numberless anonymous letters sent to various persons in high situations of the most threatening description. Infamous handbills are dropped in the streets and areas; and one yesterday was, " Mr. Perceval's ribs as a gridiron for the Prince Regent; " another, " 10,000*l*. for the Prince Regent's head."

'The price of bread and the want of work have caused the riots in the manufacturing districts, and, as far as one can see, must continue to cause them. In addition to these evils the season has been wonderfully backward, and is so still; no vegetation has taken place, and the accounts from Scotland are dreadful.'

Nor were Lady Minto's opinions of the society of London much more favourable than those she held on the state of the nation. After five years of absence, she found it more insipid than of old; the hours had grown so late, that dinners might properly be called suppers. 'Seven is the hour, and ten as early as even ladies can get away.' The heat of the rooms seemed to have increased with the multitude of Argand lamps, and the only engagement which did not deprive her of a night's rest was a dinner. In general she found a total want of animation where all came to be amused, and ' the horrid phrase *well-mannered* means silent, dull, and *no-carey*.'[1] 'It is melancholy to see the total want of character and capacity in the upper ranks; the excessive expense bestowed

---

[1] A favourite expression of the sisters Ladies Minto and Malmesbury when describing the *nil admirari* disposition which was so antagonistic to their own.

on education, and by *men*—nothing attained. A young man passes through the common routine of a public school and Oxford, and escapes acquiring any information from either; having, I fancy, only got into a variety of scrapes of every kind, and appearing to be completely a sheet of white paper.'

The severity of these remarks is occasionally tempered by the pleasure she received from the society brought together by the hosts of Holland House and Lansdowne House.

Lansdowne House was pleasant enough to compensate for much dulness elsewhere. 'There is nothing in this town half so comfortable as that house and its inhabitants.' Again: 'I have been living a great deal of late with the most agreeable people I have met with: the Smiths, who are delightful; Sir J. Mackintosh, who is not less so. I wish I could board and lodge with them.

'All London is now agog about Lord Byron, a person who three months ago was not known or thought of. The truth is, he is crazy—as all his forbears have been—not to say mad and bad; but he lately published a poem called "Childe Harold," which all London has fallen in love with, and which in good honest truth has a good deal of genius in it, with a certain portion of bad taste and bad writing; but certainly very striking from a man of five-and-twenty; and so he is all at once the thing to see and to meet. Unfortunately, he has been flattered into trying his hand at oratory, and made a ridiculous appearance. To-morrow we dine at Lord Glenbervie's to meet him.'

One more quotation we may allow ourselves from Lady Minto's letters from London; because it is always interesting to see the effect produced on contemporaries, before fame has been attained, by one destined to fill a large space in public estimation. 'Harry' (Lord Palmerston), she wrote, ' is doing very well—with a clear head and a good understanding. He will never be a great man because he has no great views; but he is painstaking and gentlemanlike to the highest degree, and will always swim where greater talents might sink. Nothing can be more amiable, and I have always regretted that he should have set out in life on the *shabby* side, which he must now stick to.'

Lord Minto returned to Calcutta towards the end of 1811. During the two years which ensued before he resigned his high office into the hands of Lord Moira, many considerable questions fell under the consideration of his Government, and led to measures of importance. Some of these referred to the relations of the Company's Government with that of the native States—of Oude, of Nagpore, and of Hyderabad—and to the irruptions of the Pindarees on the British frontier; others to the internal administration of British India, to the revenue system, and to the settlement of the ceded and conquered provinces of Bengal. But with none of these shall we attempt to deal. They find no place in Lord Minto's unofficial correspondence, and they occupy their proper one in the valuable histories of Messrs. Wilson and Marshman. The silence maintained in the private letters with regard to many of the subjects which at this period absorbed Lord Minto's most careful thoughts and laborious hours is explained by himself.

'I feel anxious to tell you why, with the same good intentions, I have fallen lately so far short of my former voluminous virtues in correspondence. One grand reason is that I have too much to do by several hours' work every day. Our conquests, among other causes, have increased our labours greatly. But since you will know my infirmities, the honest truth is that I am older every birthday, which is very common in the East; and I find, first and foremost, that writing in windy weather by candlelight is a thought more *kittle* than it was last century; secondly, and lastly, I used to write to Minto between the evening's drive and supper which is now called tea; but now-a-days getting up to open my shop at five or half-past, and slaving like a maid-of-all-work the whole day, I am ashamed to own that between 7 and 8 P.M. I am so thoroughly done up, that I *coup o'er* like a leaden statue, on a sofa ready set in the breezy verandah, and doze, and dream of Minto; but am fairly *unable* to sit up and write, fighting with the flare and with the darkness and the mosquitoes, as I was wont in my youth, a year or two ago. This is the melancholy truth.'

After his return from Java a perceptible change came over the tone of his letters. Passages in the minor key preponderate. The expressions of love and longing for home, frequent enough before, become almost painful in their repetition and intensity—the more so when a certain anxiety is discoverable shadowing the exuberance of hope.

For this there were many causes. The last two years had brought griefs such as do not leave a man without taking away great part of himself. The death of his young son, the Benjamin of the family, who by a combination of modesty and spirit had wound himself closely round his father's heart during the companionship of the long sea voyage, and the lad's subsequent adventures in his naval career, and the death of his earliest and, beyond the circle of his family, best loved friend, Mr. Windham, were events that not only enshrouded the present in gloom, but cast their shadow over the past and the future. He was wont to say that no grief should be indulged at the cost of duties to the living, or to the exclusion of a thankful acknowledgment of past happiness and of blessings untouched; and he did his best to act up to his professions; but, as he wrote to his wife, 'though their names may be seldom on my lips, their memory will be ever present to me;' and again of his long intimacy with Windham: 'The earliest fruit of friendship's tree is the sweetest, and the latest in rotting; but of it there is no second crop.'

By the side of these weightier griefs he himself would have given no place for such disappointments as arose from the neglect of his public services by ministers and directors. Yet, if they were not causes of depression, they can hardly have raised the tone of his spirits; and the climate of India and hard and anxious labour had begun to tell on the vigour of his bodily frame.

Arriving as his letters did at long intervals, it is possible that they may not have impressed those who received them, as they do ourselves, with a conviction that he had already recognised the first tones of a voice, 'no other heard, that summoned him away.'

'Calcutta: begun middle of January, ended February 7, 1812.

'I never was such a slave since I came to India as I have been since my return from Java. A great deal of additional work has fallen upon me from that quarter; and the necessity of looking back to proceedings here during my absence has also increased the demands—always greater than I can answer—upon my time. However, there is nothing saved to me by fatiguing you all with my fatigues. . . . This Barrackpore is a most happy change of scene from Batavia, and is indeed to me a kind of *little Minto,* having a faint smack of *some* virtue in it. I have kept January 3 in a grand style this year; giving a ball and supper on my wedding day, as appearing to myself more worthy of celebration than any other feast in the calendar, especially as it is also the birthday of Cicero, a gentleman who attended us faithfully through the whole campaign. Seven hundred sat down to supper, and you see how I must oppress the provinces to support such extravagance. We have had a christening of seven souls at once. . . . Five of them were presents from various Malay kings and potentates, " rich in slaves, but low in cash," like the King of Cappadocia—" Mancipiis locuples, egit æris Cappadocum rex." You have heard of them before from Malacca, where they were waiting for my gracious acceptance, and you have also heard of their arrival at Calcutta in my last. I had given the *surnames* of Man and Friend to the two eldest boys, who continue to be my own Man and Friend. I forget whether I have given you an account of these sentimental appellations; but, to save you from the chance of a second *seccatore*, I shall now refer you briefly to an amiable passage in Seneca, Epistle 47, where, preaching humanity and kindness towards slaves, he says: "Servi sunt, *imo homines*; servi sunt, imo contubernales; servi sunt, imo *humiles amici* (this I think beautiful), servi sunt, imo conservi," &c. I gave them the *truly* Christian names, therefore, of Homo and Amicus, that I may always be put in mind to treat my humble property like men and friends instead of cattle. Indeed, they deserve it; for better, gentler boys were never born in Christendom. However, they were to have Christian names in the usual sense of that word at their baptism, and one of them is Francis Man, and the other Edmund Friend; but I do not mean to part with the names given them by their godfather Seneca, and they will continue to be Man and Friend. . . . . .

'I have read seven volumes of "Madame du Deffand"[1]

---

[1] 'There is a book published, called *Correspondance de Madame de Deffand*, which contains an account of the court of Madame de Maine, greatly resembling what is to be seen at Kensington. The mixture of kindness and torment exercised towards her ladies, the violent walks and agitations of body to make up for the want of events, the jealousy about her friends, and her caprice, the shortness of her emotions, the extreme gaiety and extreme dulness of her house, are exactly like the ways of Kensington.'—Anna Maria Elliot to her father, Lord Minto, February 26, 1810.

most faithfully, which I confess is a great waste of life, especially as both her topics and her thoughts are identically the same in every letter. But I felt so much interest both in herself and in many of the persons who belonged to her society and are found in her correspondence either as parties or subjects, that I did not like to skip. Her style also is so good that I was afraid of losing a pleasure, such as good writing bestows, if I missed a sentence. I did really feel formerly a sort of affectionate veneration for her; but I knew nothing more of her real character and value than what she chose to show in the best part of her day,— that is to say, in her evening circle, which had in truth all the freshness of other people's mornings, as she was just out of bed. But now that I have seen the rest of her four-and-twenty hours, and am in all the secrets of her *insomnies* by night and her ennui by day, I confess that my veneration has much abated; and if a kind feeling still remains it is the glimmering of an old flame which a knowledge of her life, character, and opinions has not served to feed or brighten. There certainly never was anybody with talents and a good understanding whose philosophy had taught them less *de finibus*, and who had lived eighty years in greater or more childish error concerning the ends of life and the means of happiness. The only virtue she professed was sincerity, of which she has left an illustration in her correspondence with Voltaire; and her only passion friendship; witness her teasing quarrelsome connection with the President Hénault. As for Mr. Walpole, his brutality seems to have been a judgment upon her sins to others. He was a prim, precise, pretending, conceited savage, but a most *un-English* one. It is not odd that she should have thought a little incorrectly of the English character, having formed her notion of it principally from Mr. Walpole, Fish Crawfurd, and George Selwyn. I have taken of late a good course of epistolary reading, just before Madame du Deffand, having gone through the whole of Cicero's correspondence with his contemporaries, Atticus included.

'Pray never publish mine, for it is a sort of posthumous work that I think seldom does much for the fame of the writer. But Cicero repays the reader by the history, or rather memoirs, of a period more interesting than that of Louis XV., and by the charm of his style, which is always admirable. I am now reading Middleton's "Life of Cicero" for the third time. It has always entertained and interested, but not edified me, as to the character of the times, of the Roman people, of Cicero the hero of the book, or of any one of the able but universally profligate and generally detestable actors in that turbulent and calamitous though splendid scene.'

'Calcutta: March 10 1812.

'I am in perfect health, but have been less robust since my Java excursion than before. . . . My only concern is about the use of my legs. They have been so entirely confined to purposes of ornament, having touched nothing harder than a carpet or a mat, and carried their master no further than the length of a verandah, for so many years, that I have often serious doubts and anxieties about the *craigs*. If I cannot enjoy them, wherefore should I live? and at Prince of Wales' Island, scrambling up to the waterfall, my gentlemen gave themselves such fine airs that I have been rather uneasy on the subject ever since. However, I shall hope both in the climate and the exercise of the craigs, for the recovery of at least some share of what I have been losing all this time. I have long been content to *walk* through the remainder of life, and to leave the old leaping and skipping paces to my betters; but if I cannot follow my own kilted lady to Topwood or Fatlips I shall stand in need of more philosophy than any of my books have yet taught me. . . .

'January 1, 1814, is the day at which my reckonings end. It cannot probably be that identical day, but it will be as few over or under as we can contrive. "By the deep nine, and then a quarter less five," will be sung out at last, and reward our long voyage with home and perfect happiness. So man proposes; the out-turn is not our affair; and we have a right to enjoy hope till the event comes, whatever it may be.

. . . . . .

'I have received your letter of April 8; and the few words it contains concerning the Farms, the House, and other subjects of that sort, gave me the assurance that you had resumed your ordinary occupations, and that by the providential and merciful arrangements of nature, surviving cares and duties and the daily offices of life would, with the healing influences of time, soften the sharpness of recent affliction and leave only those tender impressions which are not inconsistent with the calm enjoyment of our remaining blessings, and with what may be considered the happiness of our period of life, in which, without losing our sensibilities either to good or evil, the edge at least of the latter may be less acute than when life and all its events are new. . . . I do what I can to check the pains of impatience; and in that difficult attempt I am much assisted by the total occupation of my hours and even moments in this laborious office. But I make no endeavour to weaken my notions of the happiness which I trust awaits us all, and give full scope to memory and imagination in painting the joys of home. I am sure they cannot be exaggerated, because I am sure of your love, and of my own, and of the love of every mother's son and daughter. I may be vexed a little by the injustice of the world; but I have made a true estimate of all that can happen *from without,* and the treasure of all I possess within sinks the rest to cowries, which is infinitely less than brass farthings. The one is all sterling, and the other all Birmingham, and not worth a thought, much less a care.

On June 10, 1812, the following sentence begins a letter to his wife: 'I have received from Lord Liverpool a full and handsome acknowledgment of my services with regard to all the conquests in which I have had a share, as well as of the general merit of my administration in India.'

'Calcutta: February 4 and 9, 1813.

'The whole family is in perfect health.

'If we can but take care and keep out of mischief this last year, and then find you all as perfect as ourselves, my vows and hopes will be fulfilled. A space more for you and me to witness and partake in the happiness around us, and to make up for the spoils of time by blessings which we can bestow and receive, whatever the young may think, to and from each other as long as we live, but to and from no mortal besides, will be a welcome winding up of Fortune's beautiful gifts. However she has been a good dame, and will be out of debt to us whenever our books may close.[1] My thought and fancy, having a free choice, dwell only, and that perpetually, on the bright side of the prospect.

. . . . . .

'By our latest news, Parliament was prorogued, and no change of Ministry. I am sorry for the interests, and indeed honour of the country; and one cannot see without some apprehension the inefficacy of a vote of

---

[1] To this passage Lady Minto replied: 'I agree with you that Dame Fortune has not dealt unkindly by us. The grand favour of all she has shown us, is in our family; though I do not feel insensible of her other gifts; but without the first the rest would have failed in securing the happiness we can now enjoy round us. Honours have been the result of your labours, ability, and character; but the dispositions of a family do not always go with inheritance.'

Parliament. Parliament stands between anarchy and
order, and when that defence is removed, either the
Crown or the people must be vanquished. The Crown
must probably fall in that contest, and after an interval
of blood and misery, either a foreign or domestic despotism will be the fruit of the popular triumph. These
may seem visionary notions, and I hope and pretty well
believe they are. Only one has seen in our own time
these very events run their course, and many a time in
history. Why should we be privileged against the
common laws of cause and effect? The times require
a decent, at least not a depraved and discredited,
Court; an able, firm, and well-supported Government,
not a broken, selfish, and disjointed gentry, leaving
mediocrity in possession of feeble and precarious
power.

'I have read "Portugal," by Lord Nugent, and
admire both the versification and the poetry. . . . Yet
in one point I could have wished that a sentiment
generally good, but not suited to the times, and therefore not a virtue of the day—I mean, a longing for
peace—had been withheld or expressed with less earnestness. I perceive with great concern, and sometimes
with a little *dismay*, a tone of whimpering after peace
arising gradually in England, and growing too much
into a fashion. A desire for peace, because we are tired
of war, not because its object is attained—which in the
present war is mere security against subjugation—is
little better than to call *craven*, and submit to all the
consequences of defeat. What those are we have only

to look round upon the craven-callers of Europe to understand.'¹

Lord Minto alludes in this letter to a vote of the House of Commons on a motion for an Address to the Prince Regent praying him to take measures for forming a strong and efficient Administration which was unexpectedly carried by a majority of 174 to 170. The prayer was not granted, and on June 8 Lord Liverpool assumed the first place in a Government, which was neither strong nor efficient, though it proved tough and lasting. Parliament was dissolved in the autumn, when a good harvest and the glorious victory of Salamanca had done much, in spite of exorbitant prices and scarcity of grain, to counteract the depression described in Lady Minto's letters in the early part of 1812.

The first fleet of 1813 brought to India the account of the general election, when Lord Minto's eldest son came into Parliament for Roxburghshire. In the ensuing session (1813) he had the pleasure of recording his vote in support of the very measure which had turned out Lord Grenville's ministry in 1806; a Bill to allow Roman Catholics to hold commissions as field officers. 'This,' wrote Lady Minto, ' we must devoutly hope will prove a first step in a policy of liberality and justice towards our injured fellow-subjects.'²

---

¹ 'La paix n'est rien,' said Napoleon I. 'Ce sont les conditions de la paix qui font tout.'

² In one of her letters of this summer Lady Minto gives a glimpse of Teviotdale which seems worth preserving:

'Gilbert is at Jedburgh with his troop; 640 new recruits out of

Lord Minto had intimated to the Directors his wish to be relieved from the government early in 1814. The day he had named as that of his departure from India was indeed January 1. In the summer of 1813 he learned that, six months before, it had been decided to supersede him in the government of India, and that the appointment had been bestowed on the Earl of Moira, to whom the Prince Regent conceived himself peculiarly indebted for the assistance rendered by him while a new ministry was in process of formation after Mr. Perceval's death. It was stated at the same time that Lord Moira would reach India in October 1813. The Court of Directors reluctantly submitted to the pressure put upon them by the Board of Control and accompanied their resolution of recall with another warmly acknowledging Lord Minto's eminent services. Nothing could be more undeserved, more ungracious, or more discreditable to the parties concerned, than the recall of an able and uniformly successful Governor General to make room for a personal friend of the Regent's. The calmness with which Lord Minto received

his 800 men. This is the day of inspection. We expect our cousin, Sir John Dalrymple, here, who is the inspecting General. To the honour of the race of Teviotdale, Gilbert says he never saw so fine-looking a body of men, a very great proportion, five feet ten—fine handsome fellows. The breed of men is as much changed for the better of late years as that of other stock, and we have often observed among our hosts of masons, carpenters, and labourers in the last three years the extreme good looks of the population. The men have got before the women, and are a sharp, cleanly set, though I am happy to see the younger women with cleaner, tidier houses than their grandmothers, and all are anxious to adorn their walls with roses and honeysuckles.'—August 26, 1813.

the first intelligence of the slight about to be put upon him may be seen in the following letter to Lady Minto.

'June 25, 1813.

'Your last letter, dated Minto, November 7, brought me the first notice of Lord Moira, or of any intention to supersede me earlier than the time I had myself fixed. By the same fleet I had half a page from Lord Buckinghamshire with the dry fact of Lord Moira's appointment, and of his having himself proposed an earldom to Lord Liverpool, who had concurred very readily, and in a friendly manner. By the second line from Lord Buckinghamshire in December I am informed of the Prince's assent.

. . . . . .

'I shall not launch into the question of Lord Moira's appointment to this office before I had resigned it. The feelings and opinions of us all upon this occasion must be very much alike. . . . Some circumstances, however, soften the matter so far as I am personally concerned. First, the offer of the earldom,[1] as well as what everyone knows of the motive, origin, and progress of the measure, proves that my removal from this office has no relation whatever to my conduct; and the measure is defended by its authors and instruments by arguments entirely foreign to the usual merits of such questions,—that is to say, upon the several grounds of excessive favour to another man,

[1] Lord Minto was created Viscount Melgund and Earl of Minto on February 24, 1813.

of political arrangements of office, and of commands which must be obeyed without hesitation or remonstrance. Part of this is new in England, and the remainder entirely new regarding the Government of India, but it does not touch me personally. The other softening is a vigorous protest against the measure, both on the personal and public ground, by some of the ablest and most respectable members of the Court of Directors. I might perhaps have felt mortified (though the feeling would have been false, since I have done nothing amiss) if such an affront had been passed on me through such a body without dissent. As it is, I have been well and handsomely defended, and the mere obedience of the *servum pecus* to a master ought not to humiliate me or any other man. Whether it is pleasant to their own feelings or not is their affair. It may be from this view of the subject that I cannot perhaps get myself to be quite angry enough.

. . . .

'The consequence of the arrangement might to many people be uncomfortable. I must remain at Calcutta some months after my successor will have assumed the government, but I confess this circumstance appears to me perfectly indifferent. Lord Moira is naturally disposed to act handsomely on all occasions, and I shall have no disposition to give him umbrage; so that I think the rising and setting suns may drive their chariots very peaceably and amicably round the Calcutta Course.

'. . . It is comical enough that my resignation

should have arrived just at the moment they were turning me out without leave. My answers to the thanks of the two Houses of Parliament were received by the Chancellor and the Speaker at the same critical time when the movers of the thanks were treating me like a criminal.

'We have got through the hottest hot season that anybody ever remembers in India. It has lasted longer than usual, and the rains have come so late that there has been a pretty serious scarcity in the provinces; and some apprehension of it even in this fertile quarter; for Bengal is the proper granary of India. The tanks were almost entirely dry, and the little water that remained was of course putrid and corrupted. This is a serious evil and always occasions sickness and mortality, as well as distress to those who escape disease or death.

'As the time advances, I am sorry to say it seems more tedious instead of more rapid, as I expected it would. I have opened a new account for November instead of January, and am at my old work of counting days, weeks, and decades, with painful earnestness. I dare hardly let my thoughts loose upon the end of our wanderings and separation, because it makes me downright giddy; and yet I seldom miss a night dreaming of being at home. I had been talking of the discomfort of waking out of such dreams, and the next night, three or four nights ago, I had a most lively and insidious dream of Minto. I thought we were all walking on the haugh; John was one of the party, and

I said to him in perfect confidence of the reality, and by way of triumph in that certainty, " Now, John, if I should awake this moment to find myself in India! That would be a proper job, would it not?" I said this with a sort of grin of satisfaction at my positive knowledge that I was in the midst of you on the haugh at Minto. I had hardly spoken the words when I did awake at Barrackpore. However, I shall be revenged one of these days by dreaming myself in India and waking at Minto.

'I should certainly wish to make the ash[1] that has the North Pole over it our trysting tree in preference to any elm in Carlton Gardens; and I know you will only adopt the latter plan in case of necessity.'

A letter from a friend[2] he highly valued, written when the decision to supersede him became known, finds a fit place here.

'Edinburgh: October 11, 1812.

'Your Indian administration has been thrown away upon an administration at home incapable of appreciating it, and perhaps with a selfish motive of keeping it back from the public. Either Mauritius or Batavia should have made the fortune of a Governor General; and this great success without any mixture of bad fortune, should at least afford a presumption of merit.

[1] The old ash tree which stands on the grass opposite to the entrance of the house at Minto.

[2] Mr. George Wilson, an English barrister, who resided in Edinburgh, and enjoyed the friendship of some of the most eminent men of his day.

Your peaceful administration of India, affording fewer materials for history, as happy times always do, will probably remain unknown except to a few old clerks at the India House. All this you must bear—with this consolation only, that it has been the lot of the best and wisest men in all ages, and will continue to be the lot of all those who go somewhat beyond the reach of the times they live in. There are at Minto a great quantity of letters and papers, all ready in portfolios, for you to work upon; and it is not impossible that, fifty or a hundred years hence, posterity may understand a little of these matters, and begin to do you justice. You are not of those who will say posthumous fame is of no value. But independent of that, the sons or grandsons of the present little Gilbert may feel the effect of it, and people will say, " He comes of a good stock." '

When the Governor General's recall was made known in Calcutta, surprise and indignation were loudly expressed. As the moment of his departure drew near, the manifestations of regard, of respect, and of regret, were general and cordial. Addresses poured in from all classes of the community, couched in the most gratifying terms. Not only were his brilliant services duly acknowledged, but also the fact, patent to all, that from the beginning to the end of his administration he had laboured unremittingly for the public good, and that he and his family had given an example of domestic life, not only irreproachable in its purity, but attractive by its social charm. No other circle in Calcutta contained prettier women or abler men. Youth, wit, and high spirits defied the languid atmosphere of India; and wherever the Governor General was the centre of the society it could not be otherwise than distinguished for simplicity of manners and cultivated tastes.[1] Lord Minto was at his best in the ease of private society. In London and at Vienna some of the most brilliant men and women of their time had shared his friendship and had met in familiar intercourse under his roof. The volumes of correspondence preserved at Minto testify to the regard in which he was held by friends whose signatures would rejoice the heart of a collector of autographs; and who wrote to him with the sort of easy confidence that can only co-exist with perfect social equality. At Calcutta he was a big man—bigger by head and shoulders than any one near him—yet nobody could be more unfeignedly grateful than he when some amiable person ignored the circumstance—nor more happy than when, under the shadow of the banians of Barrackpore, he gathered round him those to whom his public capacity was the least of his merits.

In the diary kept by General Malcolm for the benefit of his wife during his visit to Calcutta in 1808,

[1] During the last years of Lord Minto's residence at Calcutta, Government House was the home, not only of the family circle, but of Colonel Taylor, military secretary, who in 1809 married Miss Petrie, a lady remarkable for personal and other gifts, and of the sisters of Mrs. John Elliot, whose popularity and agreeable qualities had made their father's house at Madras a centre of pleasant society.

we find the following entry: 'Mrs. W—— happened not to have been introduced to Lord Minto when he dined here, and, mistaking him for another, she said: "Do you know the cause of General Malcolm's return to Calcutta?" "I believe I can guess," was the Lord's reply. "Pray then tell me," said the lady. Lord Minto hesitated till after we were at table, and then said: "We had better give the General plenty of wine, and we shall get this secret out of him." The lady, who had now discovered his rank, began to make apologies. "I assure you, my Lord," she said, "I did not know you." "I am delighted at that compliment," he replied; "not to be known as Governor General in private society is my ambition. I suppose you thought I looked too young, and too much of a puppy for that grave old fellow, Lord Minto, whom you had heard people talking about." I mention this anecdote as very characteristic of that playful pleasantry which makes Lord Minto's society so agreeable to those he associates with.'

In another passage Malcolm says that it had been 'an equal subject of astonishment and delight to him to find a man whose life had been passed in all the bustle of public affairs, cherishing local attachments with all the enthusiasm of a country gentleman, and resting his happiness upon the best and truest basis, natural ties, and consequently finding in the constantly increasing affection of his family that which gives success its highest zest, and brings comfort under every reverse of fortune.'[1]

[1] Kaye's *Life of Malcolm.*

The sympathy which his strong love of home excited among his brother exiles of Calcutta was gracefully displayed when, at the close of 1812, the bachelors of Calcutta gave the Governor General a ball. As he entered the door, the opposite end of the room disclosed a view of Minto House, 'the burn, the green hills all to the life, and on so large a scale as to reach from side to side of an immense room.' Mercifully, no prophetic instinct warned him that in the vision created by friendly regard he was alone to see the scene he loved so well.

CHAPTER XIV.

We have endeavoured in the preceding chapters to reproduce from Lord Minto's correspondence the most eventful transactions of his government of India. Yet that which he would himself have regarded as the most important branch of his administration, namely, its internal policy, has been altogether omitted. To enter into any details of the financial, judicial, and legislative measures which were either executed or prepared while he held the direction of public affairs in India, is beyond the competency of his present editor; but to show from his correspondence the general principles which approved themselves to his mind in connection with the subjects above named is within the province of this work. It will be remembered that when Lord Minto went to India the financial affairs of the Company were in a highly embarrassed condition. Fresh obligations had been recently incurred by the extension of their territories; an empty exchequer and high interest threatened a financial crisis; and the necessary retrenchments of expenditure consequent on the deficiency of revenue had gone far to provoke a political and social catastrophe.

During the interval between the recall of Lord Wellesley and the appointment of Lord Minto, anarchy had spread unchecked in the newly ceded provinces, and a spirit of dissatisfaction had crept over the services whose emoluments had been subjected to the pruning knife with more vigour than tact by Sir George Barlow. Lord Minto, when assuming the reins of government, was strictly charged to abstain from all political measures having a tendency to increase the expenditure of the Company, and to reduce all expenses capable of diminution. How, under these instructions, he dealt with the vexed questions which he found seething in the everboiling cauldron of Indian politics has been already told. His views concerning the advantages to be derived from further reductions in the general expenditure of the Company, especially in regard to the emoluments of their servants, may be seen in the following letter to Mr. Elliot of Wells, who had informed him of the probability that a Commission, composed of members of both Houses, would be sent out to India for the purpose of inquiring into the condition of the Company's finances and of suggesting retrenchments.

'September 4, 1809.[1]

'With regard to the Commission, the two services, civil and military, have scarcely had a breathing time from an operation precisely similar in its object, which was executed with a very steady and a very efficient

---

[1] To Mr. Elliot of Wells.

hand by the local Government under the administration of Sir G. Barlow. It is evident to me that retrenchments can no longer be classed amongst the material resources of the Company. The establishments will in reality not afford it. I do not mean that you may not lay your finger upon some isolated case of a civil office that may bear a reduction of salary, or some military staff appointment, or allowance to a military office, that might be reformed without injury to the efficiency of the service.

'I have myself constituted, and carried through, a formal inquiry of this nature with regard to the civil departments : it has terminated in some few, but in no degree considerable, reductions of charge; amongst which I may, indeed, reckon the diminution of my own salary as the principal. The investigation has nevertheless led to some alterations which, both in point of economy and *regulation* may, I hope, conduce to improvement in the prosperity both of the Company and the provinces. But it is demonstrated by the same proceeding that retrenchment of civil establishments, though not to be neglected, can afford no supply adequate to the great object of meeting the general exigency of the Company's financial situation. It is an unwelcome truth, I know, at home; but I am much inclined to believe that the general scale of legitimate emolument is perhaps already lower than is entirely consistent with justice to the Company's servants, and with sound policy, even financial, but especially with those general principles of Government on which the security and prosperity of

States are founded. The loose principles which formerly prevailed amongst the Company's servants, and the fashion, if I may so term it, of corruption which now forms the reproach of what is called the *old school*, deserved, however, a little more indulgence perhaps than, as one of its sworn enemies and persecutors, I was disposed to show it. Peculation and abuse were not merely tolerated; they were in a manner established and authorised by the parsimony of the Company in the regular remuneration of its servants. The Company, perhaps, in those older times pursued that impolitic policy upon a principle which would deserve less indulgence than the practice of its servants; I mean that of *participation*, or something like *poundage*, in abuse and even oppression; for the charge of adequate salaries is saved by the toleration of irregular emolument. If these supplementary profits had continued to be furnished only from the extortions and oppressions practised on the Princes and people of India, and had not at length—through the disorder of provinces become our own—touched the direct interests of the Company herself, we are not positively entitled to say that the abuses of the old Indian administration would have roused the vigilance of Parliament so effectually or so early, and that the only radical, as it is the only rational, remedy for abuse would have been applied. The provision of legal and authorised emoluments, corresponding with the just and fair expectations of the Company's servants, completely changed *the fashion*; and at this day I have great satisfaction in saying that a more pure and highly honourable administration does not exist than that of the E. I. Company in India; by administration, I mean the service at large.

'Now I speak from a firm conviction, founded on personal observation and knowledge, when I say that any scheme of general retrenchment, which should reduce the scale of authorised and avowed emolument materially below its present standard, would have the effect of countenancing abusive profits.

'There is another consideration, which recent events have rendered too prominent to be overlooked— I mean the effect on the public temper in India—that is to say, on the temper of the British public in India, likely to be produced by frequent and teasing renewals of odious and alarming investigations which seem to leave no man a year's security in the most moderate reward of labour. The diminution of salary is not in this country a mere loss of money, but it retards the accomplishment of that wish which is at the bottom of every heart, a return to England; and in many cases it extinguishes even hope upon that subject. . . . Anything like despondency or loss of energy in the temper of the service would cause an abatement of public zeal and public usefulness, which would seriously damage the interests of the Company, if no worse evils were to ensue.

'With regard to military retrenchments, anything short of reduction of the establishment itself will produce no essential relief to the finances of the Company; and the excited, well-nigh disaffected, state of feeling existing in large portions of the army tend to make the operation of such a Commission as that proposed of very doubtful result.

'Great injustice would be done to me if it were supposed that backwardness to incur personal odium in the performance of a duty has any influence whatever on my opinions. It is not the disaffection of the provinces over which I preside *to my person* that would deter or for a moment obstruct me in carrying through a wise and beneficial reform; it is disaffection to the Company and to the Government itself that I apprehend, and it is that apprehension that appears to me strongly to dissuade from the undertaking. These sentiments are not in any degree inconsistent with a vigilant superintendence of the public expenditure, with the suppression of all abuse and embezzlement, or even with partial and occasional reductions of charge in which the interests and feelings of individuals shall not be too harshly neglected. In this course I am proceeding, not without sensible benefit to the country, and without any sensible opposition from the public or individuals. But my views have always been more directed, because directed with better hope, to an improvement of the resources of the country and an augmentation of the Company's revenue; and I do flatter myself that, by the aid and advice of the ablest men I have ever met with, intimately acquainted with all the affairs of this country and well versed in political science, much has been effected, and more, which requires a little time to mature its fruits, is in prospect.

'A solid and substantial accession of resources to

Government will arise, coupled with material improvement in the comfort and condition of the people. In effect the present state of our finances is so much more favourable than was expected by the most sanguine when I left England, that we may wait without impatience for the benefit which rests on the fair foundation of general and permanent principles. Instead of annual deficits of three millions, which naturally alarmed Government when the Commission was proposed as a strong expedient in an urgent case, we have in this very year of account to show a *surplus* of one million.[1] Therefore I say with the best physicians, " Hands off! let Nature work."

'I cannot close this subject without saying that I have never conceived the Commission to have been proposed in *any quarter* in an unfriendly spirit to me. The apparent distress in the Company's affairs, and the necessity of going to Parliament for relief, might naturally suggest some extraordinary measure to meet the exigency; and I am satisfied that it was not a diminution of the authority of the Indian Government, but a relief from responsibility and an accession of strength, that was truly and sincerely proposed.'

The close connection between the temper of the ruling class, and the character of their rule, is briefly

---

[1] 'During the three concluding years of Lord Minto's administration the supplies remitted from India exceeded the value of the Company's investments to the extent of nearly 10 millions sterling. Of the amount so remitted nearly 2 millions were in bullion, which was unprecedented in the history of the commerce of India.'— Wilson's *History of British India*, vol. vii.

touched upon in this letter: it finds place, however, in many others. Writing to Lord Grenville on the subject of the Company's affairs, he said:—'I subscribe heartily to the advantage of a general and comprehensive view of that subject in preference to partial and individual reforms.

'To keep up establishments, or to pay them on a scale for which our funds are insufficient, is impossible on a permanent system. On the other hand, I doubt whether reductions of emoluments can ever furnish a very considerable result; for if pushed too far it extinguishes exertion and energy and creates general discontent and inaction. It produces also the danger of abusive and irregular profits, which is the greatest evil of all.'

And again to the same correspondent, writing with reference to the salary of a high legal functionary, the Recorder of Prince of Wales' Island, he says:—'It is of great moment to send a capable and respectable man to administer civil and criminal justice where he will be the only lawyer in the country; and such a man is entitled to live without penury and anxiety. He is not placed there as a step in his career; but must limit his views to the enjoyment of his office in a distant and secluded country while he holds it, and to a very moderate retreat at the close of his labours and exile.'

The peculiar conditions in which the British rule in India exists were ever present to his mind when the interests of the State or of individuals were under consideration. A few thousands of men were called upon to govern millions; between the few and the many there were no sympathies of race or of religion, no similarity in civilisation, none of the links which bind men together. Exiles from their native country, often from their families, when time and distance were evils of a magnitude which we can hardly appreciate, the dearest hope of Anglo-Indians was the achievement of such an independence as would permit them to escape from the land where the best years of their manhood had to be spent; yet the fate of India depended on the faithfulness of such men to the functions of government. To their energy and integrity England looked for safety, and India for justice. 'Destroy or even retard their hopes, and you sap their energy, and tempt their probity, and by so doing you weaken the governing power of your empire.'

In the same spirit he wrote on the general question of the suitability of a Commission to effect measures of retrenchment.

'All schemes of sound economy must be combined with other points of public policy. If simple retrenchment is ordered, without regard to other principles of government, either the economical result will itself be fallacious, and the worst as well as greatest of all prodigalities will be the real consequence, by the substitution of abuse in the room of avowed remuneration for service; or, if the economy should prove real, the State itself, for the benefit of which that economy is sought, will suffer more essentially, perhaps vitally, in its higher interests, by the inefficiency of all the branches of the public service. . . . Retrenchment is the specific object of the appointment of a Commission. It is in that branch that the public looks for the proofs of their exertion; and the accomplishment of those expectations is to be their title to public notice and approbation on their return to Europe. They are not sent out to govern India. The permanent interests of that country are not committed to them, although these objects may be recommended to their collateral regard. In this respect, therefore, I cannot help thinking a Commission of retrenchment is, by its very constitution, subject to the objection of separating those objects of public policy which ought to be combined, and of throwing an extraordinary share of the public authority and energy into a single branch of the public concerns, in a manner which is distinct from, and is on that account prejudicial to, the general interests of the State. It is in this view that I still consider the established government of India as the most convenient —I might say, as the only convenient—instrument of such economical reforms as the present conjuncture of the Company's concerns may require.

'I hope that a remedy for the disorder in our finances may be sought, in part at least, from an augmentation of resources as well as from diminution of charges. I am persuaded much may be done by an economical administration, by avoiding unnecessary expenses, and by combating abuse, fraud, and extravagance in the public expenditure.'

One source to which Lord Minto looked for an 'augmentation of resources,' was the gradual extension of free trade, in the place of the existing system of exclusion and monopoly.

In a private letter to the Hon. R. Dundas, December 1808, he wrote: 'The great question between the Company's monopoly and the private trade is too extensive and complicated for a letter. I shall only say that the circumstances on which the necessity for monopoly for the trade of India was originally founded, have passed away; and a state of the world, as well as a change in the condition of the Eastern world itself, has arrived which, so far from requiring monopoly, will I suspect, be found no longer compatible with that system. Sudden and radical changes in great institutions are however, seldom, perhaps never, free from danger and evil. My mind certainly leans to the system which appears to be in agitation—namely, that of *relaxation* in the present monopoly, rather than to its total or immediate abolition.

'Of this I will venture to assure you, looking to the Indian side of the question only, that every extension that can be given to the freedom of trade will operate most powerfully and sensibly to the instant improvement of the wealth and prosperity of India. I am strongly inclined to the opinion that the East India Company itself will find more advantage in the prosperity of its territories than in the profits of its exclusive trade; and is in reality more interested as a Stock Company in the former than in the latter. As Sovereigns of an Empire the question will admit of no doubt, and the duties arising from that relation may be thought entitled to their share in its decision.'[1]

'I should conceive that if the import and export trade is thrown open to the extent mentioned in the Articles 3rd, 4th, and 7th, of your letter, a liberty to individual traders to employ European factors, of their own appointing, in the interior of the provinces will become necessary. This will increase the number of Europeans resident in the provinces, and it will be impossible to protect the native people from oppression if Europeans residing in the provinces continue to be amenable only to the Supreme Court in Calcutta, and exempt from the local control of the Company's Courts. This inconvenience is already felt most sensibly.[2]

'Redress is in reality entirely refused if it must be sought by poor men from a foreign court at a great distance. The proper remedy will in my apprehension

[1] The exclusive monopoly by the Company of the India trade was abolished on the renewal of the East India Charter in 1813. The exclusive trade to China was confirmed to them.

[2] The system of judicature referred to was that instituted by Lord Cornwallis, of which the chief feature was the establishment of a number of courts throughout the British territory—one in the chief city of every district—over which presided a judge with one or two assistants chosen from the Company's servants. Each court was provided with a native to expound the Hindoo or Mahommedan law. All descriptions of persons, British subjects alone excepted, were amenable to these tribunals. From their decisions there were two stages of appeal; the first to the provincial courts, of which there were four; the last and highest Court of Appeal was the Sudder Dewanee Adawlet, composed of the chief members of Government assisted by natives. British subjects were amenable only to the Supreme Court at Calcutta.

be to subject Europeans at a certain distance from Calcutta to the jurisdiction of the Company's Courts, with such limitations as may be thought necessary. But I must take the liberty of cautioning you anxiously against any proposition (and such will certainly be made) for extending the administration of English law to the provinces; and consequently sending English lawyers and attorneys among the people of India. I would also caution you against any admixture of the two judicatures, by giving appeals from the Company's courts to the Supreme Court, or by placing a judge or the Chief Justice of the Supreme Court in the Sudder Dewanee Adawlet, which is the Court of Appeal from all the Company's tribunals. Our judicial system is not without defects. It is yet in an early stage, but I am persuaded it will mature itself into a good, rational, and for this country wholesome and convenient system of law, with a pure and efficient administration of justice, provided it be not perplexed by an alliance with a foreign code, and borne down by the superior authority of English and professional lawyers.'

The great burden on the finances of the Company was the size of their army. 'On all sides I am assured,' wrote Lord Minto, 'that this great expense is a necessary one.' Surrounded by rival ambitions, by populations indifferent when not hostile, the ascendancy of Great Britain could only be maintained by indisputable military supremacy.

A discussion having arisen, in connection with this

question, between the Court of Directors and the Indian Government, regarding the policy of endeavouring to restore the balance of power among the States of India, which it was assumed had been destroyed by the territorial acquisitions of the Company, Lord Minto observed in a secret despatch, that, 'as an abstract proposition, all opinions will agree that a balance of the power of States, united in political or commercial intercourse, affords the best, if not the only security which human ingenuity can devise against the projects of ambition or the ruinous effects of reciprocal enmity. But a balance of power, to be efficient, must be formed on principles of convention such as those under which it subsisted on the Continent of Europe before the French Revolution.

'It must arise out of a consentaneous submission to a system of public law, and a recognition of reciprocal rights as they respect the several States individually, and of reciprocal duties as they relate to the imposition of restraints on their own ambition, or on the ambition of their neighbours. It must be founded at least on a *declared* renunciation of views of conquest, as a principle of government; and it must operate by the apprehended, and, as the occasion may require, the actual association of several States to resist the endeavours which any one State may employ to aggrandise its power at the expense of another. At no period of the history of India do we recognise the existence of any such system of federation or balance of the power of States; nor indeed is it compatible with the character, principles, or constitution of the States which have been established on the Continent of India. With them, war, rapine, and conquest constitute an avowed and legitimate pursuit, and the chief source of public glory, sanctioned and even recommended by the ordinances of religion, and prosecuted without the semblance or pretext of justice, with a savage disregard of every obligation of humanity and public faith, and restrained alone by the power of resistance. Under the successful impulse of these principles the vast empire of the Mahommedans was established over more than the Continent of India.

'On its ruins arose the power of the Mahratta States, which subsequently branched out into a confederation of chiefs, professedly directed to objects of conquest and universal exaction, the fruits of which, by regular convention, were to be divided in specific proportions. The same views and principles animated and extended the usurpations of Hyder Ali and his successor. The checks which the Mahrattas and the rulers of Mysore occasionally received from the power of the Nizam, and from different combinations among these three States, were the result, not of a predetermined federation and balance of power, but of the prevalence of a system of conquest, violence, and usurpation. The efforts of the contending parties were directed, not to the just limitation, but to the subversion of each other's power, and the aggrandisement of their own; and it is unnecessary to refer to the testimony of specific facts, with a view to demonstrate the self-evident proposition, that the permanent existence of a balance of power is incompatible with reciprocal views of conquest and ambition.

'We shall not adduce, in proof of the existence of that spirit of insatiable conquest which we have ascribed to the native States without distinction, the various efforts which they have employed to subvert the British Government in India, since the period of its establishment. The existence of it, as the actuating principle of every Indian Power, requires no demonstration; and we found upon it this undeniable conclusion—that no extent of concession or territorial restitution on our part would have the effect of establishing any real or effectual balance of power in India, or forbearance on the part of other States when the means of aggrandisement should be placed in their hands. Your Honourable Committee has indeed justly remarked, in your letter of October 30, 1805, "that to recede is often more hazardous than to advance;" adding "that this observation is peculiarly applicable to India, where there is little probability that concession would be attributed by the native Powers to any other motives than weakness and fear." To enter more amply into this discussion would require a laborious review of events during a long course of years . . . the necessity of which is superseded by the conviction which we entertain, that no argument can be requisite to demonstrate how vain would be the expectation of augmenting our security by diminishing our power and political ascendancy on the Continent of Asia.'

It is perhaps scarcely sufficiently remembered that,

in countries where a low state of civilisation exists, military discipline is generally found to be the first and most efficient school to teach the rudiments of social order.

A curious instance of this fact is given in a passage of a journal written by Colonel Taylor, aide-de-camp to Lord Minto, while accompanying the Commander-in-chief on a visit to the Upper Provinces. After describing a visit to the ruins of Shah Soojah's palace on the Ganges, he goes on to describe a mosque some miles further on. 'We found it surrounded with jungles; in it a very picturesque and savage-looking group had taken possession of the ruins; about twenty hill-men were just taking their breakfast of venison steaks on plantain leaves; half of the deer, not skinned, lay among them; some were repairing their arrows; each had a large bamboo bow leaning against the wall, and quantities of arrows of different kinds were by them. The next day we inspected the hill rangers, a corps of about 300 men, formed entirely from the inhabitants of the hills. It is curious to see men who were, before enlisting, such as we saw in the Jumna Mesjid, or mosque near Rajemahl, with their clothes, arms, and accoutrements in high order, and going through their manœuvres by the word of command in English with more steadiness than is always to be met with in an English regiment; though I observe the native corps are generally slower in their movements.'[1]

[1] The discipline of the Sepoys was shown in a remarkable degree during a great riot at Benares in 1809.

Lord Minto's expectations as to the development of a 'wholesome and convenient system of law,' from the basis of the scheme instituted by Lord Cornwallis, do not appear to have been realised. In the year following that in which this letter was written, he had occasion, as we have seen, to deplore the lawless condition of districts at no considerable distance from Calcutta, and to trace them in part to the ignorance of European magistrates, and the corruption of the native police.

Various measures for the improvement of the administration of justice were under consideration at various periods of his tenure of office; but he himself appears to have rested his best hopes of attaining a more efficient system upon a previous amelioration in the relations of the two races, and upon the gradual instruction of the native population in those elementary principles of truth and honesty without which there can be neither law nor justice.

The mutual ignorance of each other's motives, intentions, and actions, in which Europeans and natives seemed content to live, had forcibly struck Lord Minto during his short residence at Madras in 1807. 'I do not believe that either Lord William (Bentinck) or Sir John Cradock had the slightest idea of the aversion their measures would excite. I fully believe that their intentions were totally misapprehended by the natives.' His subsequent letters show his conviction that the chief impediment to the improvement of the native race, and the chief disadvantage under which their

European rulers laboured, was to be found in their reciprocal ignorance of each other's language and modes of thought. One of the first objects of Government, he said, should be to assist them to understand each other.

In a despatch to the Home Government, written soon after his arrival in India, the following passage occurs:—' Some unnecessary mortifications experienced at present by the native officer might, I think, be removed with great propriety and advantage; and a very material and essential improvement would result from every encouragement that could be given to a closer intercourse between European officers and the Sepoys they command. To this very important object the attention of Government is now directed, and much benefit may be expected from the means of instruction in the native language which are now furnished to the younger branches of the service. It must be the care of Government to inculcate throughout the army that an intimate acquaintance and intercourse with the native soldier will constitute one of the strongest titles to the favour of their superiors, and advancement in their profession.'

In a similar spirit Lord Minto addressed himself to the students of the College of Fort William, reminding them that they were about to be employed in the administration of a great country, in which it would not be much beyond the truth to say that the English language was not known; that they would have to deal with multitudes who could only communicate with them in some one or other of the languages taught at the College of Fort William; that ignorance of the languages of India created almost unavoidable and almost unlimited dependence on the native and subordinate officers. 'How much prejudice to the interests of the Company, how much vexation, extortion, and cruelty towards our native subjects, how much individual shame and ruin have resulted from this cause, a very short acquaintance with the affairs of India will too clearly show.' He could not therefore declare too explicitly his determination to give the preference in the selection of gentlemen for public trust and employment to those who should have established a reputation for conduct, diligence, and talents during their studies at the College of Fort William.

The College of Fort William was, as is well known, founded by Lord Wellesley. The parsimony of the Directors led to several important restrictions of its original functions before Lord Minto went to India. He, however, lent it the full aid of his support, recognising in it the twofold object of promoting knowledge among the Anglo-Indian public servants and the restoration of Oriental literature to its due position among the scientific studies. A number of important and learned works on the science of language and of jurisprudence were published by the College in the years 1808, 1809, and 1810; as also others of a more literary character, reproducing the most important and esteemed productions of Hindoo, Persian, and Arabian poets and writers. A printing press, established by learned Hindoos, for the printing of books in the Sanscrit language, was munificently aided by Lord Minto, and was encouraged by the College to undertake an edition of the best Sanscrit dictionaries, and a compilation of the Sanscrit rules of grammar.

His first address in the character of Visitor to the College, in 1808, contains a passage which, emanating from the lips of the man who was shortly to open negotiations with the ruler of Afghanistan, and who later on enrolled an important portion of the Malayan race among the subjects of the Company, possibly contained more meaning than met the ear.

There were two languages which, though included in the comprehensive scheme of Oriental study embraced by the College of Fort William at an earlier period of the institution, were not provided for in the modified plan of instruction to which the College was now restricted—the Malay, and the Afghan or Pushtoo.

'Yet,' said Lord Minto, 'I cannot think either of those I have mentioned entirely devoid of interest; in the first place as branches of the general and liberal pursuit of Eastern learning which we profess; and in the next place as bearing either a present and immediate, or in the many chances of human vicissitude, a prospective, and perhaps not remote, affinity to our affairs.' Some steps had been already taken in the direction indicated, by the joint labours of a learned native of Peshawur and of a British Orientalist, of which a vocabulary, dictionary, and essay on Afghan grammar were the result.

We have seen it stated, with what truth we know not, that at the present time fewer of our officers are acquainted with the Pushtoo dialect than might be desired, and 'enlightened foreigners' have commented on the insufficient knowledge of Oriental tongues observable among British agents in the East.

Not one of his public duties, said Lord Minto in his last annual address to the College of Fort William, had excited in his mind a more cordial concern and more lively interest than those appertaining to the office of Visitor of the College.

And, perhaps, no more intellectual treat was to be obtained at Calcutta than was offered by the discourse of Lord Minto on the occasion of the annual distribution of honorary degrees, of prizes, and medals to the successful students of the College. Many went to hear him who had no other attraction than the pleasure of listening to a thoughtful address, expressed in language worthy of the thought. It is probable that none of his public appearances were so well adapted to disclose the natural bias of his tastes as this; in which the pursuit of literature in all its branches was his theme, while the almost paternal tenderness with which he sympathised in the hopes and efforts of the young gave at times a touching as well as impressive character to his exhortations.

It is pleasant to learn, on the authority of the eminent historian of British India, that Lord Minto's earnest efforts to bring into full operation the benefits intended by the illustrious founder of the College were crowned with eminent success. 'The junior members of the service were animated to honourable exertions, which formed the foundation of their future distinction; their seniors were induced to apply their knowledge and acquirements to the instruction of their younger brethren; and a number of natives of talent, exercising over their countrymen the combined influence of learning and religion, who were engaged in the service of the College, derived from their employment some compensation for that neglect to which the decay and extinction of native patrons of rank had subjected them, and learned to identify their interests with those of a foreign and intrusive race. To them and to their European associates were due a variety of useful works, tending to make the Oriental student familiar with the laws and institutions, the religion and character of the people. Every attempt so directed was encouraged and aided by Lord Minto.'

Some years' experience of the beneficial results already attained from the prosecution of Oriental studies at the College of Fort William, and through the medium of the learned works produced by the Serampore Press, induced Lord Minto to consider the propriety of instituting colleges for the two great races—the Hindoo and Mahommedan—forming the immense majority of the population over which we were called to rule. Both were races boasting histories of great renown; visible monuments of their public spirit were scattered over the land—monuments of exquisite art and refined taste. In Sanscrit literature lie imbedded some of the earliest and some of the highest theological conceptions to which the uninspired mind has attained; and with Hindoo and Mussulman—as with all men—'the natural law' of which St. Paul speaks, was capable of development under moral culture, whatever the figments of their faith.

Therefore it seemed to Lord Minto that to give a higher education on general subjects of learning through the channels by which alone they could receive it, was an object worthy of the State, and shortly before he went to Java in 1811 he wrote a minute from which the following passages are extracted.

'Fort William: March 6, 1811.[1]

'It is a common remark that science and literature are in a progressive state of decay among the natives of India. From every enquiry which I have been enabled to make on this interesting subject, that remark appears to me but too well founded. The number of the learned is not only diminished, but the circle of learning, even among those who still devote themselves to it, appears to be considerably contracted. The abstract sciences are abandoned, polite literature neglected, and no branch of learning cultivated but what is connected with the peculiar religious doctrines of the people. The immediate consequence of this state of things is the disuse, and even actual loss, of many valuable books; and it is to be apprehended that, unless Government interposes with a fostering hand, the

[1] Minute by the Governor General

revival of letters may become hopeless, from a want of books, or of persons capable of explaining them.

'The principal cause of the present neglected state of literature in India is to be traced to the want of that encouragement which was formerly afforded to it by princes, chieftains, and opulent individuals under the native governments. Such encouragement must always operate as a strong incentive to study and literary exertions, but especially in India, where the learned professions have little if any other support.

'The justness of these observations might be illustrated by a detailed consideration of the former and present state of science and literature at the three principal seats of Hindoo learning, viz. Benares, Tirhoot, and Nuddea. Such a review would bring before us the liberal patronage which was formerly bestowed, not only by princes and others in power and authority, but also by the zemindars, on persons who had distinguished themselves by the successful cultivation of letters at those places. It would equally bring to our view the present neglected state of learning at those once celebrated places; and we should have to remark with regret, that the cultivation of letters was now confined to the few surviving persons who had been patronised by the native princes and others, under the former governments, or to such of the immediate descendants of those persons as had imbibed a love of science from their parents.

'It is seriously to be lamented that a nation particularly distinguished for its love and successful cultivation of letters in other parts of the empire, should have failed to extend its fostering care to the literature of the Hindoos, and to aid in opening to the learned in Europe the repositories of that literature.

'It is not, however, the credit alone of the national character which is affected by the present neglected state of learning in the East. The ignorance of the natives in the different classes of society, arising from the want of proper education, is generally acknowledged. This defect not only excludes them as individuals from the enjoyment of all those comforts and benefits which the cultivation of letters is naturally calculated to afford, but, operating as it does throughout almost the whole mass of the population, tends materially to obstruct the measures adopted for their better government.

'Little doubt can be entertained that the prevalence of the crimes of perjury and forgery, so frequently noticed in the official reports, is in a great measure ascribable both in the Mahommedans and Hindoos, to the want of due instruction in the moral and religious tenets of their respective faiths. It has even been suggested, and apparently not without foundation, that to this uncultivated state of mind of the natives is in a great degree to be ascribed the prevalence of those crimes which were recently so great a scourge to the country.

'The latter offences against the peace and happiness of society have indeed, for the present, been materially checked by the vigilance and energy of the police; but it is probably only by the more general diffusion of knowledge among the great body of the people that the seeds of these evils can be effectually destroyed.

'Sufficient, I presume, has been already said to show the fitness of incurring some additional expense with a view to the restoration of learning in the extensive provinces subject to the immediate government of this Presidency.'

The minute indicates certain reforms which were required to adapt the existing college at Benares (for which a liberal sum was allowed by Government) to the prevailing opinions and habits of the natives, and to correct the abuses which had crept into it; it then proceeds to recommend that two other Hindoo colleges at Nuddea and at Bhour should be constituted; and ends thus:[1] 'It will be observed that in the foregoing remarks I have confined myself almost exclusively to the plan necessary to be adopted for the restoration of Hindoo science and literature. . . . With the difference only in the population of Hindoos and Mahommedans, all the arguments which have been above stated in support of the arrangements proposed to be adopted for the propagation of knowledge among the former would equally apply to similar institutions for the benefit of the Mahommedans. A sentiment, however, of deference for the Honourable Court of Directors restrains me from recommending any extension of the plan until their orders shall have been received on the subject generally of this minute. I deem it therefore sufficient to add on the present occasion that Mahommedan colleges might be beneficially established at

Bhangulpore, Juanpore (where Persian and Arabic literature formerly flourished), and at some place in the ceded and conquered provinces; and that it might be advisable to reform the Madrissa, or Mahommedan collegiate institution, at Calcutta, on the principles recommended with respect to the Hindoo colleges. The attention of the Honourable Court will be of course drawn to this interesting subject in the next despatch from the Revenue Department.'[1]

We cannot terminate this chapter more effectively than by a few extracts from an Address presented to Lord Minto on his departure from India by the British residents at Calcutta.

'The arduous and sacred trust of administering this great government devolved upon your Lordship soon after the termination of wars, which had far extended the limits of the Empire, and had raised to the highest pitch the reputation of the British councils, together with the fame of the British arms; but the mighty efforts necessary to ensure those splendid results could not be supported without proportionate sacrifices. To repair, therefore, the evils inseparable from the most

[1] This minute is quoted in an article on the 'Early or exclusively Oriental period of Government Education in Bengal,' in the *Calcutta Review*, vol. iii. 1845, and is ushered in with the remark that 'The Earl of Minto, having succeeded to his heart's content in crushing the efforts of Christian evangelists, next directed his attention to the heathenish institutions which owed their origin and support to the munificence of some of his predecessors. These he resolved not only to perpetuate but to render still more efficient. And not only so, but his purpose was consentaneously formed to add to their number at the expense of the State. . . . This document of great historical importance is little known.'

fortunate warfare, to recruit and husband our resources, to consolidate our recent conquests, to introduce among our new subjects the inestimable blessings of security, of order, and of justice, were among the first objects which called forth the exercise of your Lordship's wisdom and talents.

'The consummate prudence and complete success of the measures directed to the accomplishment of these momentous objects are attested by the flourishing condition of every branch of the public revenue; by the state of tranquillity in which these Provinces have been maintained, and by the increasing opulence and prosperity which, notwithstanding the privation of foreign commerce, they unequivocally manifest.

'At the period of your Lordship's arrival in India, the undisguised and ambitious projects of our inveterate enemy in Persia, in Turkey, and in every quarter of the East to which his agents and emissaries found means of access, threatened to interrupt the tranquillity and security of these dominions. . . . The vigilant exertions and comprehensive arrangements of that period of your Lordship's administration were commensurate with the exigency of the times, and were eminently calculated to secure those external and internal combinations of policy and power which in the season of approaching peril constitute the most efficient means of national defence.

'We have witnessed the successful exertion of promptitude, energy, and foresight in restoring tranquillity to a vast portion of the Empire; in repelling the aggression of foreign enemies; in maintaining the efficiency of our political relations, in vindicating the rights and dignity of the British Government, and in supporting the reputation of its faith and the vigour of its arms.

'These brilliant results of foresight and of energy formed a happy presage of the triumphant expeditions in which the zeal, discipline, and valour of our armies, under the guidance of your Lordship's councils, accomplished the subjugation of the Islands of Bourbon and Mauritius, and achieved the still greater conquest of the Dutch possessions in the East.

'We cannot forego the gratification of bearing our testimony to the wisdom and humanity which extended to the conquered the blessings of British protection and of British laws, and saved an ancient and populous colony from that devastation to which a less generous policy might have doomed it.'

CHAPTER XV.

Lord Minto returned to England as he had left it, on board a frigate commanded by his son, Captain George Elliot; but on this occasion accompanied by his younger son John, and the wives and infants of both brothers. All the family had assembled in London to receive him, with the exception of his wife and youngest daughter and daughter-in-law. These awaited him at Minto.

If the letters of 1812 gave us a glimpse of the gloomiest period of England's long struggle with the despotism that had enchained the Continent of Europe, those of 1814 mark the high tide of her triumph. London overflowed with Emperors, Kings, and field-marshals.

These were the heroes of the Harvest-Home, but the sheaves had been gathered by the nations in arms --from the Tyrolese Alps to the ramparts of Saragossa;

> From Moscow, self-devoted in a blaze
> Of dreadful slaughter,

to the heights where German armies paused in their headlong course to gaze upon and hail the free 'exulting' Rhine.

And in English hearts was the proud consciousness,

to which a great Whig statesman [1] has given expression, that 'the constancy, courage, and perseverance of the British people, animating the prostrate nations of the Continent, had at length achieved a triumph over the most formidable combination of military genius, warlike population, conquering armies, and political talent, which ever threatened the independence of our country.'

'Is it not quite glorious to have lived to see this holiday—this festival for all the nations under heaven?' wrote the calm Lord Webb Seymour;[2] 'yet it is humiliating to think that the bar to all this happiness—the bar we have removed—was the ascendancy of *one* baneful mind.[3] This is a sad check to those splendid contemplations which Mr. Stewart and other philosophers would encourage, respecting the influence of general causes upon the progressive improvement of the human race. Mr. Playfair will go to Paris if he finds Lord J. Russell, the Miss Berry's, or any old intimates ready to go with him.'

Another correspondent—George Eden, afterwards Lord Auckland—did go to Paris, and with all the sympathies of Holland House about him, saw nothing so interesting there as Josephine and Hortense. 'Very few of those to whom we talked disguised their admiration for Napoleon; but, with the exception of some of the army, very few would risk their internal

---

[1] Lord Russell.   [2] To Lady Minto, May 19, 1814.
[3] 'He must fall,' wrote Benjamin Constant to Sir James Mackintosh (March 1814)—'he must fall before we can think of anything else; he must fall that we may have time to think of anything else.'

quiet to have him back again. By the bye have you heard the *calembourg*? " Les Anglais nous ont vendu un cochon de dix-huit Louis qui ne vaut pas un Napoléon." His works in roads, buildings, and military establishments are magnificent beyond all idea, and I could not help being indignant at the pains taken to efface all remembrance of his being the author of them.'[1]

Into this scene of splendour and triumph arrived the returning Governor General; but to him and to those who waited for him all other feelings were swallowed up in the joy of reunion—actual, or at hand. What that moment was to them, and what too the days that followed it, their own letters will most fitly tell.

Lord Minto to Lady Minto.

'H.M.S. "Hussar" at sea: May 7, 1814.

'We are all well—off the south of Ireland—hope to land in four days. We fell in with an English frigate this forenoon with which we conversed by telegraphic signals and received the most happy intelligence. " Peace with France—the old kingdom restored," by which we understand the Bourbons restored. We now hear from the Irish boat that the Emperor of the West is sent to Elba—*relegatus ad insulas*. We are all out of our wits, and especially myself, at the thoughts of meeting you all.

---

[1] Lord Auckland to Miss Emma Elliot, who was at Madras with her father, the Rt. Hon. Hugh Elliot, Governor of the Presidency.

'London: May 19.

'I arrived yesterday, and was in a complete whirl of delight for the first two or three hours; and I was caught by the last bell, the sound and meaning of which I had forgot. I am excessively glad that you did not come to town; and the delay in our meeting will be fully compensated by the superior happiness of meeting at home. You may reckon on this day fortnight as the longest period of my stay in London. I was delighted, as you may imagine, with A. M. and Gilbert. Yesterday was indeed one of the very happiest days of my life; but there is one happier still in store, when I shall have you once more in my arms, with the certainty of having no more of those sad absences from which we have so often suffered, and Catan to kiss and to spoil, and Mary and her four upon my knee. It is in short to me, like the events of this *annus mirabilis* to the world, the commencement of a new era of happiness and repose. You will have heard from other quarters, and spare my blushes in repeating, all the compliments that are paid me, by everybody I meet, on my youth and beauty. To the latter I must plead guilty, since they all tell the same story; but of youth there is little left. I have seen crowds of old friends to-day—Glenbervies—Aucklands—Chichesters—Temples—Fred North—Henry Gally Knight—Harrises—Mrs. Robinson—Elliot of Wells—John Frere. I go to Park Place in my way to Scotland.

Lady Melgund to a Friend.

'Minto: May 20, 1814.

'The "Hussar" has arrived, and every soul on board well. They landed at Plymouth on the 14th; would get to London as yesterday or to-day. We shall probably see them in about ten days. We got this joyful news yesterday morning, and we spent such a day! It would have raised the spirit of a Dutchman to see the happiness that reigned at Minto. The news spread through the house like wildfire, everybody was running here and there, not knowing how to show their joy. When I told them to go to the top of the house to cheer, in ten minutes there were about seventy people assembled; I gave them a quantity of guns, and we had volleys and cheering from that time till one o'clock, the local militia colours flying on the house all the time. After the children's dinner we had a grand procession of all the people, with fiddles playing and colours flying, followed by Lady Minto, Gilbert, and me in the little gig, to the Rocks, to fire the cannon, which was done four times with great effect. Then we had cheering, &c. till dinner-time, when the procession returned, and we had a song from one of the workmen, made on the occasion. The moment he heard the news he ran home to make his poem, and it was all ready by two o'clock. In the evening we had dancing, and, as one of the carpenters observed, "the day ended with *the utmost hilarity.*" Lady Minto behaved admirably; she was not overcome with all this joy; but it was a long while before she durst trust herself to speak to me.'

Lady Minto to Lord Minto.

'Thursday, May 19.

'Oh, dear me! I can hardly breathe or speak or think or run about, or sit still, or *believe* that all my cares, all my wishes, and all my anxieties are whisked away in a moment by the most delightful certainty that here you are in our own little island safe and sound; and I cannot say how more than delighted I am, as a secondary feeling, to find that my having remained here proves the decision you wished for. I felt so sure of this that I have been as obstinate as any mule, and positively set my face against the opinions and advice of most of my friends, feeling sure I knew better than they could, all the feelings you must have respecting Minto itself, not to mention the everlasting delight in future years of the sweet recollections that will ever attach to the spot of our reunion. I will not say that I would not at this moment give my ears to be amongst you; but even at this moment, in all the delirium of delight, I know it is best as it is. I *can* be patient, and shall be in a more composed state than is possible just now, when all is flutter, flutter, and not one idea is settled for an instant, and every possible demonstration of joy has been made throughout the house. I was called away here by the sound of firing from the top of the house, and ran upstairs to that beautiful terrace, where I was received with three cheers, and found all the work-people assembled. The day being perfectly divine, I thought I had never seen so beautiful and interesting a scene, the air ringing with joyful sounds, and all nature gay and seeming to partake of my feelings.

Friday.—I have not slept so sound for years as I did last night.

Saturday.— You *really* are in London — only think! Comparatively speaking, I feel as if you were at Hawick or Jedburgh; and all the letters to-day, mad or sober, are full of your youthful looks and beauty, and declare you look younger and fresher than when you left England. I begin to think I did very wrong to stay at home; for I can't say our northern blasts have had the same effect on me.'

Such was the happiness and such the hopes created by Lord Minto's return. Every day brought him letters from his wife, showing that she lived in the thought of their approaching reunion, while with the unselfishness and strong sense of duty which distinguished her, she assured him she would not be miserable, and that he must not hurry away from London till all claims on his attention had been satisfied. Nothing interested her but the preparations for the moment to which all were looking forward; nothing calmed her but an active participation in them.

'I have myself been arranging the rooms, and dragging about the furniture; Gilly, who certainly expects to find you the youngest thing here, has a trap and ball ready for you.'

The poor little Malay boys brought home from Malacca were welcomed at Minto as the first detachment of the home-coming party. Lady Minto shivered for them in their ship's clothing, and at once set about clothing them in flannel. 'Are they my cousins?' asked the little son of the house, and on being told not, 'I am glad of that, as I should rather not have black cousins, but they are, *very* nice.' Then black boys and white went off to the hills together, which the little darkies climbed on all fours, chattering most excitedly in their native lingo.

'May 20, 1814.'[1]

'I breakfasted this morning with Mr. Elphinstone, the Chairman, and it is settled that I am to dine with the Court of Directors at one of their court dinners, without the fussification to both parties of an immense public dinner. The day is not fixed, but it will be very soon, which will be one step towards Minto. I am as perfectly delighted and as perfectly happy as it is possible for me to be till I see you.'

'*May* 24.—I have your letters of Thursday and Saturday, and I am thankful, my dearest love, that your cares are heaved overboard. We have nothing now to do but to be thankful and happy. The period to come will, I trust, be unshadowed by absences, or that they will be very short, and that we shall enjoy the tranquil comforts of content and of mutual love for the rest of

---

[1] Lord Minto to Lady Minto.

our time while the younger generations flourish away in the more lively joys of their period of life.'

'May 27, 1814.

'I meet a very cordial reception from everybody of all descriptions; and general esteem, sincere as it appears to be, is a satisfactory result of public life. My wish is to close it here. Indeed, young and beautiful as I am, I feel that I am not equal to the fatigues, either mental or bodily, of public business in England. My legs improve a little, and I hope to make them younger at Minto; but really young they can never be, of course; and I am not only content to toddle on with you through the rest of my journey, but shall think and find it the best part of our lives. There certainly never were happier parents, and the children who make us so, appear to be rewarded by happiness themselves.'

June 3, the day after the Drawing-room, was fixed for Lord Minto's departure from London; but on May 28 an event occurred which altered his plans, and was big with fate. Lord Auckland, who had gone to rest in perfect health, was found dead in his bed by his daughters when they went to summon him to breakfast. In order to be with his sister in her overwhelming grief, and to follow his brother-in-law to the grave, Lord Minto at once postponed his departure. Unhappily the funeral was arranged to take place at Beckenham—the parish in which Eden Farm, the happy home of the bereaved family, was situated—

and at night. The sad procession by road from London to Beckenham, and the subsequent funeral service, occupied five hours—from half-past seven till half-past twelve, in a cold drizzling rain. Four days later we have the first note of the coming tragedy. A cold, which Lord Minto had complained of before, had been greatly increased by the exposure of that fatal night. He was ordered to stay indoors. On the 8th 'he broke prison to visit Lord Melville, and obtain a nephew's well-earned promotion.' On the 13th he confessed himself so low in strength and spirits that he could not attempt a letter. In proportion to his bodily weakness was the increase of his passionate longing to reach Minto; and his family, having no apprehension of any impending danger, were equally anxious with himself to get him out of town and in the safe keeping of his home. 'With the affectionate kindness which never flagged he resolved to visit Lady Malmesbury at Park Place, although this added at least another day to the length of his journey.' There he made the greatest exertions to conceal his weakness, and his conversation was cheerful and gay; but by this time his eldest son, his constant companion and now tender nurse, was greatly, though still insufficiently, alarmed. A medical man was sent for to attend them on their journey; and from him it was for the first time ascertained that Lord Minto was suffering from an attack of a most alarming disease, which, under the treatment of those days, too frequently proved fatal.

His longing to push on was, however, too strong to be opposed. The journey was proceeded with. 'He has but one wish, to see the person on whom his thoughts are ever fixed;' one anxiety—to reach home. The rest may be guessed. From the first horrid misgiving, when the ground seems to fall away from under one's feet, to the full conviction that there is no help, no hope, no escape from an overwhelming calamity, most of us know the course.

By short stages, Stevenage on the northern road was reached; but in a state of prostration which left no room for hope; and there he quietly sank early in the night on June 21. 'Oh! my poor mother—take care of her—I know you will do all you can,' was the note sent home by his son that night.

How fearful the shock, how profound the grief, may be imagined by any reader of the letters now published; but the degree and the faithfulness of the sorrow with which he was mourned may best be told in a few affecting lines, written by his eldest son very many years after the event, and found by his children at his death. They were obviously intended to find place in the opening chapter of a biography of Lord Minto, which was, however, never proceeded with; for the date proves that the writer's own days were thenceforth but few.

'During the period of an absence of seven years, engaged in laborious and absorbing duties, there was no one day in which the evidence does not exist of the fond affection with which his mind dwelt on the domestic circle from which he was severed, and on the distant prospect of reunion with those he loved. Nor on our side was there a single day in which he was not the constant object of our thoughts, or in which we did not anxiously count the days of our separation. The one great object looked to on either side, as the greatest happiness that could await us, was his return to England, and to the tranquil enjoyment of honourable repose in the home he loved. In order to understand the intense anxiety with which we contemplated this reunion, it would be necessary to have known the feelings with which he was regarded by his family—as the friend, the companion, the playfellow, the guide and example for all ages—feelings in which were combined the warmest familiar affection, with admiration, respect, and veneration.'

Here follows an account of his gratifying reception in London; the splendid success of his government being a subject of general congratulation; and then, after some details of the course of the illness, comes the end: 'Thus at once were dashed those hopes in the moment of their accomplishment, which had been the solace of seven years of painful separation. Any attempt must be vain to describe the overwhelming weight of this blow. The first object of our affection, of our reverence, was lost in the first days of its restoration; the feelings and the mind were subdued and prostrated almost to a condition of insensibility and indifference to all the interests of life. Many, many years elapsed, chequered by other and deep affliction, before it ceased to hang as a dark cloud over our existence; nay, even now, at the distance of nearly forty years, the impressions of that sad time are fresh in my heart. Though grief may have yielded to the hand of time, the fond remembrance of affection still survives in all its warmth.'

When, in process of time, it became the part of another generation to 'open the places that were closed,' and when, upon those who did so, came the desire 'to show the image of a voice and make green the flowers that were withered,' the last year's letters from Minto to India—so full of hope, of joy—were found tied together with a black string, and inscribed 'Poor Fools.' With these was a note with unbroken seal, the last written by Lady Minto to her husband.

INDEX.

ABDULLA, extracts from Autobiography of, p. 269 *sq.*
Abercromby, Sir R., 242 (*note*)
Adair, Mr. 104
Afghanistan, British alliance with, 139 *sq.*; Mountstuart Elphinstone's mission to, 159 *sq*; troubled condition of, 162; French designs upon, 163; the king and nobility of, 169, 170; despatch on affairs of, 170; changed prospects of, *ib.*; anarchy in, 174
Amboyna, 240
Ameer Khan, 191, 192
Auchmuty, Sir Samuel, 285, 292 294, 296, 303
Auckland, Lord, 157, 390

BALLI, Rajah of, 266 *sq.*
Barasut, cadets of, 89
Barlow, Sir George, 1, 2, 23, 24, 25, 28, 32, 59, 107, 111, 144, 206, 209, 211, 212, 213, 214, 215, 216, 217, 218 (*note*), 219, 221, 226, 322
Barrackpore, 27, 28, 31, 334
Batavia, 54, 290; surrendered to the British, 286 *sq*; the Dutch in, 304 *sq.*
Bengal, natives of, 32, 33; banditti in, 185 *sq.*; mutinies in, 201, 202 (*note*)

Bentinck, Lord William, 15, 20, 21, 23, 36, 197, 206, 369
Berar, Rajah of, 191 *sq.*
Bertie, Admiral, 243
Bikaneer, 161
Bombay, mutiny in, 202 (*note*); complaints of the army of, 203
Bonaparte, counter-policy of Indian government, 52 *sq.*; his designs on the East, 54, 56, 100 *sq.*, 103 *sq.*, 163 (*note*); on treaties of peace, 342 (*note*). See Minto.
Bourbon, Isle of, 240, 243, 244, 247 *sq.*
'Brown Toast Club,' 234
Broughton, Commodore, 280 *sqq.*
Bruce, Mr., 251, 256
Buchanan, Rev. C., 72; his memorial to the Court of Directors, 73 *sq.*; charges against Lord Minto, 74 *sq.*; alleged suppression of his Sermons, 76 (*note*). See Missionaries
Bundelcund, 58 (*note*), 59 *sq.*, 193; reduction of, 60
Burke, Edmund, Lord Minto's affection for, 6; his sympathy for India, 6, 7; speech on the India Bill of 1783, 7; letter to Sir Gilbert Elliot, 9
Burke, Mrs. 10
Byron, Lord, described by Lady Minto, 330

INDEX.

CAB

CABUL, Kingdom of, 143 *sq.*; British mission to, 147 *sq.*, 159 *sq.*, 169; the King of, 162, 169 *sq.*, 172, 175. See Afghanistan. Shah Soojah.
Caffres, an intelligent chief, 170 (*note*)
Calcutta, society in, 28; Lord Minto's popularity, 348 *sq.*; address of British residents to Lord Minto, 379 *sq.*
Calcutta Review cited, 74; on Lord Minto, 379 *sq.*
Caledon, Lord, 105
Camden, Lord, 34
Canning, Mr., 34, 45, 46, 182, 239, 138 (*note*)
Capetown, French refugees in, 14
Carey, Dr. William, 64 *sq.*, 68, 72, 75
Carnatic, Nabob of the, 20 *sq.*; his present to Lord Minto, *ib.*
Caroline, Princess of Wales, 44, 179 (*note*), 180 (*note*)
Carrack, Island of, proposed occupation of, 123 *sq.*, 127 *sq.*, 131
Casamaijor, Mr. J. H., 228
Casamaijor, Miss. A., 228
Caste, marks of, 18
Castlereagh, Lord, 34, 241
Catalani, Mme., 234 *sq.*
Catholic claims, 33 (*note*), 34, 35 (*note*), 41, 45, 342
Chillinching, 284 *sq.*
Choultry plain, the, 16
Cicero, Lord Minto's partiality for, 300; passage from the 'Somnium Scipionis,' *ib.*; from the 'De Finibus,' 301 (*note*); cited, 334, 337
Clerks, the, of Eldin, 234
Clive, Lord, 201, 218 (*note*)
Close, Colonel (Sir Barry) 50 (*note*), 51 *sq.*, 52, 192, 215, 216
Cockburn, H., 234
Cole, Captain, 276
Colebrooke, Mr., 210
Constant, Benjamin, cited, 383 (*note*)

EDG

Cornelis, 288, 289; storming of, 291
Cornwallis, Lord, death of, 1, 2; his Indian system of judicature, 363 (*note*)
Coulaincourt M., 104
Councils, Indian, 27
Court of Directors, in collision with the Cabinet, 3; despatch on religious toleration in India, 63 *sq.*; appoint an envoy to Persia, 99; on Lord Minto's military policy, 194, 198, 200; instructions concerning Java, 306 *sq.*; silence on Lord Minto's measures, 318 *sq.*, 323 *sq.* See India. Minto, Lord.
Cradock, Sir John, 19, 199 *sq.*, 206, 369
Crewe, Lady, letter to Lord Minto, 179 (*note*); on the affairs of Spain, 181

DACOITS, in Bengal, 185 *sq.*
D'Aendels, Marshal, 283, 302 *sq*
Davy, Lady, 233
Deccan, the wild tribes of, 191
Deffand, Mme. du, *Correspondence* of, 355 *sq.*
Drury, Admiral, 250, 274, 280 (*note*)
Dugald Stewart, 233
Duncan, J., Governor of Bombay, 203
Dundas, Right Hon. R., 34, 108 (*note*), 246, 247, 362
Dutch, the, in Batavia, 304 *sq.*

EAST India Company. See Court of Directors. Minto, Lord, India
Eden, Miss, her letters from *Up the Country* cited, 157
Eden, Mr. G. (afterwards Lord Auckland), 383 *sq.*
Edgell, Captain, 276, 278

INDEX.

EDI

Edinburgh, the winter of 1809-10 in, 233 *sqq.*
Edmonstone, Mr., 23, 65, 69, 116, 137
Egypt, British troops from India in, 242 (*note*)
Eldon, Lord, 34, 44, 45
Elliot, Sir Gilbert. See Minto, Lord
Elliot, Hon. Gilbert (2nd Earl of Minto) 12 (*note*), 85. 86, 297, 300, 342: on the death of his father, 392
Elliot, Hon. George, 13, 231, 249, 263, 268, 277, 281, 283
Elliot, Hon. John, 15 (*note*), 16, 17, 228, 251, 253
Elliot, Right Hon. Hugh, 384 (*note*)
Elliot, Right Hon. W., 37, 48, 317
Elliot, Mr., of Wells, letter to, from Lord Minto, 353 *sq.*
Elliot, Miss A. M., letters to her father, 137 (*note*), 232 *sq.*, 335 (*note*)
Elphinstone, Mountstuart, 129; sent as envoy to Afghanistan, 159 *sq.*; difficulties of his mission, 160; line of march, 161 *sq.*; letters to Governor-General, 162 *sq.*; asks for increased powers, 163 *sq.*; delays, 165; progress to Peshawur, 166; arrival at his destination, 168; reception, 169; interviews with king and nobles, 169, 170 *sq.*; despatches to and from Indian Government, *ib.*; signs a treaty, 172 *sq.*; treaty ratified at Calcutta, 175; withdrawal of mission, *ib.*; the treaty, 175 (*note*); his *History of Cabul,* 176. See Cabul. Shah Soojah.
England, Administration of the 'Talents,' 1; the Duke of Portland's Cabinet, 34; Lord Grenville on home politics, 34 *sqq.*; state of parties in, 45; Lady Malmesbury on the Duke of

GWI

Portland's Administration, 43 *sq.*, 46; diplomatic relations with Persia, 138; foreign acquisitions of, 239 *sq.*; state of in 1811-12, 326 *sqq.*; triumphs in 1814, 382 *sqq.* See Minto.
Europe, state of, after the Peace of Tilsit, 97

FARQUHAR, Mr., 248
Fisher, Dr., 237
Fitzharris, Lord, 45
Fitzherbert, Mrs., 45
Fort St. George. See Madras.
Fort William, College of, 371 *sq.*
Fox, Mr., 3, 4, 8, 46
Fox, Miss, 181
France, ascendancy of, 97 *sq.*; capture of British Indiamen, 242; expeditions against the Eastern settlements of, 243 *sq.*, 318 *sqq.*
France, Isle of. See Mauritius.
Frere, Mr., 179 (*note*)

GEORGE III., dismisses his Ministry, 34; new Cabinet, *ib.*
Gillespie, Colonel, 289, 296
Goa, 239
Gowdie, General, 226
Greig, Admiral, 278 *sq.*, 279
Grenville, Lord, 37, 43, 44, 45, 46, 99, 100, 103, 241; his approval of Lord Wellesley's administration of India, 3; nominates Lord Minto to Governor-Generalship, 4; conferences with the new Viceroy, 5; fall of his Administration, 33, 34; letters to and from Lord Minto, 34 *sq.*, 41 *sq.*, 359; his hostility to the Duke of Portland's Cabinet, 35
Grenville, Lady, 45
Grey, Lord, 241
Gwillin, Sir H., 23

INDEX.

HAR

HARIANA, 193
Hawkesbury, Lord, 34
Hewitt, General (Commander-in-Chief of India), 23, 114 *sq.*, 122, 147 *sq.*, 210, 223, 226
Holland, Lord, letter from, to Lord Minto, 326
Hope, Mr., 251, 292 *sq.*
Howick, Lord, 44
Huguenots, at Capetown, 14
Hyder Ali, 152

IMPEY, Sir Elijah, 9
India, successive Governors-General of, 1 *sq.*; action of the Cabinet in relation to, 3; Burke's speech on the Bill of 1783, 7; native sovereigns, 8; Lord Minto's first impressions of, 16 *sq.*; the Gentoos of Madras, 17 *sq.*; Caste, 18, 19; Pariahs, 19; results of Caste, *ib.*; Nabob of the Carnatic, 20 *sq.*; prickly heat, 23; famine in, 22; condition of, on arrival of Lord Minto, 25; routine of government, 26; climate, 28; financial prospects of, 53, 56 *sq.*, 247, 353 *sqq.*; French designs on, 54 *sq.*, 56, 100 *sq.*, 163 (*note*); British tenure of, 55; disaffection among the Mohamedans, 61 *sq*; religious toleration proclaimed, 63 *sq.*; Christian missionaries in, 64 *sq.*; conflict of the Government and the missionaries, 65 *sq.*; an ecclesiastical hierarchy demanded for, 73; licensed missionaries, 81, 82; Government accused of persecution, 82; inconveniences of life in, 83 *sq.*; prodigality of European residents, 92; alternations of climate, 94; differences of religion in, 95; apprehended French invasion of, 103; letters of Lord Minto on defence of, 105 *sqq.*; disposition of the

JAV

Native States, 106 *sq.*; Lord Minto on the powers of the Governors-General of, 135 *sq.*; alliance with the States of the North-West, 141 *sq.*; missions to Lahore and Cabul, 147 *sq.*; relations with Runjeet Singh, 154 *sq.*; Mountstuart Elphinstone's mission to Afghanistan, 159 *sq.*; results of Lord Minto's scheme for defence of, 176; news of British victory in Spain, 179 *sq.*; Lord Minto on the possibility of a French invasion of, 182; the rains in, 183; the natives, 184; dacoity in, 185 *sqq.*; mutinies in, 201 (*note*); strife between the military and civil authorities, 201, 208; Lord Minto's foreign policy, 239 *sq.*; expeditions sent from, 240 *sq.*; troops despatched to Egypt from, 242 (*note*); finances of, 247, 354; indifference of Home Government to, 297 *sq.*, 318 *sqq.*, 323 *sqq.*; last years of Lord Minto's rule, 331 *sq.*; Viceroy's account of his civil administration of, 353 *sqq.*; the Company's monopoly, 362 *sq.*; balance of power among Native States, 365 *sq.*; administration of justice, 369; obstacles to the improvement of, *ib.*; Native officers, 370; Lord Minto's Minute on education in, 375 *sq.*; address to the Viceroy from the British residents in Calcutta, 379 *sq.* See Minto
Ireland, the Catholics of, 35 (*note*)

JANSSENS, General, 283, 287, 288, 291, 294, 302
Java, British expedition to, 240, 249 *sq.*, 269 *sq.*, 284 *sq.*, 287 *sq.*, 294; arrival of French troops in, 281; surrender of Batavia, 286; action at Weltevreeden,

288; storming of Cornelis by the British, 291 *sq.*; made a British dependancy, 296; the Dutch in, 304 *sq.* 310; instructions concerning, from Court of Directors, 306 *sq.*; Lord Minto's settlement of, 310 *sq.*; slavery in, 312; Lord Minto's care for, 316 *sq.* See Minto
Jeffrey, Mr., 232 *sq.*, 234
Jones, Sir Harford, envoy to the court of Persia, 99 *sq.*, 108, 110 *sq.*, 113, 126 *sqq.*, 129 *sq.*; Lord Minto on his diplomatic powers, 132 *sqq.*; his treaty with Persia, 137, 139; disavowed by Lord Minto, 138. See Persia. Malcolm. Minto
Jumelle, General, 291
Junot, Marshal, 179, 181

KAYE, Sir John, his *Life* and *Correspondence* of Sir John Malcolm cited, 121 (*note*), 216 (*note*), 350; *Correspondence of Lord Metcalfe* cited, 151 (*note*)
Keating, Lieutenant-Colonel, 243 *sq.*
Khyberees, the, 168, 174
Kohat, 166, 167

LAHORE, Government of. See Runjeet Singh
Lake, Lord, 58, 98
Lanfrey, M., his *Histoire de Napoléon I.* cited, 104 (*note*)
Lauderdale, Lord, appointed Governor-General of India, 3; resigns, 4
Leyden, Dr., 67 *sq.*, 251, 253 *sq.*, 255 (*note*), 278, 295, 339, 342
London, condition and society in, in 1812, 328 *sqq.*
Lumsden, Mr., 23, 210

MACAO, 240
Macartney, Lord, 202 (*note*)
Machery, Rajah of, 185 (*note*)
Mackintosh, Sir J., 126, 218, 219, 330
Macleod, Colonel M., 89 *sq.*
Madras, Government of and Vellore mutiny, 15 (*note*); Lord Minto's impressions of, 16 *sqq.*; affairs of, 197 *sq.*; mutiny in the army, 202 (*note*), 205 *sqq.*; grievances of officers, 206 *sqq.*; conflict of civil and military authorities, 208; memorial of officers, 212 *sqq.*; Lord Minto's answer to the memorial, 213 *sq.*; progress of insubordination, 215 *sq.*; energetic action of Sir G. Barlow, 217; effect of the Viceroy's letter, 219; General order to the army, 220; termination of the revolt, 221; Lord Minto on the revival of discipline, 223 *sq.*; conflicting opinions on the mutiny, 227, 230, 321. See Minto. Barlow
Madrassees, the, 17, 18 *sqq.*
Mahommed Shah, 173, 174
Malacca, 260 *sq.*; slavery in, 265 *sq.*; British expedition at, 269 *sq.*; debtors' prison in, 273
Malcolm, Colonel (Sir John), 50 (*note*), 99, 103, 112, 113, 128, 129, 137, 152, 215, 216, 218, 219; sent as envoy to Persia, 108 *sq.*; instructions from the Indian Government, 110 *sq.*; account of his mission to Persia, 114 *sq.*; failure of his embassy, 120 *sq.*; his scheme for the defence of India, 123 *sq.*; made brigadier-general, 126 (*note*); again deputed to Persia, 139; his *History of Persia* and *Sketches in Persia*, 176; his *History of India*, 115 (*note*); his Diary quoted, 350. See Persia. Jones, Sir Harford. Minto, Lord

MAL

Malmesbury, Lady, letters to Lord Minto, 11, 12, 43 *sq.*, 46, 181, 282 (*note*); to Lady Minto, 43; to her sister, 44, 45; on the death of Mr. Windham, 236
Malmesbury, Lord, 213
Maria Louisa, empress, 282
Marshman, Mr., 68, 72; his *History of India* cited, 206, 217
Masulipatam, military revolt at, 216, 219, 222
Mauritius, 240, 242 (*note*), 318, 320; British expedition sent against, 244 *sq.*; surrender of, 248
McDowell, General, 207 *sq.*
Melgund, Lady, 386
Melgund, Lord, 167, 176 (*note*)
Menou, General, 100
Metcalfe, Lord, 97 *sq.*, 149 *sq.*; sent as envoy to Runjeet Singh, 151; his services and instructions, *ib.*; proceeds on his mission, 152; progress of negotiations, 152; conclusion of treaty, 156 *sq.*; his relations to Lord Minto, 158. See Runjeet Singh
Milman, Dean, cited, 66, 67
Milton, Lord, 47
Minto, Lord (Sir Gilbert Elliot), assumes the government of India 1; President of the Board of Control, *ib.*; letters to Sir G Barlow and Lord William Bentinck, 3, 4, 5; on Lord Lauderdale's appointment, 4; his Indian policy and character, 5; early intimacy with Burke, 6; designated Parliamentary Director, 8; speech at trial of Warren Hastings, 9; letter from Burke, *ib.*; moves the impeachment of Sir Elijah Impey, *ib.*; his visit to Beaconsfield, 10; letters from Lord and Lady Malmesbury, 11; letters to his wife, 12, 24, 91 *sq.*, 93 *sq.*, 185 *sq.*, 225, 229 *sq.*, 384; voyage to India, 13; at Madeira, *ib.*; log

MIN

on board the 'Modeste,' 14; at Capetown, 14, 15; at Madras, 15; his first impressions of India, 16 *sqq.*; reception by the Nabob of the Carnatic, 20 *sq.*; description of an Indian famine, 22; arrives at Calcutta, 23; letter to his son, 24 *sq.*; condition of India, 25; routine of business, 26 *sq.*; Councils, 27; absence of opposition to his government, 28; his mode of life and *entourage*, 29 *sq.*, 87; his conditional resignation, 37; on the office of Governor-General, 38 *sq.*; confirmed by the new Ministry, 39; letter to Lord Grenville, 39 *sqq.*; his reputation in India, 49; letter to Colonel Barry Close, 51 *sq.*; to Sir E. Pellew, 52 *sq.*; correspondence on Indian and Persian affairs. 53 *sq.*; on the state of Bundelcund, 59 *sq.*; causes of Indian sedition, 62; dispute with the missionaries, 65 *sq.*, 67 *sq.*, 70 *sq.*, liberality to the missionaries 71; charges against him, 74 *sq.*; on the Serampore press, 78 *sq.*; letters to and from home, 84; letter to Colonel Macleod, 99 *sq.*; on French designs on India, 100 *sq.*; on the defence of India, 105 *sq.*, 109 *sq.*, 123 *sq.*; letter to Right Hon. R. Dundas, 108; to Colonel Malcolm, 113; to General Hewitt, 114 *sq.*, 122; memorandum to Colonel Malcolm, 116 *sq.*; on Sir Harford Jones's mission to Persia, 128, 132 *sq.*; ratifies treaty with Persia, 138, 139; letter to Board of Control, 142; on intervention in the affairs of Native States, 146; on the missions to Lahore and Peshawur, 147 *sq.*; relations with Runjeet Singh, 154 *sq.*; opinion of Mr. Metcalfe, 158; change

MIN

in the policy of his government, 165; instructions to Mr. Elphinstone, *ib.*; despatch on the affairs of Afghanistan, 170; private despatch from Mr. Elphinstone, 172 *sq.*; results of his scheme for defence of India, 176; receives news of the battle of Vimiero, 180; on Caroline, Princess of Wales, 180 (*note*); on the possibility of French invasion of India, 182; his administration during the years 1808-9, 184 *sq.*; on the campaign against Ameer Khan, 193 *sq.*; sends an expedition to the Persian Gulf, 195; on the affairs of Madras, 197 *sq.*; on the exclusion of the Commanders-in-Chief from seats in Council, 199 *sq.*; on the subordination of the military to the civil power, 201: on the complaints of the Bombay army, 203 *sqq.*; on the military disturbances in Madras, 207 *sq.*; on the conflict of authorities in Madras, 209 *sq.*; his reply to the memorial of the Madras officers, 213; goes to Madras, 219; his stay at Fort St. George, 220, 221, 228; despatches and letters on the Madras mutiny, 222 *sq.*; returns to Calcutta, 231; his daughters-in-law, *ib.*; letter to his daughter, 235; receives news of Mr. Windham's death, 236 *sq.*; his foreign policy, 239 *sq.*; plans for the acquisition of the French settlements, 241 *sq.*; expeditions for the purpose, 243 *sq.*; expedition to Java, 249 *sq.*; reasons for going to Java, 250; his suite, 251; occupations during his voyage thither in the 'Modeste,' 252 *sq.*; arrives at Penang, 256; his description of Malacca, 260 *sq.*; receives at present of slaves, 267 *sq.*;

MIR

correspondence on the Java expedition, 273 *sqq.*, 284 *sqq.*, 285; storming of Cornelis and scenes after the battle, 291 *sq.*; on his relations with the Home Government, 297 *sq.*; the 'Minto Vision,' 301; on the annexation of Java, 307 *sqq.*; settlement of the island, 310 *sq.*; his care for Java, 316 *sq.*; Home Government and his foreign policy, 318 *sqq.*; returns to Calcutta, 318, 331; correspondence from Calcutta, 318 *sq.*; letter from his daughter, 323 *sqq.*; last years of his Viceroyalty, 331 *sqq.*: longing for home, 332, 346; his Malay slaves, 334 *sq.*, 389; recognition of his services, 339; recalled, 343, 348; created Viscount Melgund and Earl of Minto, 344; correspondence on Lord Moira's appointment, 344 *sqq.*; his popularity in Calcutta 348; his social circle at Government House, 349; Sir John Malcolm's anecdote of him, 350; bachelors' ball given to him in Calcutta, 351; his internal policy, 352 *sqq.*; correspondence on his civil administration of India, 353 *sqq.*; addresses to the students of the College of Fort William, 370 *sq.*; minute on education, 375 *sq.*; his return and arrival in England, 382, 385; correspondence with Lady Minto after his return, 385 *sqq.*; his reception in London, 390; falls ill, 391; his journey northward, 392; and death, *ib.* See India.

Minto, Lady, descended from a Huguenot family, 15; letters to her husband, 183, 386 *sqq.*, 391: on the state of England, social and political, in 1812, 327 *sqq.* See Minto, Lord

Mir Hashan Khan, 176 (*note*)

MIS

Missionaries in India, 63 *sq.*, 81 : action of the Government regarding, 65 *sq.* ; interviews with Lord Minto, 68 ; their partisans in England, 70. See Serampore.
'Modeste' frigate, voyage of, to India, 13, 14, 15 ; voyage to Java, 252 *sq.*
Mohamedans, 76. See India
Moira, Lord, 331 ; appointed Lord Minto's successor, 343
Moluccas, the, 240
Mooltan, 161
Morier, Mr., 137
Munro, Colonel, 206 *sq.*
Murray, J., 233
Mutinies in India, 201 (*note*). See Madras. Vellore.

N APIER, Sir W., his *History of the Peninsular War* quoted by a Caffre chief, 170 (*note*)
Napoleon I. See Bonaparte
Nautches, 22, 92
Ness, Miss, 231
North-West, British alliances with the States of the, 141 *sqq.*; rivalries of the States of the, *ib.* See Cabul. Runjeet Singh
Nugent, Lord, his *Portugal,* 341

O ODYPORE, beautiful daughter of the Rajah of, 191 (*note*)
Ool Moolk, Ameer, 173 *sq.*
Ophir, Mount, 262
Ouseley, Sir Gore, 138 (*note*), 139

P ALMERSTON, Lord, 45, 331
Palmerston, Lady, 184
Panambangan, Island of, 277 *sqq.*
Pariahs, 19
Parry, Mr., 78, 80, 81
Pasley, Captain, 114 *sq.*, 128
Pellew, Sir E. (Lord Exmouth), 23, 52

RUN

Penang, Lord Minto's arrival at, and account of, 257 *sq.*
Percival, Mr., 34, 44, 326, 328
Persia, French intrigues in, 51 *sq.*, 54 *sq.*, 98 *sq.*, 100 *sq.*, 120, 121 *sq.*; British mission to, 56, 99, 108 *sq.*, 114 *sq.*, 130 *sqq.*, 131 ; an ambassador sent from the Shah to London, 137 (*note*); letter from Shah to Lord Minto, 137 ; treaty, 138 (*note*), 175. See Jones, Sir Harford. Malcolm. Minto.
Persian Gulf, expedition against brigands of the, 195
Peshawur, British mission at, 161 ; banditti of, *ib.*; withdrawal of mission from, 175
Petrie, Miss, 349 (*note*)
Phillips, Mr., 256
Pigot, Lord, 202 (*note*)
Pindarries, the, 191, 195
Playfair, Mr., 233, 383
Pontiana, Rajah of, 268, 281 (*note*)
Port St. Paul, capture of, 244
Portland, Duke of, 34
Pottinger, Sir H., 176
Press, Indian missionary, 64 *sqq.* 71, 72. See Missionaries. Serampore
Prickly heat, the, 23
Prince of Wales's Island, Recorder of, 359
Punjaub frontier force, 167 (*note*). See Cabul. Runjeet Singh. Afghanistan
Punkahs, 95

R AFFLES, Sir S., 251, 264, 268, 296, 307, 310, 316, 317
Rewa, Rajah of, 185 (*note*)
Robison, Captain, 251, 288, 291
Rodriguez, Island of, 243
Rowley, Commodore, 243
Runjeet Singh, 143, 144, 180 ; ambitious designs of, 145 ; proposed mission to, 147 *sq.*; his reception of Lord Metcalfe's em-

bassy 152; progress of negotiations with, 152 *sq*; treaty concluded with, 156 *sq*., 175; his conquests, 157; his reception by the British, and death, *ib*; his jealousy of the embassy to Afghanistan, 160 See. Metcalfe.

Russell, Lord, on the humiliation of Bonaparte, 383

SALAMANCA, victory of, 342
Sayer, Captain, 282
Scinde, French and Persian intrigues in, 177 *sq*.; British treaty with, 178
Scott, Sir William, 179 (*note*)
Scott, Sir Walter, his *Lady of the Lake*, 232
Sebastiani, M., 104
Seneca, quotation from, 335
Sepoys, discipline of, 368. See Minto.
Serampore press and missionaries, 32, 64 *sq*., 70, 71, 72, 78, 80, 81
Seringapatam, military revolt at, 216, 222
Seton, Mr., 251, 259
Seton, Captain, his engagements with the Ameer of Scinde repudiated, 177 *sq*.
Seymour, Lord Webb, 233, 383
Shah Soojah, British mission to, 152 *sq*., 162, 169, 170; treaty with, 172 *sq*., 175 (*note*); turn in affairs of, 172; his defeat and exile, 175. See Cabul. Afghanistan, Elphinstone
Sikhs, the, 143, 144
Slavery in Malacca, 265 *sq*.; in Java, 312
 ith, Mr. Bobus, 88 (*note*)
Smith, Mr. H., envoy in Scinde, 177

Spain, affairs of, 179 *sq*.
Spice Islands, 240
Stopford, Admiral, 282, 287
Stuart, Major-General, 202 (*note*)

'TALENTS,' Ministry of the, 1, 3, 8, 33. See Whigs
Talleyrand, on non-intervention, 194
Tatties, 94
Taylor, Colonel, 251, 289, 349 (*note*); citation from his Journal, 368
Teignmouth, Lord, 201
Teviotdale, the men of, 342 (*note*)
Theatricals at sea, 279 *sq*.
Thomson, Mr., 234, 269
Tilsit, Peace of, 97, 103 *sq*.
Tippoo Sultan, 242 (*note*)

VELLORE, mutiny of, 15 (*note*), 62, 197 *sq*.
Vimiero, battle of, 179

WALES, Prince of, 44. See Caroline, Princess of Wales
Ward, Rev. Mr., 81
Warren Hastings, trial of, 9
Wellesley, Lord, 2, 3, 98, 151, 183, 194, 202, 241, 242, 371
Wellesley, Sir Arthur, 99, 103, 179 *sq*., 180, 181
Weltevreeden, battle at, 288 *sq*.
Whigs, the, 1, 33, 43, 46, 47 *sq*., 323
Whitbread, Mr., 182
Widows, burning of, in India, 96
Wilson, Mr. G., on Lord Minto's administration, 347 *sq*.
Windham, Mr., 179 (*note*), 180 (*note*), 236, 237, 333

39 PATERNOSTER ROW, E.C.
LONDON, *July* 1879.

GENERAL LIST OF WORKS

PUBLISHED BY

MESSRS. LONGMANS, GREEN & CO

HISTORY, POLITICS, HISTORICAL MEMOIRS, &c.

A History of England from the Conclusion of the Great War in 1815. By SPENCER WALPOLE, Author of 'Life of the Rt. Hon. Spencer Perceval.' VOLS. I. & II. 8vo. 36s.

History of England in the 18th Century. By W. E. H. LECKY, M.A. VOLS. I. & II. 1700-1760. 2 vols. 8vo. 36s.

The History of England from the Accession of James II. By the Right Hon. Lord MACAULAY.
STUDENT'S EDITION, 2 vols. cr. 8vo. 12s.
PEOPLE'S EDITION, 4 vols. cr. 8vo. 16s.
CABINET EDITION, 8 vols. post 8vo. 48s.
LIBRARY EDITION, 5 vols. 8vo. £4.

Critical and Historical Essays contributed to the Edinburgh Review. By the Right Hon. Lord MACAULAY.
CHEAP EDITION, crown 8vo. 3s. 6d.
STUDENT'S EDITION, crown 8vo. 6s.
PEOPLE'S EDITION, 2 vols. crown 8vo. 8s.
CABINET EDITION, 4 vols. 24s.
LIBRARY EDITION, 3 vols. 8vo. 36s.

Lord Macaulay's Works. Complete and uniform Library Edition. Edited by his Sister, Lady TREVELYAN. 8 vols. 8vo. with Portrait £5. 5s.

The History of England from the Fall of Wolsey to the Defeat of the Spanish Armada. By J. A. FROUDE, M.A.
CABINET EDITION, 12 vols. cr. 8vo. £3. 12s.
LIBRARY EDITION, 12 vols. 8vo. £8. 18s.

The English in Ireland in the Eighteenth Century. By J. A. FROUDE, M.A. 3 vols. 8vo. £2. 8s.

Journal of the Reigns of King George IV. and King William IV. By the late C. C. F. GREVILLE, Esq. Edited by H. REEVE, Esq. Fifth Edition. 3 vols. 8vo. price 36s.

The Life of Napoleon III. derived from State Records Unpublished Family Correspondence, and Personal Testimony. By BLANCHARD JERROLD. In Four Volumes, 8vo. with numerous Portraits and Facsimiles. VOLS. I. to III. price 18s. each.

The Constitutional History of England since the Accession of George III. 1760-1870. By Sir THOMAS ERSKINE MAY, K.C.B. D.C.L. Fifth Edition. 3 vols. crown 8vo. 18s.

Democracy in Europe; a History. By Sir THOMAS ERSKINE MAY, K.C.B. D.C.L. 2 vols. 8vo. 32s.

Introductory Lectures on Modern History delivered in 1841 and 1842. By the late Rev. T. ARNOLD, D.D. 8vo. price 7s. 6d.

On Parliamentary Government in England; its Origin, Development, and Practical Operation. By ALPHEUS TODD. 2 vols. 8vo. price £1. 17s.

History of Civilisation in England and France, Spain and Scotland. By HENRY THOMAS BUCKLE. 3 vols. crown 8vo. 24s.

Lectures on the History of England from the Earliest Times to the Death of King Edward II. By W. LONGMAN, F.S.A. Maps and Illustrations. 8vo. 15s.

History of the Life & Times of Edward III. By W. LONGMAN, F.S.A. With 9 Maps, 8 Plates, and 16 Woodcuts. 2 vols. 8vo. 28s.

History of the Life and Reign of Richard III. To which is added the Story of PERKIN WARBECK, from Original Documents. By JAMES GAIRDNER. With Portrait and Map. Second Edition. Crown 8vo. 10s. 6d.

Memoirs of the Civil War in Wales and the Marches, 1642-1649. By JOHN ROLAND PHILLIPS, of Lincoln's Inn, Barrister-at-Law. Second Edition, in One Volume. 8vo. 16s.

The Life of Simon de Montfort, Earl of Leicester, with special reference to the Parliamentary History of his time. By G. W. PROTHERO. Crown 8vo. Maps, 9s.

History of England under the Duke of Buckingham and Charles I. 1624-1628. By S. R. GARDINER. 2 vols. 8vo. Maps, 24s.

The Personal Government of Charles I. from the Death of Buckingham to the Declaration in favour of Ship Money, 1628-1637. By S. R. GARDINER. 2 vols. 8vo. 24s.

Popular History of France, from the Earliest Times to the Death of Louis XIV. By ELIZABETH M. SEWELL. With 8 Maps. Crown 8vo. 7s. 6d.

The Famine Campaign in Southern India, (Madras, Bombay, and Mysore,) in 1876-78. By WILLIAM DIGBY, Secretary of the Madras Famine Committee. With Maps and many Illustrations. 2 vols. 8vo. 32s.

A Student's Manual of the History of India from the Earliest Period to the Present. By Col. MEADOWS TAYLOR, M.R.A.S. Third Thousand. Crown 8vo. Maps, 7s. 6d.

Indian Polity; a View of the System of Administration in India. By Lieut.-Col. G. CHESNEY. 8vo. 21s.

Waterloo Lectures; a Study of the Campaign of 1815. By Colonel C. C. CHESNEY, R.E. 8vo. 10s. 6d.

The Oxford Reformers—John Colet, Erasmus, and Thomas More; a History of their Fellow-Work. By F. SEEBOHM. 8vo. 14s.

General History of Rome from B.C. 753 to A.D. 476. By Dean MERIVALE, D.D. Crown 8vo. Maps, price 7s. 6d.

The Fall of the Roman Republic; a Short History of the Last Century of the Commonwealth. By Dean MERIVALE, D.D. 12mo. 7s. 6d.

Carthage and the Carthaginians. By R. BOSWORTH SMITH, M.A. Second Edition. Maps, Plans, &c. Crown 8vo. 10s. 6d.

History of the Romans under the Empire. By Dean MERIVALE, D.D. 8 vols. post 8vo. 48s.

The History of Rome. By WILHELM IHNE. VOLS. I. to III. 8vo. price 45s.

The Sixth Oriental Monarchy; or, the Geography, History, and Antiquities of Parthia. By G. RAWLINSON, M.A. With Maps and Illustrations. 8vo. 16s.

The Seventh Great Oriental Monarchy; or, a History of the Sassanians. By G. RAWLINSON, M.A. With Map and 95 Illustrations. 8vo. 28s.

The History of European Morals from Augustus to Charlemagne. By W. E. H. LECKY, M.A. 2 vols. crown 8vo. 16s.

History of the Rise and Influence of the Spirit of Rationalism in Europe. By W. E. H. LECKY, M.A. 2 vols. crown 8vo. 16s.

The History of Philosophy, from Thales to Comte. By GEORGE HENRY LEWES. Fourth Edition. 2 vols. 8vo. 32s.

Zeller's Stoics, Epicureans, and Sceptics. Translated by the Rev. O. J. REICHEL, M.A. Cr. 8vo. 14s.

Zeller's Socrates & the Socratic Schools. Translated by the Rev. O. J. REICHEL, M.A. Second Edition. Crown 8vo. 10s. 6d.

Zeller's Plato & the Older Academy. Translated by S. FRANCES ALLEYNE and ALFRED GOODWIN, B.A. Crown 8vo. 18s.

Epochs of Modern History. Edited by C. COLBECK, M.A.
Church's Beginning of the Middle Ages, 2s. 6d.
Cox's Crusades, 2s. 6d.
Creighton's Age of Elizabeth, 2s. 6d.
Gairdner's Houses of Lancaster and York, 2s. 6d.
Gardiner's Puritan Revolution, 2s. 6d.
——— Thirty Years' War, 2s. 6d.
Hale's Fall of the Stuarts, 2s. 6d.
Johnson's Normans in Europe, 2s. 6d.
Ludlow's War of American Independence, 2s. 6d.
Morris's Age of Anne, 2s. 6d.
Seebohm's Protestant Revolution, price 2s. 6d.
Stubbs's Early Plantagenets, 2s. 6d.
Warburton's Edward III. 2s. 6d.

Epochs of Ancient History. Edited by the Rev. Sir G. W. COX, Bart. M.A. & C. SANKEY, M.A.
Beesly's Gracchi, Marius & Sulla, 2s. 6d.
Capes's Age of the Antonines, 2s. 6d.
——— Early Roman Empire, 2s. 6d.
Cox's Athenian Empire, 2s. 6d.
——— Greeks & Persians, 2s. 6d.
Curteis's Macedonian Empire, 2s. 6d.
Ihne's Rome to its Capture by the Gauls, 2s. 6d.
Merivale's Roman Triumvirates, 2s. 6d.
Sankey's Spartan & Theban Supremacies, 2s. 6d.

Epochs of English History. Edited by the Rev. MANDELL CREIGHTON, M.A. Fcp. 8vo. 5s.
Browning's Modern England, 1820-1874, 9d.
Cordery's Struggle against Absolute Monarchy, 1603-1688, 9d.
Creighton's (Mrs.) England a Continental Power, 1066-1216, 9d.
Creighton's (Rev. M.) Tudors and the Reformation, 1485-1603, 9d.
Rowley's Rise of the People, 1215-1485, 9d.
Rowley's Settlement of the Constitution, 1688-1778, 9d.
Tancock's England during the American & European Wars, 1778-1820, 9d.
York-Powell's Early England to the Conquest, 1s.

Creighton's Shilling History of England, introductory to the above. Fcp. 8vo. 1s.

The Student's Manual of Modern History; the Rise and Progress of the Principal European Nations. By W. COOKE TAYLOR, LL.D. Crown 8vo. 7s. 6d.

The Student's Manual of Ancient History; the Political History, Geography and Social State of the Principal Nations of Antiquity. By W. COOKE TAYLOR LL.D. Cr. 8vo. 7s. 6d.

BIOGRAPHICAL WORKS.

Memoirs of the Life of Anna Jameson, Author of 'Sacred and Legendary Art' &c. By her Niece, GERARDINE MACPHERSON. 8vo. with Portrait, price 12s. 6d.

Memorials of Charlotte Williams-Wynn. Edited by her Sister. Crown 8vo. with Portrait, price 10s. 6d.

The Life and Letters of Lord Macaulay. By his Nephew, G. OTTO TREVELYAN, M.P.

CABINET EDITION, 2 vols. crown 8vo. 12s.
LIBRARY EDITION, 2 vols. 8vo. 36s.

The Life of Sir Martin Frobisher, Knt. containing a Narrative of the Spanish Armada. By the Rev. FRANK JONES, B.A. Portrait, Maps, and Facsimile. Crown 8vo. 6s.

Gotthold Ephraim Lessing, his Life and Works. By HELEN ZIMMERN. Crown 8vo. 10s. 6d.

The Life, Works, and Opinions of Heinrich Heine. By WILLIAM STIGAND. 2 vols. 8vo. Portrait, 28s.

The Life of Mozart. Translated from the German Work of Dr. LUDWIG NOHL by Lady WALLACE. 2 vols. crown 8vo. Portraits, 21s.

Life of Robert Frampton, D.D. Bishop of Gloucester, deprived as a Non-Juror in 1689. Edited by T. S. EVANS, M.A. Crown 8vo. 10s. 6d.

The Life of Simon de Montfort, Earl of Leicester, with special reference to the Parliamentary History of his time. By G. W. PROTHERO. Crown 8vo. Maps, 9s.

Maunder's Biographical Treasury; a Dictionary of Universal Biography. Latest Edition, thoroughly revised and for the most part re-written, with over Fifteen Hundred additional Memoirs, by WILLIAM L. R. CATES. Fcp. 8vo. 6s.

Felix Mendelssohn's Letters, translated by Lady WALLACE. 2 vols. crown 8vo. 5s. each.

Autobiography. By JOHN STUART MILL. 8vo. 7s. 6d.

Apologia pro Vitâ Suâ; Being a History of his Religious Opinions by JOHN HENRY NEWMAN, D.D. New Edition. Crown 8vo. 6s.

Isaac Casaubon, 1559-1614. By MARK PATTISON, Rector of Lincoln College, Oxford. 8vo. 18s.

Leaders of Public Opinion in Ireland; Swift, Flood, Grattan, O'Connell. By W. E. H. LECKY, M.A. Crown 8vo. 7s. 6d.

Essays in Ecclesiastical Biography. By the Right Hon. Sir J. STEPHEN, LL.D. Crown 8vo. 7s. 6d.

Cæsar; a Sketch. By JAMES ANTHONY FROUDE, M.A. formerly Fellow of Exeter College, Oxford. With Portrait and Map. 8vo. 16s.

Life of the Duke of Wellington. By the Rev. G. R. GLEIG, M.A. Crown 8vo. Portrait, 6s.

Memoirs of Sir Henry Havelock, K.C.B. By JOHN CLARK MARSHMAN. Crown 8vo. 3s. 6d.

Vicissitudes of Families. By Sir BERNARD BURKE, C.B. Two vols. crown 8vo. 21s.

MENTAL and POLITICAL PHILOSOPHY.

Comte's System of Positive Polity, or Treatise upon Sociology:—

Vol. I. **General View of Positivism** and Introductory Principles. Translated by J. H. Bridges, M.B. 8vo. 21s.

Vol. II. **The Social Statics,** or the Abstract Laws of Human Order. Translated by F. Harrison, M.A. 8vo. 14s.

Vol. III. **The Social Dynamics,** or the General Laws of Human Progress (the Philosophy of History). Translated by E. S. Beesly, M.A. 8vo. 21s.

Vol. IV. **The Theory of the Future of Man;** with Comte's Early Essays on Social Philosophy. Translated by R. Congreve, M.D. and H. D. Hutton, B.A. 8vo. 24s.

De Tocqueville's Democracy in America, translated by H. Reeve. 2 vols. crown 8vo. 16s.

Analysis of the Phenomena of the Human Mind. By James Mill. With Notes, Illustrative and Critical. 2 vols. 8vo. 28s.

On Representative Government. By John Stuart Mill. Crown 8vo. 2s.

On Liberty. By John Stuart Mill. Post 8vo. 7s. 6d. crown 8vo. 1s. 4d.

Principles of Political Economy. By John Stuart Mill. 2 vols. 8vo. 30s. or 1 vol. crown 8vo. 5s.

Essays on some Unsettled Questions of Political Economy. By John Stuart Mill. 8vo. 6s. 6d.

Utilitarianism. By John Stuart Mill. 8vo. 5s.

The Subjection of Women. By John Stuart Mill. Fourth Edition. Crown 8vo. 6s.

Examination of Sir William Hamilton's Philosophy. By John Stuart Mill. 8vo. 16s.

A System of Logic, Ratiocinative and Inductive. By John Stuart Mill. 2 vols. 8vo. 25s.

Dissertations and Discussions. By John Stuart Mill. 4 vols. 8vo. price £2. 6s. 6d.

Philosophical Fragments written during intervals of Business. By J. D. Morell, LL.D. Crown 8vo. 5s.

The Philosophy of Reflection. By S. H. Hodgson, Hon. LL.D. Edin. 2 vols. 8vo. 21s.

The Law of Nations considered as Independent Political Communities. By Sir Travers Twiss, D.C.L. 2 vols. 8vo. £1. 13s.

A Systematic View of the Science of Jurisprudence. By Sheldon Amos, M.A. 8vo. 18s.

A Primer of the English Constitution and Government. By S. Amos, M.A. Crown 8vo. 6s.

A Sketch of the History of Taxes in England from the Earliest Times to the Present Day. By Stephen Dowell. Vol. I. to the Civil War 1642. 8vo. 10s. 6d.

Principles of Economical Philosophy. By H. D. Macleod, M.A. Second Edition in 2 vols. Vol. I. 8vo. 15s. Vol. II. Part I. 12s.

The Institutes of Justinian; with English Introduction, Translation, and Notes. By T. C. Sandars, M.A. 8vo. 18s.

Lord Bacon's Works, collected & edited by R. L. Ellis, M.A. J. Spedding, M.A. and D. D. Heath. 7 vols. 8vo. £3. 13s. 6d.

Letters and Life of Francis Bacon, including all his Occasional Works. Collected and edited, with a Commentary, by J. Spedding. 7 vols. 8vo. £4. 4s.

The Nicomachean Ethics of Aristotle, translated into English by R. WILLIAMS, B.A. Crown 8vo. price 7s. 6d.

Aristotle's Politics, Books I. III. IV. (VII.) Greek Text, with an English Translation by W. E. BOLLAND, M.A. and Short Essays by A. LANG, M.A. Crown 8vo. 7s. 6d.

The Politics of Aristotle; Greek Text, with English Notes. By RICHARD CONGREVE, M.A. 8vo. 18s.

The Ethics of Aristotle; with Essays and Notes. By Sir A. GRANT, Bart. LL.D. 2 vols. 8vo. 32s.

Bacon's Essays, with Annotations. By R. WHATELY, D.D. 8vo. 10s. 6d.

Picture Logic; an Attempt to Popularise the Science of Reasoning. By A. SWINBOURNE, B.A. Post 8vo. 5s.

Elements of Logic. By R. WHATELY, D.D. 8vo. 10s. 6d. Crown 8vo. 4s. 6d.

Elements of Rhetoric. By R. WHATELY, D.D. 8vo. 10s. 6d Crown 8vo. 4s. 6d.

On the Influence of Authority in Matters of Opinion. By the late Sir. G. C. LEWIS, Bart. 8vo. 14s.

The Senses and the Intellect. By A. BAIN, LL.D. 8vo. 15s.

The Emotions and the Will. By A. BAIN, LL.D. 8vo. 15s.

Mental and Moral Science; a Compendium of Psychology and Ethics. By A. BAIN, LL.D. Crown 8vo. 10s. 6d.

An Outline of the Necessary Laws of Thought; a Treatise on Pure and Applied Logic. By W. THOMSON, D.D. Crown 8vo. 6s.

Essays in Political and Moral Philosophy. By T. E. CLIFFE LESLIE, Hon. LL.D. Dubl. of Lincoln's Inn, Barrister-at-Law; late Examiner in Polit. Econ. in the Univ. of London; Prof. of Jurisp. and Polit. Econ. in the Queen's University. 8vo. price 10s. 6d.

Hume's Philosophical Works. Edited, with Notes, &c. by T. H. GREEN, M.A. and the Rev. T. H. GROSE, M.A. 4 vols. 8vo. 56s. Or separately, Essays, 2 vols. 28s. Treatise on Human Nature, 2 vols. 28s.

The Schools of Charles the Great, and the Restoration of Education in the Ninth Century. By J. BASS MULLINGER, M.A. 8vo. price 7s. 6d.

MISCELLANEOUS & CRITICAL WORKS.

The London Series of English Classics. Edited by JOHN W. Hales, M.A. and by CHARLES S. JERRAM, M.A. Fcp. 8vo.

Bacon's Essays, annotated by E. A. ABBOT, D.D. 2 vols. 6s. or in 1 vol. without Notes, 2s. 6d.

Ben Jonson's Every Man in His Humour, by H. B. WHEATLEY, F.S.A. Price 2s. 6d.

Macaulay's Clive, by H. C. BOWEN, M.A. 2s. 6d.

Marlowe's Doctor Faustus, by W. WAGNER, Ph.D. 2s.

Milton's Paradise Regained, by C. S. JERRAM, M.A. 2s. 6d.

Pope's Select Poems, by T. ARNOLD, M.A. 2s. 6d.

Miscellaneous Writings of J. Conington, M.A. Edited by J. A. SYMONDS, M.A. 2 vols. 8vo. 28s.

Selected Essays, chiefly from Contributions to the Edinburgh and Quarterly Reviews. By A. HAYWARD, Q.C. 2 vols. crown 8vo. 12s.

Literary Studies. By the late WALTER BAGEHOT, M.A. and Fellow of University College, London. With a Prefatory Memoir. Edited by R. H. HUTTON. 2 vols. 8vo. with Portrait, 28s.

Short Studies on Great Subjects. By J. A. FROUDE, M.A. 3 vols. crown 8vo. 18s.

Manual of English Literature, Historical and Critical. By T. ARNOLD, M.A. Crown 8vo. 7s. 6d.

Lord Macaulay's Miscellaneous Writings:—
LIBRARY EDITION, 2 vols. 8vo. 21s.
PEOPLE'S EDITION, 1 vol. cr. 8vo. 4s. 6d.

Lord Macaulay's Miscellaneous Writings and Speeches. Student's Edition. Crown 8vo. 6s.

Speeches of the Right Hon. Lord Macaulay, corrected by Himself. Crown 8vo. 3s. 6d.

Selections from the Writings of Lord Macaulay. Edited, with Notes, by G. O. TREVELYAN, M.P. Crown. 8vo. 6s.

The Wit and Wisdom of the Rev. Sydney Smith. Crown 8vo. 3s. 6d.

Miscellaneous and Posthumous Works of the late Henry Thomas Buckle. Edited by HELEN TAYLOR. 3 vols. 8vo. 52s. 6d.

Miscellaneous Works of Thomas Arnold, D.D. late Head Master of Rugby School. 8vo. 7s. 6d.

German Home Life; a Series of Essays on the Domestic Life of Germany. Crown 8vo. 6s.

Realities of Irish Life. By W. STEUART TRENCH. Crown 8vo. 2s. 6d. boards, or 3s. 6d. cloth.

Max Müller and the Philosophy of Language. By LUDWIG NOIRÉ. 8vo. 6s.

Lectures on the Science of Language. By F. MAX MÜLLER, M.A. 2 vols. crown 8vo. 16s.

Chips from a German Workshop; Essays on the Science of Religion, and on Mythology, Traditions & Customs. By F. MAX MÜLLER, M.A. 4 vols. 8vo. £2. 18s.

Language & Languages. A Revised Edition of Chapters on Language and Families of Speech. By F. W. FARRAR, D.D. F.R.S. Crown 8vo. 6s.

The Essays and Contributions of A. K. H. B. Uniform Cabinet Editions in crown 8vo.

Recreations of a Country Parson, Three Series, 3s. 6d. each.

Landscapes, Churches, and Moralities, price 3s. 6d.

Seaside Musings, 3s. 6d.

Changed Aspects of Unchanged Truths, 3s. 6d.

Counsel and Comfort from a City Pulpit, 3s. 6d.

Lessons of Middle Age, 3s. 6d.

Leisure Hours in Town, 3s. 6d.

Autumn Holidays of a Country Parson, price 3s. 6d.

Sunday Afternoons at the Parish Church of a University City, 3s. 6d.

The Commonplace Philosopher in Town and Country, 3s. 6d.

Present-Day Thoughts, 3s. 6d.

Critical Essays of a Country Parson, price 3s. 6d.

The Graver Thoughts of a Country Parson, Three Series, 3s. 6d. each.

DICTIONARIES and OTHER BOOKS of REFERENCE.

Dictionary of the English Language. By R. G. LATHAM, M.A. M.D. Abridged from Dr. Latham's Edition of Johnson's English Dictionary. Medium 8vo. 24s.

A Dictionary of the English Language. By R. G. LATHAM, M.A. M.D. Founded on Johnson's English Dictionary as edited by the Rev. H. J. TODD. 4 vols. 4to. £7.

Roget's Thesaurus of English Words and Phrases, classified and arranged so as to facilitate the expression of Ideas, and assist in Literary Composition. Revised and enlarged by the Author's Son, J. L. ROGET. Crown 8vo. 10s. 6d.

English Synonymes. By E. J. WHATELY. Edited by R. WHATELY, D.D. Fcp. 8vo. 3s.

Handbook of the English Language. By R. G. LATHAM, M.A. M.D. Crown 8vo. 6s.

Contanseau's Practical Dictionary of the French and English Languages. Post 8vo. price 7s. 6d.

Contanseau's Pocket Dictionary, French and English, abridged from the Practical Dictionary by the Author. Square 18mo. 3s. 6d.

A New Pocket Dictionary of the German and English Languages. By F. W. LONGMAN, Ball. Coll. Oxford. Square 18mo. 5s.

A Practical Dictionary of the German and English Languages. By Rev. W. L. BLACKLEY, M.A. & Dr. C. M. FRIEDLÄNDER. Post 8vo. 7s. 6d.

A Dictionary of Roman and Greek Antiquities. With 2,000 Woodcuts illustrative of the Arts and Life of the Greeks and Romans. By A. RICH, B.A. Crown 8vo. 7s. 6d.

The Critical Lexicon and Concordance to the English and Greek New Testament. By the Rev. E. W. BULLINGER. Medium 8vo. 30s.

A Greek-English Lexicon. By H. G. LIDDELL, D.D. Dean of Christchurch, and R. SCOTT, D.D. Dean of Rochester. Crown 4to. 36s.

Liddell & Scott's Lexicon, Greek and English, abridged for Schools. Square 12mo. 7s. 6d.

An English-Greek Lexicon, containing all the Greek Words used by Writers of good authority. By C. D. YONGE, M.A. 4to. 21s.

Mr. Yonge's Lexicon, English and Greek, abridged from his larger Lexicon. Square 12mo. 8s. 6d.

A Latin-English Dictionary. By JOHN T. WHITE, D.D. Oxon. and J. E. RIDDLE, M.A. Oxon. Sixth Edition, revised. 1 vol. 4to. 28s.

White's College Latin-English Dictionary, for the use of University Students. Medium 8vo. 15s.

A Latin-English Dictionary for the use of Middle-Class Schools. By JOHN T. WHITE, D.D. Oxon. Square fcp. 8vo. 3s.

White's Junior Student's Latin-English and English-Latin Dictionary. Square 12mo.
ENGLISH-LATIN DICTIONARY, 5s. 6d.
LATIN-ENGLISH DICTIONARY, 7s. 6d.
COMPLETE, 12s.

M'Culloch's Dictionary of Commerce and Commercial Navigation. Re-edited by HUGH G. REID. With 11 Maps and 30 Charts. 8vo. 63s.

Keith Johnston's General Dictionary of Geography, Descriptive, Physical, Statistical, and Historical; a complete Gazetteer of the World. Medium 8vo. 42s.

The Public Schools Atlas of Ancient Geography, in 28 entirely new Coloured Maps. Edited by the Rev. G. BUTLER, M.A. Imperial 8vo. or imperial 4to. 7s. 6d.

The Public Schools Atlas of Modern Geography, in 31 entirely new Coloured Maps. Edited by the Rev. G. BUTLER, M.A.

ASTRONOMY and METEOROLOGY.

Outlines of Astronomy.
By Sir J. F. W. Herschel, Bart. M.A. Latest Edition, with Plates and Diagrams. Square crown 8vo. 12s.

Essays on Astronomy.
A Series of Papers on Planets and Meteors, the Sun and Sun-surrounding Space, Star and Star Cloudlets. By R. A. Proctor, B.A. With 10 Plates and 24 Woodcuts. 8vo. 12s.

The Moon; her Motions, Aspects, Scenery, and Physical Condition. By R. A. Proctor, B.A. With Plates, Charts, Woodcuts, and Lunar Photographs. Crown 8vo. 10s. 6d.

The Sun; Ruler, Light, Fire, and Life of the Planetary System. By R. A. Proctor, B.A. With Plates & Woodcuts. Crown 8vo. 14s.

The Orbs Around Us;
a Series of Essays on the Moon & Planets, Meteors & Comets, the Sun & Coloured Pairs of Suns. By R. A. Proctor, B.A. With Chart and Diagrams. Crown 8vo. 7s. 6d.

Other Worlds than Ours;
The Plurality of Worlds Studied under the Light of Recent Scientific Researches. By R. A. Proctor, B.A. With 14 Illustrations. Cr. 8vo. 10s. 6d.

The Universe of Stars;
Presenting Researches into and New Views respecting the Constitution of the Heavens. By R. A. Proctor, B.A. Second Edition, with 22 Charts (4 Coloured) and 22 Diagrams. 8vo. price 10s. 6d.

The Transits of Venus;
A Popular Account of Past and Coming Transits. By R. A. Proctor, B.A. 20 Plates (12 Coloured) and 27 Woodcuts. Crown 8vo. 8s. 6d.

Saturn and its System.
By R. A. Proctor, B.A. 8vo. with 14 Plates, 14s.

The Moon, and the Condition and Configurations of its Surface. By E. Neison, F.R.A.S. With 26 Maps & 5 Plates. Medium 8vo. 31s. 6d.

A New Star Atlas, for the Library, the School, and the Observatory, in 12 Circular Maps (with 2 Index Plates). By R. A. Proctor, B.A. Crown 8vo. 5s.

Larger Star Atlas, for the Library, in Twelve Circular Maps, with Introduction and 2 Index Plates. By R. A. Proctor, B.A. Folio, 15s. or Maps only, 12s. 6d.

A Treatise on the Cycloid, and on all forms of Cycloidal Curves, and on the use of Cycloidal Curves in dealing with the Motions of Planets, Comets, &c. and of Matter projected from the Sun. By R. A. Proctor, B.A. With 161 Diagrams. Crown 8vo. 10s. 6d.

Dove's Law of Storms, considered in connexion with the Ordinary Movements of the Atmosphere. Translated by R. H. Scott, M.A. 8vo. 10s. 6d.

Air and Rain; the Beginnings of a Chemical Climatology. By R. A. Smith, F.R.S. 8vo. 24s.

Schellen's Spectrum Analysis, in its Application to Terrestrial Substances and the Physical Constitution of the Heavenly Bodies. Translated by Jane and C. Lassell, with Notes by W. Huggins, LL.D. F.R.S. 8vo. Plates and Woodcuts, 28s.

NATURAL HISTORY and PHYSICAL SCIENCE.

Professor Helmholtz' Popular Lectures on Scientific Subjects. Translated by E. ATKINSON, F.C.S. With numerous Wood Engravings. 8vo. 12s. 6d.

Professor Helmholtz on the Sensations of Tone, as a Physiological Basis for the Theory of Music. Translated by A. J. ELLIS, F.R.S. 8vo. 36s.

Ganot's Natural Philosophy for General Readers and Young Persons; a Course of Physics divested of Mathematical Formulæ and expressed in the language of daily life. Translated by E. ATKINSON, F.C.S. Third Edition. Plates and Woodcuts. Crown 8vo. 7s. 6d.

Ganot's Elementary Treatise on Physics, Experimental and Applied, for the use of Colleges and Schools. Translated and edited by E. ATKINSON, F.C.S. Eighth Edition. Plates and Woodcuts. Post 8vo. 15s.

Arnott's Elements of Physics or Natural Philosophy. Seventh Edition, edited by A. BAIN, LL.D. and A. S. TAYLOR, M.D. F.R.S. Crown 8vo. Woodcuts, 12s. 6d.

The Correlation of Physical Forces. By the Hon. Sir W. R. GROVE, F.R.S. &c. Sixth Edition, revised and augmented. 8vo. 15s.

Weinhold's Introduction to Experimental Physics; including Directions for Constructing Physical Apparatus and for Making Experiments. Translated by B. LOEWY, F.R.A.S. With a Preface by G. C. FOSTER, F.R.S. 8vo. Plates & Woodcuts 31s. 6d.

A Treatise on Magnetism, General and Terrestrial. By H. LLOYD, D.D. D.C.L. 8vo. 10s. 6d.

Elementary Treatise on the Wave-Theory of Light. By H. LLOYD, D.D. D.C.L. 8vo. 10s. 6d.

Fragments of Science. By JOHN TYNDALL, F.R.S. Sixth Edition, revised and augmented. 2 vols. crown 8vo. 16s.

Heat a Mode of Motion. By JOHN TYNDALL, F.R.S. Fifth Edition in preparation.

Sound. By JOHN TYNDALL, F.R.S. Third Edition, including Recent Researches on Fog-Signalling. Crown 8vo. price 10s. 6d.

Researches on Diamagnetism and Magne-Crystallic Action; including Diamagnetic Polarity. By JOHN TYNDALL, F.R.S. New Edition in preparation.

Contributions to Molecular Physics in the domain of Radiant Heat. By JOHN TYNDALL, F.R.S. Plates and Woodcuts. 8vo. 16s.

Six Lectures on Light, delivered in America in 1872 and 1873. By JOHN TYNDALL, F.R.S. Second Edition. Portrait, Plate, and Diagrams. Crown 8vo. 7s. 6d.

Lessons in Electricity at the Royal Institution, 1875-6. By JOHN TYNDALL, F.R.S. With 58 Woodcuts. Crown 8vo. 2s. 6d.

Notes of a Course of Seven Lectures on Electrical Phenomena and Theories, delivered at the Royal Institution. By JOHN TYNDALL, F.R.S. Crown 8vo. 1s. sewed, or 1s. 6d. cloth.

Notes of a Course of Nine Lectures on Light, delivered at the Royal Institution. By JOHN TYNDALL, F.R.S. Crown 8vo. 1s. sewed, or 1s. 6d. cloth.

Principles of Animal Mechanics. By the Rev. S. HAUGHTON F.R.S. Second Edition. 8vo. 21s.

Text-Books of Science,
Mechanical and Physical, adapted for the use of Artisans and of Students in Public and Science Schools. Small 8vo. with Woodcuts, &c.

Abney's Photography, 3s. 6d.
Anderson's (Sir John) Strength of Materials, 3s. 6d.
Armstrong's Organic Chemistry, 3s. 6d.
Barry's Railway Appliances, 3s. 6d.
Bloxam's Metals, 3s. 6d.
Goodeve's Mechanics, 3s. 6d.
——— Mechanism, 3s. 6d.
Gore's Electro-Metallurgy, 6s.
Griffin's Algebra & Trigonometry, 3/6.
Jenkin's Electricity & Magnetism, 3/6.
Maxwell's Theory of Heat, 3s. 6d.
Merrifield's Technical Arithmetic, 3s. 6d.
Miller's Inorganic Chemistry, 3s. 6d.
Preece & Sivewright's Telegraphy, 3/6.
Rutley's Study of Rocks, 4s. 6d.
Shelley's Workshop Appliances, 3s 6d.
Thomé's Structural and Physiological Botany, 6s.
Thorpe's Quantitative Analysis, 4s. 6d.
Thorpe & Muir's Qualitative Analysis, price 3s. 6d.
Tilden's Systematic Chemistry, 3s. 6d.
Unwin's Machine Design, 3s. 6d.
Watson's Plane & Solid Geometry, 3/6.

Light Science for Leisure
Hours; Familiar Essays on Scientific Subjects, Natural Phenomena, &c. By R. A. PROCTOR, B.A. 2 vols. crown 8vo. 7s. 6d. each.

An Introduction to the
Systematic Zoology and Morphology of Vertebrate Animals. By A. MACALISTER, M.D. Professor of Comparative Anatomy and Zoology, University of Dublin. With 28 Diagrams. 8vo. 10s. 6d.

The Comparative Anatomy and Physiology of the Vertebrate Animals. By RICHARD OWEN, F.R.S. With 1,472 Woodcuts. 3 vols. 8vo. £3. 13s. 6d.

Homes without Hands;
a Description of the Habitations of Animals, classed according to their Principle of Construction. By the Rev. J. G. WOOD, M.A. With about 140 Vignettes on Wood. 8vo. 14s.

Wood's Strange Dwellings; a Description of the Habitations of Animals, abridged from 'Homes without Hands.' With Frontispiece and 60 Woodcuts. Crown 8vo. 7s. 6d.

Wood's Insects at Home;
a Popular Account of British Insects, their Structure, Habits, and Transformations. With 700 Woodcuts. 8vo. 14s.

Wood's Insects Abroad;
a Popular Account of Foreign Insects, their Structure, Habits, and Transformations. With 700 Woodcuts. 8vo. 14s.

Wood's Out of Doors; a
Selection of Original Articles on Practical Natural History. With 6 Illustrations. Crown 8vo. 7s. 6d.

Wood's Bible Animals; a
description of every Living Creature mentioned in the Scriptures, from the Ape to the Coral. With 112 Vignettes. 8vo. 14s.

The Sea and its Living
Wonders. By Dr. G. HARTWIG. 8vo. with numerous Illustrations, price 10s. 6d.

Hartwig's Tropical
World. With about 200 Illustrations. 8vo. 10s. 6d.

Hartwig's Polar World;
a Description of Man and Nature in the Arctic and Antarctic Regions of the Globe. Chromoxylographs, Maps, and Woodcuts. 8vo. 10s. 6d.

Hartwig's Subterranean
World. With Maps and Woodcuts. 8vo. 10s. 6d.

Hartwig's Aerial World;
a Popular Account of the Phenomena and Life of the Atmosphere. Map, Chromoxylographs, Woodcuts. 8vo. price 10s. 6d.

Kirby and Spence's Introduction to Entomology, or Elements of the Natural History of Insects. Crown 8vo. 5s.

A Familiar History of Birds. By E. STANLEY, D.D. Fcp. 8vo. with Woodcuts, 3s. 6d.

Rocks Classified and Described. By BERNHARD VON COTTA. An English Translation, by P. H. LAWRENCE (with English, German, and French Synonymes), revised by the Author. Post 8vo. 14s.

The Geology of England and Wales; a Concise Account of the Lithological Characters, Leading Fossils, and Economic Products of the Rocks. By H. B. WOODWARD, F.G.S. Crown 8vo. Map & Woodcuts, 14s.

Keller's Lake Dwellings of Switzerland, and other Parts of Europe. Translated by JOHN E. LEE, F.S.A. F.G.S. New Edition, enlarged, with 206 Illustrations. 2 vols. royal 8vo. 42s.

The Primæval World of Switzerland. By Professor OSWAL HEER, of the University of Zurich. Edited by JAMES HEYWOOD, M.A. F.R.S. With Map, 19 Plates, & 372 Woodcuts. 2 vols. 8vo. 16s.

The Puzzle of Life and How it Has Been Put Together; a Short History of Praehistoric Vegetable and Animal Life on the Earth. By A. NICOLS, F.R.G.S. With 12 Illustrations. Crown 8vo. 3s. 6d.

The Origin of Civilisation, and the Primitive Condition of Man; Mental and Social Condition of Savages. By Sir J. LUBBOCK, Bart. M.P. F.R.S. 8vo. Woodcuts, 18s.

A Dictionary of Science, Literature, and Art. Re-edited by the late W. T. BRANDE (the Author) and the Rev. Sir G. W. COX, Bart., M.A. 3 vols. medium 8vo. 63s.

The History of Modern Music, a Course of Lectures delivered at the Royal Institution. By JOHN HULLAH, LL.D. 8vo. 8s. 6d.

The Transition Period of Musical History, from the Beginning of the 17th to the Middle of the 18th Century. A Second Series of Lectures. By the same Author. 8vo. 10s. 6d.

Loudon's Encyclopædia of Plants; comprising the Specific Character, Description, Culture, History, &c. of all the Plants found in Great Britain. With upwards of 12,000 Woodcuts. 8vo. 42s.

De Caisne & Le Maout's System of Descriptive and Analytical Botany. Translated by Mrs. HOOKER; edited and arranged according to the English Botanical System, by J. D. HOOKER, M.D. With 5,500 Woodcuts. Imperial 8vo. 31s. 6d.

The Treasury of Botany, or Popular Dictionary of the Vegetable Kingdom; with which is incorporated a Glossary of Botanical Terms. Edited by J. LINDLEY, F.R.S., and T. MOORE, F.L.S. With 274 Woodcuts and 20 Steel Plates. Two Parts, fcp. 8vo. 12s.

Rivers's Orchard-House; or, the Cultivation of Fruit Trees under Glass. Sixteenth Edition, re-edited by T. F. RIVERS. Crown 8vo. with 25 Woodcuts, price 5s.

The Rose Amateur's Guide. By THOMAS RIVERS. Latest Edition. Fcp. 8vo. 4s. 6d.

Town and Window Gardening, including the Structure, Habits and Uses of Plants; a Course of Sixteen Lectures given out of School-Hours to Pupil Teachers and Children attending the Leeds Board Schools. By Mrs. BUCKTON, Member of the Leeds School Board. With 127 Woodcuts. Crown 8vo. 2s.

WORKS *published by* LONGMANS & CO.   13

CHEMISTRY and PHYSIOLOGY.

Miller's Elements of Chemistry, Theoretical and Practical. Re-edited, with Additions, by H. MACLEOD, F.C.S. 3 vols. 8vo.
PART I. CHEMICAL PHYSICS. 16s.
PART II. INORGANIC CHEMISTRY, 24s.
PART III. ORGANIC CHEMISTRY, New Edition in the press.

Animal Chemistry, or the Relations of Chemistry to Physiology and Pathology: a Manual for Medical Men and Scientific Chemists. By CHARLES T. KINGZETT, F.C.S. 8vo. price 18s.

Health in the House: Twenty-five Lectures on Elementary Physiology in its Application to the Daily Wants of Man and Animals. By Mrs. BUCKTON. Crown 8vo. Woodcuts, 2s.

A Dictionary of Chemistry and the Allied Branches of other Sciences. By HENRY WATTS, F.C.S. assisted by eminent Scientific and Practical Chemists. 7 vols. medium 8vo. £10. 16s. 6d.

Third Supplement, completing the Record of Chemical Discovery to the year 1877. PART I. 8vo. 36s. PART II. completion, in the press.

Select Methods in Chemical Analysis, chiefly Inorganic. By WM. CROOKES, F.R.S. With 22 Woodcuts. Crown 8vo. 12s. 6d.

The History, Products, and Processes of the Alkali Trade, including the most recent Improvements. By CHARLES T. KINGZETT, F.C.S. With 32 Woodcuts. 8vo. 12s.

The FINE ARTS and ILLUSTRATED EDITIONS.

In Fairyland; Pictures from the Elf-World. By RICHARD DOYLE. With a Poem by W. ALLINGHAM. With 16 coloured Plates, containing 36 Designs. Folio, 15s.

Lord Macaulay's Lays of Ancient Rome. With Ninety Illustrations on Wood from Drawings by G. SCHARF. Fcp. 4to. 21s.

Miniature Edition of Macaulay's Lays of Ancient Rome, with Scharf's 90 Illustrations reduced in Lithography. Imp. 16mo. 10s. 6d.

Moore's Lalla Rookh. TENNIEL'S Edition, with 68 Woodcut Illustrations. Fcp. 4to. 21s.

Moore's Irish Melodies, MACLISE'S Edition, with 161 Steel Plates. Super-royal 8vo. 21s.

Lectures on Harmony, delivered at the Royal Institution. By G. A. MACFARREN. 8vo. 12s.

Sacred and Legendary Art. By Mrs. JAMESON. 6 vols. square crown 8vo. price £5. 15s. 6d.

Jameson's Legends of the Saints and Martyrs. With 19 Etchings and 187 Woodcuts. 2 vols. 31s. 6d.

Jameson's Legends of the Monastic Orders. With 11 Etchings and 88 Woodcuts. 1 vol. 21s.

Jameson's Legends of the Madonna. With 27 Etchings and 165 Woodcuts. 1 vol. 21s.

Jameson's History of the Saviour, His Types and Precursors. Completed by Lady EASTLAKE. With 13 Etchings and 281 Woodcuts. 2 vols. 42s.

The Three Cathedrals dedicated to St. Paul in London. By W. LONGMAN, F.S.A. With numerous Illustrations. Square crown 8vo. 21s.

The USEFUL ARTS, MANUFACTURES, &c.

The Art of Scientific Discovery. By G. GORE, LL.D. F.R.S. Author of 'The Art of Electro-Metallurgy.' Crown 8vo. 15s.

The Amateur Mechanics' Practical Handbook; describing the different Tools required in the Workshop. By A. H. G. HOBSON. With 33 Woodcuts. Crown 8vo. 2s. 6d.

The Engineer's Valuing Assistant. By H. D. HOSKOLD, Civil and Mining Engineer, 16 years Mining Engineer to the Dean Forest Iron Company. 8vo. 31s. 6d.

Industrial Chemistry; a Manual for Manufacturers and for Colleges or Technical Schools; a Translation (by Dr. T. H. BARRY) of Stohmann and Engler's German Edition of PAYEN's 'Précis de Chimie Industrielle;' with Chapters on the Chemistry of the Metals, &c. by B. H. PAUL, Ph.D. With 698 Woodcuts. Medium 8vo. 42s.

Gwilt's Encyclopædia of Architecture, with above 1,600 Woodcuts. Revised and extended by W. PAPWORTH. 8vo. 52s. 6d.

Lathes and Turning, Simple, Mechanical, and Ornamental. By W. H. NORTHCOTT. Second Edition, with 338 Illustrations. 8vo. 18s.

The Theory of Strains in Girders and similar Structures, with Observations on the application of Theory to Practice, and Tables of the Strength and other Properties of Materials. By B. B. STONEY, M.A. M. Inst. C.E. Royal 8vo. with 5 Plates and 123 Woodcuts, 36s.

A Treatise on Mills and Millwork. By the late Sir W. FAIRBAIRN, Bart. C.E. Fourth Edition, with 18 Plates and 333 Woodcuts. 1 vol. 8vo. 25s.

Useful Information for Engineers. By the late Sir W. FAIRBAIRN, Bart. C.E. With many Plates and Woodcuts. 3 vols. crown 8vo. 31s. 6d.

The Application of Cast and Wrought Iron to Building Purposes. By the late Sir W. FAIRBAIRN, Bart. C.E. With 6 Plates and 118 Woodcuts. 8vo. 16s.

Hints on Household Taste in Furniture, Upholstery, and other Details. By C. L. EASTLAKE. Fourth Edition, with 100 Illustrations. Square crown 8vo. 14s.

Handbook of Practical Telegraphy. By R. S. CULLEY, Memb. Inst. C.E. Seventh Edition. Plates & Woodcuts. 8vo. price 16s.

A Treatise on the Steam Engine, in its various applications to Mines, Mills, Steam Navigation, Railways and Agriculture. By J. BOURNE, C.E. With Portrait, 37 Plates, and 546 Woodcuts. 4to. 42s.

Recent Improvements in the Steam Engine. By J. BOURNE, C.E. Fcp. 8vo. Woodcuts, 6s.

Catechism of the Steam Engine, in its various Applications. By JOHN BOURNE, C.E. Fcp. 8vo. Woodcuts, 6s.

Handbook of the Steam Engine, a Key to the Author's Catechism of the Steam Engine. By J. BOURNE, C.E. Fcp. 8vo. Woodcuts, 9s.

Examples of Steam and Gas Engines of the most recent Approved Types as employed in Mines, Factories, Steam Navigation, Railways and Agriculture, practically described. By JOHN BOURNE, C.E. With 54 Plates and 356 Woodcuts. 4to. 70s.

Encyclopædia of Civil Engineering, Historical, Theoretical, and Practical. By E. CRESY, C.E. With above 3,000 Woodcuts. 8vo. 42s.

Ure's Dictionary of Arts, Manufactures, and Mines. Seventh Edition, re-written and enlarged by R. HUNT, F.R.S. assisted by numerous contributors. With 2,604 Woodcuts. 4 vols. medium 8vo. £7. 7s.

Practical Treatise on Metallurgy. Adapted from the last German Edition of Professor KERL'S Metallurgy by W. CROOKES, F.R.S. &c. and E. RÖHRIG, Ph.D. 3 vols. 8vo. with 625 Woodcuts. £4. 19s.

Anthracen; its Constitution, Properties, Manufacture, and Derivatives, including Artificial Alizarin, Anthrapurpurin, &c. with their Applications in Dyeing and Printing. By G. AUERBACH. Translated by W. CROOKES, F.R.S. 8vo. 12s.

On Artificial Manures, their Chemical Selection and Scientific Application to Agriculture; a Series of Lectures given at the Experimental Farm at Vincennes in 1867 and 1874-75. By M. GEORGES VILLE. Translated and edited by W. CROOKES, F.R.S. With 31 Plates. 8vo. 21s.

Practical Handbook of Dyeing and Calico-Printing. By W. CROOKES, F.R.S. &c. With numerous Illustrations and specimens of Dyed Textile Fabrics. 8vo. 42s.

Mitchell's Manual of Practical Assaying. Fourth Edition, revised, with the Recent Discoveries incorporated, by W. CROOKES, F.R.S. Crown 8vo. Woodcuts, 31s. 6d.

Loudon's Encyclopædia of Gardening; the Theory and Practice of Horticulture, Floriculture, Arboriculture & Landscape Gardening. With 1,000 Woodcuts. 8vo. 21s.

Loudon's Encyclopædia of Agriculture; the Laying-out, Improvement, and Management of Landed Property; the Cultivation and Economy of the Productions of Agriculture. With 1,100 Woodcuts. 8vo. 21s.

RELIGIOUS and MORAL WORKS.

Four Lectures on some Epochs of Early Church History. By the Very Rev. C. MERIVALE, D.D. Dean of Ely. Crown 8vo. 5s.

A History of the Church of England; Pre-Reformation Period. By the Rev. T. P. BOULTBEE, LL.D. late Fellow of St. John's College, Cambridge. 8vo. 15s.

Sketch of the History of the Church of England to the Revolution of 1688. By T. V. SHORT, D.D. Crown 8vo. 7s. 6d.

The English Church in the Eighteenth Century. By CHARLES J. ABBEY, late Fellow of University College, Oxford; and JOHN H. OVERTON, late Scholar of Lincoln College, Oxford. 2 vols. 8vo. 36s.

The Human Life of Christ revealing the Order of the Universe, being the Hulsean Lectures for 1877; with an APPENDIX. By G. S. DREW, M.A. Vicar of Holy Trinity, Lambeth. 8vo. 8s.

An Exposition of the 39 Articles, Historical and Doctrinal. By E. H. BROWNE, D.D. Bishop of Winchester. Eleventh Edition. 8vo. 16s.

A Commentary on the 39 Articles, forming an Introduction to the Theology of the Church of England. By the Rev. T. P. BOULTBEE, LL.D. New Edition. Crown 8vo. 6s.

Historical Lectures on the Life of Our Lord Jesus Christ. By C. J. ELLICOTT, D.D. 8vo. 12s.

Sermons preached mostly in the Chapel of Rugby School by the late T. ARNOLD, D.D. Collective Edition, revised by the Author's Daughter, Mrs. W. E. FORSTER. 6 vols. crown 8vo. 30s. or separately, 5s. each.

The Eclipse of Faith; or a Visit to a Religious Sceptic. By HENRY ROGERS. Fcp. 8vo. 5s.

Defence of the Eclipse of Faith. By H. ROGERS. Fcp. 8vo. 3s. 6d.

Nature, the Utility of Religion and Theism. Three Essays by JOHN STUART MILL. 8vo. 10s. 6d.

A Critical and Grammatical Commentary on St. Paul's Epistles. By C. J. ELLICOTT, D.D. 8vo. Galatians, 8s. 6d. Ephesians, 8s. 6d. Pastoral Epistles, 10s. 6d. Philippians, Colossians, & Philemon, 10s. 6d. Thessalonians, 7s. 6d.

Conybeare & Howson's Life and Epistles of St. Paul. Three Editions, copiously illustrated.

Library Edition, with all the Original Illustrations, Maps, Landscapes on Steel, Woodcuts, &c. 2 vols. 4to. 42s.

Intermediate Edition, with a Selection of Maps, Plates, and Woodcuts. 2 vols. square crown 8vo. 21s.

Student's Edition, revised and condensed, with 46 Illustrations and Maps. 1 vol. crown 8vo. 9s.

The Jewish Messiah; Critical History of the Messianic Idea among the Jews, from the Rise of the Maccabees to the Closing of the Talmud. By JAMES DRUMMOND, B.A. 8vo. 15s.

The Prophets and Prophecy in Israel; an Historical and Critical Inquiry. By Prof. A. KUENEN, Translated from the Dutch by the Rev. A. MILROY, M.A. with an Introduction by J. MUIR, D.C.L. 8vo. 21s.

Mythology among the Hebrews and its Historical Development. By IGNAZ GOLDZIHER, Ph.D. Translated by RUSSELL MARTINEAU, M.A. 8vo. 16s.

Bible Studies. By M. M. KALISCH, Ph.D. PART I. *The Prophecies of Balaam.* 8vo. 10s. 6d. PART II. *The Book of Jonah.* 8vo. 10s. 6d.

Historical and Critical

Ewald's History of Israel. Translated from the German by J. E. CARPENTER, M.A. with Preface by R. MARTINEAU, M.A. 5 vols. 8vo. 63s.

Ewald's Antiquities of Israel. Translated from the German by H. S. SOLLY, M.A. 8vo. 12s. 6d.

The Types of Genesis, briefly considered as revealing the Development of Human Nature. By A. JUKES. Crown 8vo. 7s. 6d.

The Second Death and the Restitution of all Things; with some Preliminary Remarks on the Nature and Inspiration of Holy Scripture. By A. JUKES. Crown 8vo. 3s. 6d.

Commentaries, by the Rev. W. A. O'CONOR, B.A. Rector of St. Simon and St. Jude, Manchester.

Epistle to the Romans, crown 8vo. 3s. 6d.
Epistle to the Hebrews, 4s. 6d.
St. John's Gospel, 10s. 6d.

Supernatural Religion; an Inquiry into the Reality of Divine Revelation. Complete Edition, thoroughly revised, with New Preface and Conclusions. 3 vols. 8vo. 36s.

Lectures on the Origin and Growth of Religion, as illustrated by the Religions of India; being the Hibbert Lectures for 1878, delivered at the Chapter House, Westminster Abbey, in 1878, by F. MAX MÜLLER, M.A. Second Edition. 8vo. price 10s. 6d.

Introduction to the Science of Religion, Four Lectures delivered at the Royal Institution; with Two Essays on False Analogies and the Philosophy of Mythology. By MAX MÜLLER, M.A. Crown 8vo.

Thoughts for the Age. by ELIZABETH M. SEWELL. New Edition. Fcp. 8vo. 3s. 6d.

Preparation for the Holy Communion; the Devotions chiefly from the works of Jeremy Taylor. By ELIZABETH M. SEWELL. 32mo. 3s.

Bishop Jeremy Taylor's Entire Works; with Life by Bishop Heber. Revised and corrected by the Rev. C. P. EDEN. 10 vols. £5. 5s.

Hymns of Praise and Prayer. Corrected and edited by Rev. JOHN MARTINEAU, LL.D. Crown 8vo. 4s. 6d. 32mo. 1s. 6d.

Spiritual Songs for the Sundays and Holidays throughout the Year. By J. S. B. MONSELL, LL.D. Fcp. 8vo. 5s. 18mo. 2s.

Christ the Consoler; a Book of Comfort for the Sick. By ELLICE HOPKINS. With a Preface by the Bishop of Carlisle. Second Edition. Fcp. 8vo. 2s. 6d.

Lyra Germanica; Hymns translated from the German by Miss C. WINKWORTH. Fcp. 8vo. 5s.

The Temporal Mission of the Holy Ghost; or, Reason and Revelation. By HENRY EDWARD MANNING, D.D. Crown 8vo. 8s. 6d.

Hours of Thought on Sacred Things; a Volume of Sermons. By JAMES MARTINEAU, D.D. LL.D. Crown 8vo. Price 7s. 6d.

Endeavours after the Christian Life; Discourses. By JAMES MARTINEAU, D.D. LL.D. Fifth Edition. Crown 8vo. 7s. 6d.

The Pentateuch & Book of Joshua Critically Examined. By J. W. COLENSO, D.D. Bishop of Natal. Crown 8vo. 6s.

Lectures on the Pentateuch and the Moabite Stone; with Appendices. By J. W. COLENSO, D.D. Bishop of Natal. 8vo. 12s.

TRAVELS, VOYAGES, &c.

A Voyage in the 'Sunbeam,' our Home on the Ocean for Eleven Months. By Mrs. BRASSEY. Cheaper Edition, with Map and 65 Wood Engravings. Crown 8vo. 7s. 6d.

A Freak of Freedom; or, the Republic of San Marino. By J. THEODORE BENT, Honorary Citizen of the same. With a Map and 15 Woodcuts. Crown 8vo. 7s. 6d.

One Thousand Miles up the Nile; a Journey through Egypt and Nubia to the Second Cataract. By AMELIA B. EDWARDS. With Plans, Maps & Illustrations. Imperial 8vo. 42s.

The Indian Alps, and How we Crossed them; Two Years' Residence in the Eastern Himalayas, and Two Months' Tour into the Interior. By a LADY PIONEER. With Illustrations. Imperial 8vo. 42s.

Discoveries at Ephesus, Including the Site and Remains of the Great Temple of Diana. By J. T. WOOD, F.S.A. With 27 Lithographic Plates and 42 Wood Engravings. Medium 8vo. 63s.

Memorials of the Discovery and Early Settlement of the Bermudas or Somers Islands, from 1615 to 1685. By Major-General Sir J. H. LEFROY, R.A. With Maps, &c. 2 vols. Imp. 8vo. 60s.

Eight Years in Ceylon. By Sir SAMUEL W. BAKER, M.A. Crown 8vo. Woodcuts. 7s. 6d.

The Rifle and the Hound in Ceylon. By Sir SAMUEL W. BAKER, M.A. Crown 8vo. Woodcuts. 7s. 6d.

Guide to the Pyrenees, for the use of Mountaineers. By CHARLES PACKE. Crown 8vo. 7s. 6d.

The Alpine Club Map of Switzerland, with parts of the Neighbouring Countries, on the scale of Four Miles to an Inch. Edited by R. C. NICHOLS, F.R.G.S. 4 Sheets in Portfolio, 42s. coloured, or 34s. uncoloured.

The Alpine Guide. By JOHN BALL, M.R.I.A. Post 8vo. with Maps and other Illustrations.

The Eastern Alps, 10s. 6d.

Central Alps, including all the Oberland District, 7s. 6d.

Western Alps, including Mont Blanc, Monte Rosa, Zermatt, &c. Price 6s. 6d.

On Alpine Travelling and the Geology of the Alps. Price 1s. Either of the 3 Volumes or Parts of the 'Alpine Guide' may be had with this Introduction prefixed, 1s. extra.

The Fenland Past and Present. By S. H. MILLER, F.R.A.S. F.M.S.; and S. B. J. SKERTCHLEY, F.G.S. of H.M. Geological Survey. With numerous Illustrations and Maps. Royal 8vo. 31s. 6d. Large Paper, fcp. folio, 50s. half-morocco.

WORKS of FICTION.

Novels and Tales. By the Right Hon. the EARL of BEACONSFIELD, K.G. Cabinet Editions, complete in Ten Volumes, crown 8vo. 6s. each.

Lothair, 6s.	Venetia, 6s.
Coningsby, 6s.	Alroy, Ixion, &c. 6s.
Sybil, 6s.	Young Duke &c. 6s.
Tancred, 6s.	Vivian Grey, 6s.
Henrietta Temple, 6s.	
Contarini Fleming, &c. 6s.	

Tales from Euripides; Iphigenia, Alcestis, Hecuba, Helen, Medea. By VINCENT K. COOPER, M.A. late Scholar of Brasenose College, Oxford. Fcp. 8vo. 3s. 6d.

Whispers from Fairyland. By the Right Hon. E. H. KNATCHBULL-HUGESSEN, M.P. With 9 Illustrations. Crown 8vo. 3s. 6d.

Higgledy-Piggledy; or, Stories for Everybody and Everybody's Children. By the Right Hon. E. H. KNATCHBULL-HUGESSEN, M.P. With 9 Illustrations. Cr. 8vo. 3s. 6d.

Stories and Tales. By ELIZABETH M. SEWELL. Cabinet Edition, in Ten Volumes, each containing a complete Tale or Story:—

Amy Herbert, 2s. 6d. Gertrude, 2s. 6d. The Earl's Daughter, 2s. 6d. The Experience of Life, 2s. 6d. Cleve Hall, 2s. 6d. Ivors, 2s. 6d. Katharine Ashton, 2s. 6d. Margaret Percival, 3s. 6d. Laneton Parsonage, 3s. 6d. Ursula, 3s. 6d.

The Modern Novelist's Library. Each work complete in itself, price 2s. boards, or 2s. 6d. cloth.

By Lord BEACONSFIELD.
 Lothair.
 Coningsby.
 Sybil.
 Tancred.
 Venetia.
 Henrietta Temple.
 Contarini Fleming.
 Alroy, Ixion, &c.
 The Young Duke, &c.
 Vivian Grey.

THE MODERN NOVELIST'S LIBRARY—*continued*.

By ANTHONY TROLLOPE.
  Barchester Towers.
  The Warden.

By Major WHYTE-MELVILLE.
  Digby Grand.
  General Bounce.
  Kate Coventry.
  The Gladiators.
  Good for Nothing.
  Holmby House.
  The Interpreter.
  The Queen's Maries.

By the Author of 'The Rose Garden.'
  Unawares.

By the Author of 'Mlle. Mori.'
  The Atelier du Lys.
  Mademoiselle Mori.

By Various Writers.
  Atherstone Priory.
  The Burgomaster's Family.
  Elsa and her Vulture.
  The Six Sisters of the Valleys.

The Novels and Tales of the Right Honourable the Earl of Beaconsfield, K.G. Complete in Ten Volumes, crown 8vo. cloth extra, gilt edges, price 30s.

POETRY and THE DRAMA.

Lays of Ancient Rome; with Ivry and the Armada. By LORD MACAULAY. 16mo. 3s. 6d.

Horatii Opera. Library Edition, with English Notes, Marginal References & various Readings. Edited by Rev. J. E. YONGE, M.A. 8vo. 21s.

Poems by Jean Ingelow.
2 vols. fcp. 8vo. 10s.
FIRST SERIES, containing 'Divided,' 'The Star's Monument,' &c. Fcp. 8vo. 5s.
SECOND SERIES, 'A Story of Doom,' 'Gladys and her Island,' &c. 5s.

Poems by Jean Ingelow. First Series, with nearly 100 Woodcut Illustrations. Fcp. 4to. 21s.

Brian Boru, a Tragedy. By J. T. B. Crown 8vo. 6s.

Festus, a Poem. By PHILIP JAMES BAILEY. 10th Edition, enlarged & revised. Crown 8vo. 12s. 6d.

The Iliad of Homer, Homometrically translated by C. B. CAYLEY, Translator of Dante's Comedy, &c. 8vo. 12s. 6d.

The Æneid of Virgil. Translated into English Verse. By J. CONINGTON, M.A. Crown 8vo. 9s.

Bowdler's Family Shakspeare. Genuine Edition, in 1 vol. medium 8vo. large type, with 36 Woodcuts, 14s. or in 6 vols. fcp. 8vo. 21s.

Southey's Poetical Works, with the Author's last Corrections and Additions. Medium 8vo. with Portrait, 14s.

RURAL SPORTS, HORSE and CATTLE MANAGEMENT, &c.

Annals of the Road; or, Notes on Mail and Stage-Coaching in Great Britain. By Captain MALET. With 3 Woodcuts and 10 Coloured Illustrations. Medium 8vo. 21s.

Down the Road; or, Reminiscences of a Gentleman Coachman. By C. T. S. BIRCH REYNARDSON. Second Edition, with 12 Coloured Illustrations. Medium 8vo. 21s.

Blaine's Encyclopædia of Rural Sports; Complete Accounts, Historical, Practical, and Descriptive, of Hunting, Shooting, Fishing, Racing, &c. With 600 Woodcuts. 8vo. 21s.

A Book on Angling; or, Treatise on the Art of Fishing in every branch; including full Illustrated Lists of Salmon Flies. By FRANCIS FRANCIS. Post 8vo. Portrait and Plates, 15s.

Wilcocks's Sea-Fisherman: comprising the Chief Methods of Hook and Line Fishing, a glance at Nets, and remarks on Boats and Boating. Post 8vo. Woodcuts, 12s. 6d.

The Fly-Fisher's Entomology. By ALFRED RONALDS. With 20 Coloured Plates. 8vo. 14s.

Horses and Riding. By GEORGE NEVILE, M.A. With 31 Illustrations. Crown 8vo. 6s.

Horses and Stables. By Colonel F. FITZWYGRAM, XV. the King's Hussars. With 24 Plates of Illustrations. 8vo. 10s. 6d.

Youatt on the Horse. Revised and enlarged by W. WATSON, M.R.C.V.S. 8vo. Woodcuts, 12s. 6d.

Youatt's Work on the Dog. Revised and enlarged. 8vo. Woodcuts, 6s.

The Dog in Health and Disease. By STONEHENGE. With 78 Wood Engravings. Square crown 8vo. 7s. 6d.

The Greyhound. By STONEHENGE. Revised Edition, with 25 Portraits of Greyhounds, &c. Square crown 8vo. 15s.

Stables and Stable Fittings. By W. MILES. Imp. 8vo. with 13 Plates, 15s.

The Horse's Foot, and How to keep it Sound. By W. MILES. Imp. 8vo. Woodcuts, 12s. 6d.

A Plain Treatise on Horse-shoeing. By W. MILES. Post 8vo. Woodcuts, 2s. 6d.

Remarks on Horses' Teeth, addressed to Purchasers. By W. MILES. Post 8vo. 1s. 6d.

The Ox, his Diseases and their Treatment; with an Essay on Parturition in the Cow. By J. R. DOBSON, M.R.C.V.S. Crown 8vo. Illustrations, 7s. 6d.

WORKS of UTILITY and GENERAL INFORMATION.

Maunder's Treasury of Knowledge and Library of Reference; comprising an English Dictionary and Grammar, Universal Gazetteer, Classical Dictionary, Chronology, Law Dictionary, Synopsis of the Peerage, Useful Tables, &c. Fcp. 8vo. 6s.

Maunder's Biographical Treasury. Latest Edition, reconstructed and partly re-written, with above 1,600 additional Memoirs, by W. L. R. CATES. Fcp. 8vo. 6s.

Maunder's Treasury of Natural History; or, Popular Dictionary of Zoology. Revised and corrected Edition. Fcp. 8vo. with 900 Woodcuts, 6s.

Maunder's Scientific and Literary Treasury; a Popular Encyclopædia of Science, Literature, and Art. Latest Edition, partly re-written, with above 1,000 New Articles, by J. Y. JOHNSON. Fcp. 8vo. 6s.

Maunder's Treasury of Geography, Physical, Historical, Descriptive, and Political. Edited by W. HUGHES, F.R.G.S. With 7 Maps and 16 Plates. Fcp. 8vo. 6s.

Maunder's Historical Treasury; Introductory Outlines of Universal History, and Separate Histories of all Nations. Revised by the Rev. Sir G. W. COX, Bart. M.A. Fcp. 8vo. 6s.

The Treasury of Botany, or Popular Dictionary of the Vegetable Kingdom; with which is incorporated a Glossary of Botanical Terms. Edited by J. LINDLEY, F.R.S. and T. MOORE, F.L.S. With 274 Woodcuts and 20 Steel Plates. Two Parts, fcp. 8vo. 12s.

The Treasury of Bible Knowledge; being a Dictionary of the Books, Persons, Places, Events, and other Matters of which mention is made in Holy Scripture. By the Rev. J. AYRE, M.A. Maps, Plates & Woodcuts. Fcp. 8vo. 6s.

A Practical Treatise on Brewing; with Formulæ for Public Brewers & Instructions for Private Families. By W. BLACK. 8vo. 10s. 6d.

The Theory of the Modern Scientific Game of Whist. By W. POLE, F.R.S. Tenth Edition. Fcp. 8vo. 2s. 6d.

The Correct Card; or, How to Play at Whist; a Whist Catechism. By Captain A. CAMPBELL-WALKER, F.R.G.S. New Edition. Fcp. 8vo. 2s. 6d.

The Cabinet Lawyer; a Popular Digest of the Laws of England, Civil, Criminal, and Constitutional. Twenty-Fifth Edition, corrected and extended. Fcp. 8vo. 9s.

Chess Openings. By F.W. LONGMAN, Balliol College, Oxford. Second Edition. Fcp. 8vo. 2s. 6d.

Pewtner's Comprehensive Specifier; a Guide to the Practical Specification of every kind of Building-Artificer's Work. Edited by W. YOUNG. Crown 8vo. 6s.

The English Manual of Banking. By ARTHUR CRUMP. Second Edition, revised and enlarged. 8vo. 15s.

Modern Cookery for Private Families, reduced to a System of Easy Practice in a Series of carefully-tested Receipts. By ELIZA ACTON. With 8 Plates and 150 Woodcuts. Fcp. 8vo. 6s.

Food and Home Cookery. A Course of Instruction in Practical Cookery and Cleaning, for Children in Elementary Schools, as followed in the Schools of the Leeds School Board. By Mrs. BUCKTON, Member of the Leeds School Board. With 11 Woodcuts. Crown 8vo. 2s.

Hints to Mothers on the Management of their Health during the Period of Pregnancy and in the Lying-in Room. By THOMAS BULL, M.D. Fcp. 8vo. 2s. 6d.

The Maternal Management of Children in Health and Disease. By THOMAS BULL, M.D. Fcp. 8vo. 2s. 6d.

The Farm Valuer. By JOHN SCOTT, Land Valuer. Crown 8vo. price 5s.

Economics for Beginners By H. D. MACLEOD, M.A. Small crown 8vo. 2s. 6d.

The Elements of Banking. By H. D. MACLEOD, M.A. Fourth Edition. Crown 8vo. 5s.

The Theory and Practice of Banking. By H. D. MACLEOD, M.A. 2 vols. 8vo. 26s.

The Resources of Modern Countries; Essays towards an Estimate of the Economic Position of Nations and British Trade Prospects. By ALEX. WILSON. 2 vols. 8vo. 24s.

Willich's Popular Tables for ascertaining, according to the Carlisle Table of Mortality, the value of Lifehold, Leasehold, and Church Property, Renewal Fines, Reversions, &c. Also Interest, Legacy, Succession Duty, and various other useful tables. Eighth Edition. Post 8vo. 10s.

The Patentee's Manual; a Treatise on the Law and Practice of Letters Patent, for the use of Patentees and Inventors. By J. JOHNSON, Barrister-at-Law; and J. H. JOHNSON, Assoc. Inst. C.E. Solicitor and Patent Agent, Lincoln's Inn Fields and Glasgow. Fourth Edition, enlarged. 8vo. 10s. 6d.

INDEX.

Abbey & Overton's English Church History	15
———*'s* Photography	11
Acton's Modern Cookery	21
Alpine Club Map of Switzerland	18
Alpine Guide (The)	18
Amos's Jurisprudence	5
——— Primer of the Constitution	5
Anderson's Strength of Materials	11
Armstrong's Organic Chemistry	11
Arnold's (Dr.) Lectures on Modern History	2
——————— Miscellaneous Works	7
——————— Sermons	15
——————— (T.) English Literature	7
Arnott's Elements of Physics	10
Atelier (The) du Lys	19
Atherstone Priory	19
Autumn Holidays of a Country Parson	7
Ayre's Treasury of Bible Knowledge	21
Bacon's Essays, by *Abbott*	6
——————— by *Whately*	6
——————— Life and Letters, by *Spedding*	5
——————— Works	5
Bagehot's Literary Studies	7
Bailey's Festus, a Poem	19
Bain's Mental and Moral Science	6
——— on the Senses and Intellect	6
——— Emotions and Will	6
Baker's Two Works on Ceylon	17
Ball's Alpine Guides	18
Barry on Railway Appliances	11
Beaconsfield's (Lord) Novels and Tales	18
Beesly's Gracchi, Marius, and Sulla	3
Bent's Republic of San Marino	17
Black's Treatise on Brewing	21
Blackley's German-English Dictionary	8
Blaine's Rural Sports	20
Bloxam's Metals	11
Bolland and *Lang's* Aristotle's Politics	6
Boultbee on 39 Articles	15
——————*'s* History of the English Church	15
Bourne's Works on the Steam Engine	14
Bowdler's Family *Shakespeare*	19
Bramley-Moore's Six Sisters of the Valleys	19
Brande's Dictionary of Science, Literature, and Art	12
Brassey's Voyage of the Sunbeam	17
Brian Boru, a Tragedy	19
Browne's Exposition of the 39 Articles	15
Browning's Modern England	3
Buckle's History of Civilisation	2
——————— Posthumous Remains	7
Buckton's Food and Home Cookery	21
——————— Health in the House	13
——————— Town and Window Gardening	12
Bull's Hints to Mothers	21
——— Maternal Management of Children	21
Bullinger's Lexicon to the Greek Testament	8
Burgomaster's Family (The)	19
Burke's Vicissitudes of Families	4
Cabinet Lawyer	21
Capes's Age of the Antonines	3
——— Early Roman Empire	3
Cayley's Iliad of Homer	19
Changed Aspects of Unchanged Truths	7
Chesney's Indian Polity	2
——————— Waterloo Campaign	2
Church's Beginning of the Middle Ages	3
Colenso on Moabite Stone &c.	17
——————*'s* Pentateuch and Book of Joshua	17
Commonplace Philosopher	7
Comte's Positive Polity	5
Congreve's Politics of Aristotle	6
Conington's Translation of Virgil's Æneid	19
——————— Miscellaneous Writings	6
Contanseau's Two French Dictionaries	8
Conybeare and *Howson's* St. Paul	16
Cooper's Tales from Euripides	18
Cordery's Struggle against Absolute Monarchy	3
Cotta on Rocks, by *Lawrence*	12
Counsel and Comfort from a City Pulpit	7
Cox's (G. W.) Athenian Empire	3
——————— Crusades	3
——————— Greeks and Persians	3
Creighton's Age of Elizabeth	3
——————— England a Continental Power	3
——————— Shilling History of England	3
——————— Tudors and the Reformation	3
Cresy's Encyclopædia of Civil Engineering	14
Critical Essays of a Country Parson	7
Crookes's Anthracen	15
——————— Chemical Analyses	13
——————— Dyeing and Calico-printing	15
Crump's Manual of Banking	21
Culley's Handbook of Telegraphy	14
Curteis's Macedonian Empire	3
De Caisne and *Le Maout's* Botany	12
De Tocqueville's Democracy in America	5
Digby's Indian Famine Campaign	2
Dobson on the Ox	20
Dove's Law of Storms	9
Dowell's History of Taxes	5
Doyle's (R.) Fairyland	13
Drew's Hulsean Lectures	15
Drummond's Jewish Messiah	16
Eastlake's Hints on Household Taste	14
Edwards's Nile	17
Ellicott's Scripture Commentaries	16
——————— Lectures on Life of Christ	15
Elsa and her Vulture	19
Epochs of Ancient History	3
——————— English History	3
——————— Modern History	3
Ewald's History of Israel	16
——————— Antiquities of Israel	16
Fairbairn's Applications of Iron	14
——————— Information for Engineers	14
——————— Mills and Millwork	14
Farrar's Language and Languages	7
Fitzwygram on Horses and Stables	20
Frampton's (Bishop) Life	4
Francis's Fishing Book	20
Frobisher's Life by *Jones*	4
Froude's Cæsar	4
——————— English in Ireland	1
——————— History of England	1
——————— Short Studies	7
Gairdner's Houses of Lancaster and York	3
——————— Richard III. & Perkin Warbeck	2

Ganot's Elementary Physics	10
—— Natural Philosophy	10
Gardiner's Buckingham and Charles	2
—— Personal Government of Charles I.	2
—— First Two Stuarts	3
—— Thirty Years' War	3
German Home Life	7
Goldziher's Hebrew Mythology	16
Goodeve's Mechanics	11
—— Mechanism	11
Gore's Art of Scientific Discovery	14
—— Electro-Metallurgy	11
Grant's Ethics of Aristotle	6
Graver Thoughts of a Country Parson	7
Greville's Journal	1
Griffin's Algebra and Trigonometry	11
Grove on Correlation of Physical Forces	10
Gwilt's Encyclopædia of Architecture	14
Hale's Fall of the Stuarts	3
Hartwig's Works on Natural History and Popular Science	11
Haughton's Animal Mechanics	10
Hayward's Selected Essays	6
Heer's Primeval World of Switzerland	12
Heine's Life and Works, by Stigand	4
Helmholtz on Tone	10
Helmholtz's Scientific Lectures	10
Herschel's Outlines of Astronomy	9
Hobson's Amateur Mechanic	14
Hodgson's Philosophy of Reflection	5
Hopkins's Christ the Consoler	17
Hoskold's Engineer's Valuing Assistant	14
Hullah's History of Modern Music	12
—— Transition Period	12
Hume's Essays	6
—— Treatise on Human Nature	6
Ihne's Rome to its Capture	3
—— History of Rome	2
Indian Alps	17
Ingelow's Poems	19
Jameson's Sacred and Legendary Art	13
—— Memoirs	4
Jenkin's Electricity and Magnetism	11
Jerrold's Life of Napoleon	1
Johnson's Normans in Europe	3
—— Patentee's Manual	21
Johnston's Geographical Dictionary	8
Jonson's (Ben) Every Man in his Humour	6
Jukes's Types of Genesis	16
—— on Second Death	16
Kalisch's Bible Studies	16
—— Commentary on the Bible	16
Keller's Lake Dwellings of Switzerland	12
Kerl's Metallurgy, by Crookes and Röhrig	15
Kingzett's Alkali Trade	13
—— Animal Chemistry	13
Kirby and Spence's Entomology	12
Knatchbull-Hugessen's Fairy-Land	18
—— Higgledy-Piggledy	18
Kuenen's Prophets and Prophecy in Israel	16
Landscapes, Churches, &c.	7
Latham's English Dictionaries	8
—— Handbook of English Language	8
Lecky's History of England	1
—— European Morals	3
—— Rationalism	3
—— Leaders of Public Opinion	4
Lefroy's Bermudas	17
Leisure Hours in Town	7
Leslie's Essays in Political and Moral Philosophy	6
Lessons of Middle Age	7
Lewes's Biographical History of Philosophy	3
Lewis on Authority	6
Liddell and Scott's Greek-English Lexicons	8
Lindley and Moore's Treasury of Botany	21
Lloyd's Magnetism	10
—— Wave-Theory of Light	10
London Series of English Classics	6
Longman's (F. W.) Chess Openings	21
—— German Dictionary	8
—— (W.) Edward the Third	2
—— Lectures on History of England	2
—— Old and New St. Paul's	13
Loudon's Encyclopædia of Agriculture	15
—— Gardening	15
—— Plants	12
Lubbock's Origin of Civilisation	12
Ludlow's American War	3
Lyra Germanica	17
Macalister's Vertebrate Animals	11
Macaulay's (Lord) Clive, by Bowen	6
—— Essays	1
—— History of England	1
—— Lays, Illus. Editions	13
—— Cheap Edition	19
—— Life and Letters	4
—— Miscellaneous Writings	7
—— Speeches	7
—— Works	1
—— Writings, Selections from	7
McCulloch's Dictionary of Commerce	8
Macfarren on Musical Harmony	13
Macleod's Economical Philosophy	5
—— Economics for Beginners	21
—— Theory and Practice of Banking	21
—— Elements of Banking	21
Mademoiselle Mori	19
Malet's Annals of the Road	19
Manning's Mission of the Holy Spirit	17
Marlowe's Doctor Faustus, by Wagner	6
Marshman's Life of Havelock	4
Martineau's Christian Life	17
—— Hours of Thought	17
—— Hymns	17
Maunder's Popular Treasuries	20
Maxwell's Theory of Heat	11
May's History of Democracy	1
—— History of England	1
Melville's (Whyte) Novels and Tales	19
Memorials of Charlotte Williams-Wynn	4
Mendelssohn's Letters	4
Merivale's Early Church History	15
—— Fall of the Roman Republic	2
—— General History of Rome	2
—— Roman Triumvirates	2
—— Romans under the Empire	2
Merrifield's Arithmetic and Mensuration	11
Miles on Horse's Foot and Horse Shoeing	20
—— on Horse's Teeth and Stables	20
Mill (J.) on the Mind	5
Mill's (J. S.) Autobiography	4
—— Dissertations & Discussions	5
—— Essays on Religion	16
—— Hamilton's Philosophy	5
—— Liberty	5
—— Political Economy	5
—— Representative Government	5

WORKS published by LONGMANS & CO.

Mill's (J. S.) Subjection of Women	5
——— System of Logic	5
——— Unsettled Questions	5
——— Utilitarianism	5
Miller's Elements of Chemistry	13
——— Inorganic Chemistry	11
——— & *Skertchley's* Fenland	18
Mitchell's Manual of Assaying	15
Milton's Paradise Regained, by *Jerram*	6
Modern Novelist's Library	18–19
Monsell's Spiritual Songs	17
Moore's Irish Melodies, Illustrated Edition	13
——— Lalla Rookh, Illustrated Edition	13
Morell's Philosophical Fragments	5
Morris's Age of Anne	3
Mozart's Life, by *Nohl*	4
Müller's Chips from a German Workshop	7
——— Hibbert Lectures on Religion	16
——— Science of Language	7
——— Science of Religion	16
Mullinger's Schools of Charles the Great	6
Neison on the Moon	9
Nevile's Horses and Riding	20
Newman's Apologia pro Vitâ Suâ	4
Nicols's Puzzle of Life	12
Noiré's Müller & Philosophy of Language	7
Northcott's Lathes & Turning	14
O'Conor's Scripture Commentary	16
Owen's Comparative Anatomy and Physiology of Vertebrate Animals	11
Packe's Guide to the Pyrenees	18
Pattison's Casaubon	4
Payen's Industrial Chemistry	14
Pewtner's Comprehensive Specifier	21
Phillips's Civil War in Wales	2
Pole's Game of Whist	21
Pope's Select Poems, by *Arnold*	6
Powell's Early England	3
Preece & *Sivewright's* Telegraphy	11
Present-Day Thoughts	7
Proctor's Astronomical Works	9
——— Scientific Essays (Two Series)	11
Prothero's De Montfort	2
Public Schools Atlas of Ancient Geography	8
——— Atlas of Modern Geography	8
Rawlinson's Parthia	3
——— Sassanians	3
Recreations of a Country Parson	7
Reynardson's Down the Road	19
Rich's Dictionary of Antiquities	8
Rivers's Orchard House	12
——— Rose Amateur's Guide	12
Rogers's Eclipse of Faith	15
——— Defence of Eclipse of Faith	15
Roget's English Thesaurus	8
Ronalds' Fly-Fisher's Entomology	20
Rowley's Rise of the People	3
——— Settlement of the Constitution	3
Rutley's Study of Rocks	11
Sandars's Justinian's Institutes	5
Sankey's Sparta and Thebes	3
Schellen's Spectrum Analysis	9
Seaside Musings	7
Scott's Farm Valuer	21
Seebohm's Oxford Reformers of 1498	2
Seebohm's Protestant Revolution	3
Sewell's History of France	
——— Passing Thoughts on Religion	
——— Preparation for Communion	
——— Stories and Tales	
——— Thoughts for the Age	
Shelley's Workshop Appliances	
Short's Church History	
Smith's (*Sydney*) Wit and Wisdom	
——— (Dr. R. A.) Air and Rain	
——— (R. B.) Carthage & the Carthaginians	
Southey's Poetical Works	
Stanley's History of British Birds	
Stephen's Ecclesiastical Biography	
Stonehenge, Dog and Greyhound	
Stoney on Strains	
Stubbs's Early Plantagenets	
Sunday Afternoons, by A. K. H. B.	
Supernatural Religion	
Swinbourne's Picture Logic	
Tancock's England during the Wars, 1778–1820	
Taylor's History of India	
——— Ancient and Modern History	
——— (*Jeremy*) Works, edited by *Eden*	
Text-Books of Science	
Thomé's Botany	
Thomson's Laws of Thought	
Thorpe's Quantitative Analysis	
Thorpe and *Muir's* Qualitative Analysis	
Tilden's Chemical Philosophy	
Todd on Parliamentary Government	
Trench's Realities of Irish Life	
Trollope's Warden and Barchester Towers	
Twiss's Law of Nations	
Tyndall's (Professor) Scientific Works	
Unawares	
Unwin's Machine Design	
Ure's Arts, Manufactures, and Mines	
Ville on Artificial Manures	
Walker on Whist	
Walpole's History of England	
Warburton's Edward the Third	
Watson's Geometry	
Watts's Dictionary of Chemistry	
Weinhold's Experimental Physics	
Wellington's Life, by *Gleig*	
Whately's English Synonymes	
——— Logic	
——— Rhetoric	
White's Four Gospels in Greek	
——— and *Riddle's* Latin Dictionaries	
Wilcocks's Sea-Fisherman	
Williams's Aristotle's Ethics	
Willich's Popular Tables	
Wilson's Resources of Modern Countries	
Wood's (J. G.) Popular Works on Natural History	
——— (J. T.) Ephesus	
Woodward's Geology	
Yonge's English-Greek Lexicons	
——— Horace	
Youatt on the Dog	
——— on the Horse	
Zeller's Plato, Socrates, &c.	
Zimmern's Lessing	

www.ingramcontent.com/pod-product-compliance
Lightning Source LLC
Chambersburg PA
CBHW051725300426
44115CB00007B/471